The Sunbelt/Snowbelt Controversy

THE SUNBELT/SNOWBELT CONTROVERSY:
The War over Federal Funds

by Robert Jay Dilger

New York University Press 1982 NEW YORK AND LONDON

Library of Congress Cataloging in Publication Data

Dilger, Robert Jay, 1954–
    The sunbelt/snowbelt controversy.

    Bibliography: p.
    Includes index.
    1. United States. Congress. House.
2. Caucus.   3. Pressure groups—United States.
4. Grants-in-aid—United States.   5. United
States—Appropriations and expenditures.   I. Title.
JK1323 1982   328.73'077   82-3463
ISBN 0-8147-1774-8   AACR2

Manufactured in the United States of America

To Gloria and Chris

Contents

Acknowledgments

I would like to thank the congressional members and staff of the Northeast–Midwest Congressional Coalition, the Southern Growth Policies Board, and all those in the Washington community who were kind enough to subject themselves to what often turned into quite lengthy and sometimes repeated interviews. Without their assistance this book would not have been possible. I am particularly grateful to John Moriarty, Laurence Zabar, and Shelly Amdur of the coalition and David Peterson and Bud Weinstein of the board.

For reading early versions of this work and providing numerous suggestions that served to strengthen my arguments I would like to thank Jeffrey Berry, Samuel Krislov, Martin Levin, Robert Peabody, and especially my dissertation adviser, Christopher Leman.

For financial support, both in the preparation of the dissertation from which this book emerged and for my graduate education at Brandeis University, I would like to thank the James Gordon Foundation of Chicago. Also, a special thanks to the Brookings Institution for designating me a Research Fellow in 1979. Brookings provided not only needed financial support but also an ideal intellectual atmosphere in which to complete work on my dissertation.

I also owe a special intellectual debt to Milton Cummings, Jr., and Robert Peabody who, by their example, convinced me as an undergraduate at Johns Hopkins to pursue political science as my profession.

Finally, for her moral, financial, editorial, and typing assistance, a very special thanks to Gloria.

The Sunbelt/Snowbelt Controversy

INTRODUCTION: *The Birth of a Caucus*

Politics, according to the title of Harold Lasswell's classic, concerns who gets what, when, and how.[1] On September 1, 1976, two dozen members of the U.S. House of Representatives from the New England states and the industrialized Midwest attended a meeting called and presided over by Democratic Representative Michael Harrington of Massachusetts. The congressmen had become convinced that they were being shortchanged in the determination of who got what share of the federal government's economic resources. By the time the meeting adjourned, they had formed the Northeast–Midwest Congressional Coalition and elected Harrington the coalition's chairman. In addition, each had volunteered two of his most precious resources to the cause—his time and a portion of his clerk-hire fees to fund a staff to support the coalition's activities.[2] This book documents these congressmen's efforts to get more federal economic aid for their region—dubbed the Snowbelt by the press—during the Ninety-fifth Congress. The purpose of this work, however, is not to ennoble the coalition or its accomplishments but to analyze its effect on congressional policymaking structures and the intergovernmental system.

The formation of the Northeast-Midwest Congressional Coalition in 1976 was not the first time a caucus had been formed as a means of creating a voting bloc. But the practice of organizing a select group of members, hiring a staff, and electing a chairman was a new congressional development in the 1970s. Between 1971 and 1976, eight new caucuses were formed, including the coalition, that followed this pattern of organization, and six more caucuses were formed in 1977.[3] By 1980 more than thirty special-issue-oriented caucuses were functioning on Capitol Hill.[4] Most of these caucuses serve only as an informational resource for their members, publishing periodic newsletters on what is happening on the Hill. Some do not have paid staff, and still others exist merely to attract media attention either to the cause of the caucus or to its organizers. There are several caucuses, however, such as the New England Caucus, the Congressional Black Caucus and the coalition that not only monitor the legislative process but actively intercede in the federal policymaking process. These caucuses are not only altering federal policy decisions but are changing the federal policymaking process as well.

No attempt has been made to document the activities of all these caucuses here. Instead, the Northeast–Midwest Congressional Coalition's activities during the Ninety-fifth Congress are highlighted. It will be argued that the coalition's activities, independent of these other caucuses, has adversely altered the federal policymaking process. Yet the existence of these other caucuses suggests that the coalition's fostering of computer politics (the use of information generated by computers to build coalition support for a given policy stance, discussed in detail in Chapter 9) and the problem of leadership that computer politics generates may be more acute than even this analysis suggests.

The Northeast-Midwest Congressional Coalition had eight salaried staff members in 1980, plus an additional eighteen undergraduate and graduate student interns to help with the workload. When the coalition was formed in 1976, it had only three salaried staff members and no student interns, but its activities in 1976 and 1977 nevertheless generated considerable publicity. The press began to produce numerous articles concerning the Sunbelt/Snowbelt controversy—the political clash between the representatives of the cold weather states of the Northeast-Great Lakes region (the Snowbelt) and the warm weather states of the Southeast and the Southwest (the Sunbelt).

Press accounts of the controversy, unfortunately, used the terms "Sunbelt" and "Snowbelt" rather loosely, lumping together states like Montana and Washington with Arizona and Florida into the Sunbelt. It is difficult to imagine Montana as a Sunbelt state. In an effort to develop a more accurate definition of these terms, several distinguishing criteria emerged, involving primarily economic development, climate, and energy resources. Although there are numerous ways to divide the nation into regions, these three factors produced a fourteen-state Sunbelt consisting of the southeastern states stretching into Oklahoma and Texas and westward to California. Most of the states of the West, it was discovered, had little in common with either the "booming" economies of the South-

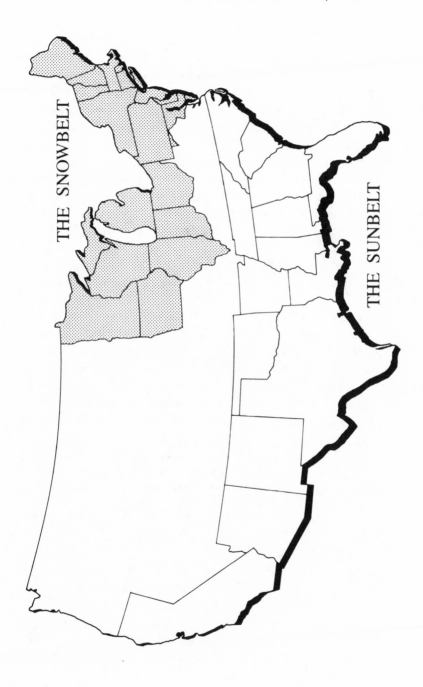

east-California corridor or the economically stagnant Northeast-Great Lakes region. Thus, most of the western states, Alaska, and Hawaii are not considered Sunbelt states in this analysis. Snowbelt states, on the other hand, were readily identifiable as those eighteen states holding membership in the Northeast-Midwest Congressional Coalition. Even these states are not completely homogeneous in every respect, however, Iowa differs in many ways from New York for example.

No effort is made here to take sides in this "war over federal funds." Both sides, as will be demonstrated, have real, discernible needs, which not only deserve to be, but must be met for the continued economic prosperity of the nation as a whole. In an era of governmental retrenchment, it is difficult to imagine that both regions' needs will be accommodated. The issue I hope to raise is that the current process—the computer and formulamanship politics (defined in Chapter 1, p. 22)—is counterproductive to both regions' goals.

Before examining how this Sunbelt/Snowbelt controversy began, who is winning or losing the war over federal funds, and what effect the coalition's activities have had on congressional decision-making structures and the intergovernmental system, I wish to state that I believe an era is coming to a close. As Kirkpatrick Sale points out in *Power Shift*, from 1870 to 1940 this nation was dominated by the economic and political interests of the Northeast.

> In practically every aspect of life this country was dominated by a nexus of industrial, financial, political, academic and cultural centers based in the Northeast, stretching from Chicago to New York, from Boston to Philadelphia. . . . It was this nexus that influenced the selection of Presidential candidates (between 1869 and 1945 only two Presidents were born outside of the Northeast), that controlled the houses of Congress, that determined American foreign policy, that set economic priorities and directives, that more or less determined who were to be the powerful and the powerless.[5]

Sale argued, however, that since World War II the dominance of the Northeast has been slipping while a rival nexus has emerged that is based in the southern and western states, stretching from California to Texas and into the southeastern states. According to Sale, this region (the Sunbelt) experienced an economic revolution based upon the postwar growth of such industries as defense, aerospace technology, electronics, agribusiness, oil and gas extraction, and services. As a region of increased economic power, Sale argued, the influence of the southern half of the nation in national politics has increased dramatically. The Sunbelt now plays a decisive role in the selection of presidential candidates of both major parties, and it still controls the major congressional committees and much of the inner workings of the Congress. As a result, according to Sale, by the mid-1970s the balance of power in American politics had already begun to shift away from the Northeast and toward the South.[6]

At the same time that the economic condition of the Sunbelt was improving, the economic condition of the Snowbelt was worsening. In 1979 the Northeast–Midwest Congressional Coalition published a list of the economic ailments besetting the Northeast:

—Almost 90 percent of the nation's population growth between 1970 and 1977 has been outside the Northeast-Midwest region.

—The region experienced a net out-migration of 2.4 million persons in the seven year period.

—The Census Bureau projects that the population of the South and West may grow at three times the rate of the Northeast-Midwest region between 1975 and 2000.

—For every nonagricultural job gained in the Northeast and Midwest between 1970 and 1977, the South and West gained three.

—Northeastern and Midwestern states lost nearly three-quarters of a million manufacturing jobs between 1970 and 1977.

—The 10 U.S. Cities with the worst job-growth prospects are all older, industrialized centers in the Northeast, according to *Money* magazine.

—Unemployment in the Northeast and Midwest was as high as 125 percent of the national average in 1977.

—Investment growth in nonresidential structures between 1970 and 1977 was only one-third in the Northeast and Midwest what it was in the South and West; the Northeast-Midwest region's growth in investment in new capital equipment was less than half the growth rate in the South and West.[7]

On top of these economic ailments, the Northeast-Midwest region will lose fifteen congressional seats in 1982 as a result of the 1980 census.

D. L. Jusenius and L. C. Ledebur, in "A Myth in the Making," provide an excellent rebuttal concerning the coalition's claim of economic calamity. They point out that whereas the economies of the Sunbelt states are growing at a much more rapid rate than those of the Snowbelt states, they have not yet reached the Snowbelt's level of economic attainment and, therefore, continue to deserve more federal aid than the Snowbelt states.[8] The following chart depicting regional per capita income trends substantiates Jusenius' and Ledebur's argument. The southeastern and southwestern states are catching up with the northeastern and midwestern states ("Mideast" on the chart) but have not yet caught up. While their argument is convincing with respect to the short term, what about

Regional per Capita Income as a Percent of U.S. Average, Selected Years, 1900–79

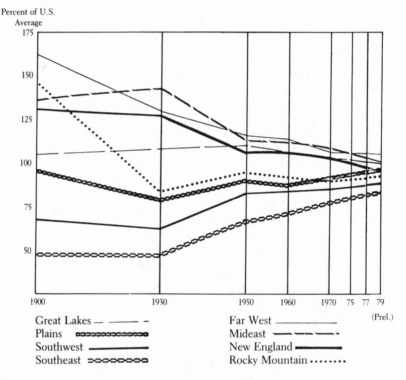

Great Lakes — ——— –   Far West ————   (Prel.)
Plains ◖◖◖◖◖◖◖◖◖◖   Mideast ——— —— ——·
Southwest ————   New England ■———■
Southeast ◁◇◇◇◇◇◇◁   Rocky Mountain ········

SOURCE: Advisory Commission on Intergovernmental Relations, *Significant Features of Fiscal Federalism* (Washington, D.C.: U.S. Government Printing Office, October 1980), p. 188.

NOTE: This chart does not take cost of living into account.

the long term? There are few who would deny the likelihood that the Sunbelt's economic status will exceed the Snowbelt's by the year 2000 and that, because of population trends, by 2000 the Sunbelt will in all probability have many more representatives than the Snowbelt in the U.S. House of Representatives. Thus, indications are that the era of northeastern hegemony is drawing to a close both economically and politically. Among other things the Sunbelt/Snowbelt controversy examined here may very well be the last gasps of a region being passed by.

CHAPTER ONE *Necessity Is the Mother of Invention: The Rise of a Regional Caucus*

As an incoming freshman representative from Massachusetts in 1971, Michael Harrington had not yet recognized the subtle shifting of sectional dominance that Kirkpatrick Sale would later argue was, and still is, taking place. Sale had the advantage of historical perspective as he reviewed the course of thirty years of economic development. He did not have the immediate responsibility, as Harrington did, of dealing with the results of that shift. Harrington, while not yet decided on the long-term causes of his district's, state's, and region's economic difficulties, could clearly see in 1971 symptoms of some deep, underlying causes of the economic problems of the area. The number one symptom—and the one most on Harrington's mind at the time—was the fact that the rest of the nation's unemployment rate was no more than 5 percent while his district's and that of the entire New England region as a whole exceeded 7 percent.[1]

In June 1971, Harrington, convinced that something had to be done to revitalize what he perceived to be a decline in the economic base of the New England region, wrote to his fellow New England representatives urging them to form a bipartisan New England Caucus whose purpose would be to address the economic decline of the New England region; exchange their views on the subject; and, ultimately, pool their political resources to achieve desired changes in federal policy that would provide the region with needed economic relief.

Harrington's letter drew a favorable response from many of his New England colleagues, especially from Representatives Silvio Conte (R-Mass.) and F. Bradford Morse (R-Mass.). Soon after the letter circulated, several informal meetings of the New England delegation took place to discuss the establishment of a formal regional caucus. In these discussions the private sector was included when Morse enlisted the help of James Howell, vice-president and chief economist of the First National Bank of Boston. Howell, along with another economist, John Buckley, vice-president of Boston's Northeast Petroleum Corporation, and James Hostetler, a member of the New England Council (a business group), proposed on July 7, 1972, not only that the New England House delegation meet regularly on a bipartisan basis as proposed by Harrington but that it also establish a permanent research office assisted by an advisory committee consisting of seven members—three from the private sector generally, two from the public sector, one from labor, and another from the academic community.[2] On August 8, 1972, Representatives Thomas P. O'Neill (D-Mass.), then majority leader; Conte, and Harrington wrote to the New England delegation informing them that the Howell plan would be implemented and the New England Caucus was officially born.[3]

The objective of what was to be called the New England Economic Research Office was to provide the New England Caucus with information concerning the region's economic interests. Conte was quoted at the time as saying that the caucus and the research group were formed to make sure "that New England gets what's coming to it" in the allocation of federal grants.[4] Howell commented that the caucus-research organization, the first of its kind, was also aimed at the larger issue of questioning the "evolution of national economic policy," which "we think [is] being aimed at growing parts of the country . . . leaving large chunks of New England out of it."[5]

On January 29, 1973, the joint caucus-research office was formally established as two separate entities sharing the same telephone number and four-room suite of offices just a few blocks from the Capitol. Jill Schuker, a former Harrington aide, was selected to head the caucus office; Paul London, an economist, was picked to head the research office. At the same time, Conte and O'Neill, the senior Republican and Democrat, respectively, in the New England delegation, were named acting cochairmen of the caucus.[6]

Whereas in 1973 Harrington was extremely encouraged by, and optimistic about, the possibilities the formation of the New England Caucus presented for providing economic relief to the New England area, he had become disillusioned with the organization by 1976.

Conte and O'Neill, the caucus' cochairmen, repeatedly frustrated his efforts to push it into taking aggressive political action on various federal policies. The cochairmen, who had both served for many years in Congress, could not bring themselves to attack from outside the structural process by which decisions were reached in committee. In their view, politics allowed for private consultation and compromise among congressional members as drafts of legislation were processed through the committee structure. They did not see as acceptable Harrington's desire for direct confrontation during congressional consideration of an issue, and especially after it had taken place. Nor did they approve of Harrington's desire to use the media to enhance their position. Conte and O'Neill believed that these kinds of tactics would not be conducive to maintaining viable long-term relationships with noncaucus members whose votes would be needed on other issues. And Conte and O'Neill also knew that many caucus members felt as they did on this question. Undertaking the aggressive actions suggested by Harrington would, in their opinion, destroy the caucus.

THE RECESSION AND THE NORTHEAST

Harrington grew increasingly frustrated with the New England Caucus both because he had become convinced that the foundation of the New England economy had reached a crisis point and because of his aggressive, straightforward personality that demands action.[7] In 1972–73 the national economy, which had just begun to recover from an economic slowdown in 1969, suddenly nose-dived into a recession. In many areas of the New England–Great Lakes region unemployment threatened to approach the record levels of the depression of the 1930s, while the Arab oil embargo of 1973–74 promoted double-digit inflation nationally. Harrington recognized that the recession affected all regions of the country, but he was also well aware that no region was more devastated by the economic downturn than the Northeast. Northern industries, already hit hard by high labor and energy costs, were suddenly faced with staggering increases in operating expenses as the cost of oil (which accounts for more than 60 percent of the region's energy use) jumped from the official OPEC price of $2 per barrel to $14 per barrel on the world open market.[8] To make matters worse, New England was, and remains, nearly totally dependent for its oil on expensive imports, importing approximately 88 percent of its oil from countries belonging to OPEC, a much higher proportion than any other region in the United States.[9]

Northern industries, no longer certain of a supply of cheap oil and faced with a declining national and international market as the recession became worldwide, laid off thousands of employees. Many smaller businesses were forced to close their operations. As these closings mounted, a fundamental question stuck in Harrington's mind: Why was it that the Northeast's economy had been hit so much harder by the recession than the South or the West? As he

Figure 1.1   Nonagricultural Employment
(as a percent of U.S. total, 1950–78)

	No. of States	1950	1960	1970	1975	1978
Northeast	(11)	33.2	30.7	28.4	26.2	24.8
Great Lakes	(7)	23.0	21.6	20.6	19.7	20.4
Southeast	(9)	13.4	14.9	16.5	17.6	18.2
Southwest	(5)	13.1	15.8	17.2	18.4	19.5

SOURCE: Advisory Commission on Intergovernmental Relations, *Regional Growth: Historical Perspective* (Washington, D.C.: U.S. Government Printing Office, June 1980), pp. 124 and 125.

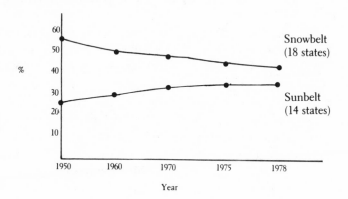

Figure 1.2   Population
(as a percent of U.S. total, 1950–78)

	No. of States	1950	1960	1970	1975	1978
Northeast	(11)	27.9	26.9	26.3	25.0	24.7
Great Lakes	(7)	20.2	20.2	19.8	19.2	19.0
Southeast	(9)	18.8	18.4	18.4	19.2	19.4
Southwest	(5)	14.6	16.7	18.0	18.5	19.1

SOURCE: Advisory Commission on Intergovernmental Relations, *Regional Growth: Historical Perspective* (Washington, D.C.: U.S. Government Printing Office, June 1980), pp. 116 and 117.

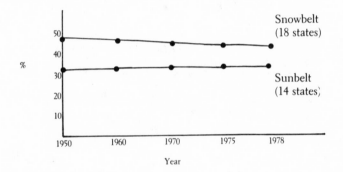

What Harrington discovered was that during the previous two decades the northeastern states were falling far behind the southern and western states in almost every economic category. The western states had added five times more new jobs to their economies than the northeastern states; the population growth rate in the south was almost twice that in the Northeast; and the per capita income of the southeastern states, which stood at only half the national average in 1930, had risen to 84 percent by 1970 and was nearly equal to the national average by 1976.[11] Figures 1.1 and 1.2 provide some of the data Harrington had at his disposal (plus some updated data).

searched for the answer to this question, he became increasingly aware, as he would later refer to it, on the "gut level," that there had been an economic and political shift of power within the United States.[10]

The growth of the Sunbelt states in both nonagricultural employment and population is clearly evident.

Harrington was convinced that the industrial and manufacturing economic base that had made the Northeast the dominant economic power during the previous two generations was slipping and that the recession was part of a long-term economic decline of the Northeast rather than a short-term business downturn. Figure 1.3 indicates that the Snowbelt states were even losing their share of the nation's manufacturing labor force.

Harrington outlined, in his own mind, the causes behind the decline of the Northeast's economy and the rapid growth of the Sunbelt's. First, in an era of scarce and expensive energy resources,

*Figure 1.3   U.S. Manufacturing Labor Force
(regional distribution as a percent, 1950–78)*

	No. of States	1950	1960	1970	1975	1978
Northeast	(11)	38.7	35.2	30.7	27.9	26.2
Great Lakes	(7)	28.9	26.8	26.0	25.2	24.8
Southeast	(9)	12.6	14.3	17.6	19.0	19.5
Southwest	(5)	8.0	11.7	13.1	14.4	15.5

SOURCE: Advisory Commission on Intergovernmental Relations, *Regional Growth: Historical Perspective* (Washington, D.C.: U.S. Government Printing Office, June 1980), pp. 120 and 121.

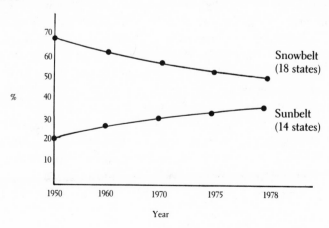

the warmer southern climate, coupled with the natural gas and oil deposits located in the Sunbelt, promised not only to encourage industrial expansion within the Sunbelt but to attract northern industries that were heavily dependent upon the uncertain and increasingly expensive energy supplies of OPEC. The relocation of several major corporate headquarters, including Coca-Cola and the Shell and Mobil oil companies, in the Sunbelt convinced Harrington that he was witnessing a potential mass exodus. Second, the Sunbelt, having industrialized later than the Northeast, had built its industries with later, more modern technologies. Not only were Sunbelt industries more efficient than Northern-based firms, but owing to the energy crunch northern firms lacked the funds to retool their factories in order to become effectively competitive on either the national or the international market. Also, many Sunbelt cities built major portions of their infrastructure networks in the past thirty years and do not face the immediate necessity of expending billions of dollars as northern cities do, to replace rapidly deteriorating infrastructures.

Collectively, these economic problems signaled in Harrington's mind the need for drastic political action. In 1975–76, however, few other northern representatives viewed the recession as an omen of a permanent, long-term economic decline of the northeastern region. Most expected that the recession would end in a relatively short period of time and that the Northeast's economy would regain its former stature. As the recession dragged on, however, many northern representatives began to realize that their political futures were directly tied to their ability to provide added economic relief to their constituencies. Programs were adopted, such as the countercyclical general revenue-sharing program, that provided federal aid to communities hardest hit by the recession. These programs did not increase economic activity in the Northeast, however, they merely prevented the region's economy from worsening. As studies began to appear indicating that despite this federal assistance the Northeast's economy continued to flounder while the economies of the South and West were flourishing, many northeastern representatives began to wonder what was happening. In the manufacturing sector, for example, which had been the backbone of the

Northeast's economy for generations, the northeastern states lost 533,000 jobs between 1973 and 1978, whereas the southern states gained nearly 600,000 manufacturing jobs during this period.[12]

As the northeastern states' economies failed to rebound from the recession, the region's representatives began to come under increasing pressure by their constituents to solve the economic problems. In response to this pressure, these representatives began to look for what Harrington would later refer to as a thematic and political means of helping their constituencies.[13] The thematic means was provided, perhaps unintentionally, by the press, and the political means was provided by Harrington.

MILITARY BASES AND THE PRESS: THE CATALYSTS

In March and April 1976, President Gerald Ford announced that 160 military bases, many located in the New England–Great Lakes region, would be closed or their personnel drastically reduced as an economy move. Shortly after Ford's announcement, Majority Leader Thomas O'Neill, Jr., on behalf of the economically troubled northeastern states, offered a series of amendments to the 1977 fiscal weapons procurement authorization bill that would have increased congressional control over military base changes. If adopted, these amendments would have provided the opportunity for northeastern representatives to prevent base reductions that promised to substantially increase unemployment in the Northeast. The amendments drew heavy bipartisan support from Snowbelt representatives and heavy bipartisan opposition from Sunbelt representatives, who feared that any revisions made in the president's policy would increase the number and severity of base closings and reductions in the Sunbelt.[14] While the congressional battle between the two regions ended with the Northeast attaining only the requirement that the president provide the Congress with sixty days' notice of any base realignments, Harrington realized that once the northeastern states' representatives recognized their common interest, they could forget party, personal, and ideological differences and vote as a bloc—one powerful enough to challenge the Sunbelt representatives. It was this series of votes that prompted Harrington to think about forming a permanent organization like the New England Caucus that would unite the representatives of New England with the representatives of the Great Lakes states.

The military base issue, however, was an isolated example of regional solidarity. The issue was clearly defined; all parties knew if they were helped or hurt by the president's directive.[15] The pending economic difficulties, although directly affecting all constituents in the Northeast, was a much less visible issue. Unlike the military base issue, for which the president could be blamed, who could be blamed for the Northeast's economic difficulties? The southern states may have been able to weather the storm better than the Northeast, but had they caused the North's economy to flounder? Until a common theme emerged, such as the president's directive on military bases, Harrington's dream of uniting the Northeast representatives into a cohesive bloc would have to remain a dream.

Shortly before the vote on the military base closing both the *New York Times* and *Business Week* reported that the South was the fastest-growing region in the nation and suggested that much of its growth was a result of a favorable balance of payments with the federal government. Then, on June 26, 1976, a report appeared in the *National Journal*, a self-professed trade magazine of the federal policymaking community, that provided in detail the political theme Harrington needed. The article, entitled "Federal Spending: The North's Loss Is the Sunbelt's Gain," indicated that in fiscal 1975 the Snowbelt states sent $29.4 billion more to Washington than they received in federal spending, whereas the Sunbelt states (broadly defined to include the west), received $23 billion more in federal expenditures than they paid in federal taxes.[16] Table 1.1 indicates, according to the *National Journal's* figures, the federal return per each dollar paid in federal taxes by state and region in fiscal year 1975. The table clearly indicates that most of the states in the Northeast and Midwest received less from the federal government than they paid in federal taxes, whereas most of the Sunbelt states received more from the federal government than they paid in.

From this table, which soon became widely known, Harrington could now approach the northeastern representatives and present them with evidence that this "inequitable" flow of federals funds

Table 1.1

Northeast	$ .86	Midwest	$ .76
Connecticut	$ .92	Illinois	$ .72
Maine	$1.12	Indiana	$ .73
Massachusettes	$ .95	Iowa	$ .69
New Hampshire	$1.00	Michigan	$ .65
New Jersey	$ .66	Minnesota	$ .83
New York	$ .89	Ohio	$ .70
Pennsylvania	$ .87	Wisconsin	$ .73
Rhode Island	$ .92		
Vermont	$1.17		
South	$1.14	West	$1.20
Alabama	$1.34	Alaska	$2.60
Arkansas	$1.37	Arizona	$1.41
Delaware	$ .66	California	$1.11
District of Columbia	$7.67	Colorado	$1.20
Florida	$1.00	Hawaii	$1.58
Georgia	$1.16	Idaho	$1.25
Kentucky	$1.21	Kansas	$ .98
Louisiana	$1.16	Montana	$1.28
Maryland	$1.20	Nebraska	$ .84
Mississippi	$1.76	Nevada	$ .96
Missouri	$1.10	New Mexico	$1.93
North Carolina	$ .98	North Dakota	$1.35
Oklahoma	$1.22	Oregon	$ .94
South Carolina	$1.19	South Dakato	$1.29
Tennessee	$1.13	Utah	$1.35
Texas	$1.03	Washington	$1.40
Virginia	$1.34	Wyoming	$1.21
West Virginia	$1.21		

SOURCE: Joel Havemann and Rochelle Stanfield, "Federal Spending: The North's Loss Is the Sunbelt's Gain," *National Journal* (June 26, 1976), p. 881.

was causing their states' economies to worsen. It was their task as representatives of the Northeast, Harrington would argue, to protect the economic interests of their constituents. Clearly, he would continue, it was their duty to reverse this flow of federal funds so that more would be spent in the area of greatest need—the Northeast. It was a theme, Harrington was convinced, that was not only right but that would unite the entire Northeast.

HENRY REUSS AND THE HOUSE BANKING
COMMITTEE

The Banking, Finance and Urban Affairs Committee in the U.S. House of Representatives has jurisdiction over many federal assistance programs and was one of the few committees during the Ninety-fifth Congress dominated by representatives of the Northeast.[17] It was clear to Harrington that if he was ever going to formally organize a caucus whose purpose was to help better the economic situation of the Northeast by redirecting the flow of federal funds, he would need the support of the northeastern representatives on this committee and of its chairman, Henry Reuss (D-Wis.). Thus, Harrington's first step in building his regional caucus was to enlist the support of the three leading Democrats on the Banking Committee: Reuss; Thomas Ashley (D-Ohio), who chaired the Banking Committee's Subcommittee on Housing and Urban Development; and William Moorhead (D-Pa.), who chaired the Banking Committee's Subcommittee on Economic Stabilization. Harrington had achieved a reputation as somewhat of an ultraliberal maverick in the House because of his past voting record and his efforts to disclose information concerning CIA activities in Chile. He was considered an outcast by many in the Congress. Thus, adding these more moderate, House-respected members to his regional coalition was necessary to provide it with a solid nucleus of support that would give it a quality of legitimacy and respect, which in turn would attract northeastern representatives from all ideological and partisan persuasions.

Henry Reuss represented the North Side of Milwaukee, Wisconsin, a district that like most others in the Northeast suffered greatly from the recession and had been slow to recover. Consequently, it might have been expected that Reuss would be very interested in joining Harrington's coalition. But, as a committee chairman, Reuss was already in a good position to protect his district's interests. For this reason, it might have been surprising to see Reuss join any coalition because, in all likelihood, his district would have little to gain by doing so. Reuss's joining Harrington's coalition would enhance the bargaining position of the coalition rather than the reverse. Reuss, however, was no ordinary committee chairman. He was, and still is, one of the most intellectually distinguished liberals in the House of Representatives. He was a thinking man, a man who could, like Harrington, perceive that something was happening to the national economy that did not promise better economic news for Milwaukee, Wisconsin, or for the entire Northeast. Reuss, like Harrington, did not fully comprehend exactly what that something was that was happening to the national economy, but perhaps, Reuss thought, Harrington's coalition could provide some of the answers. Also, Wisconsin had been designated as a regional loser in the federal spending, federal tax burden question, getting back only 73 cents on each dollar paid in federal taxes. Perhaps this coalition, Reuss must have thought, could help alleviate that problem as well.

Once Reuss made the decision to join the coalition, Harrington knew that it had a chance of turning into something of importance. As John Moriarty, who would later be designated executive director of the Northeast–Midwest Congressional Coalition, and was at this time (early summer, 1976) one of Harrington's legislative assistants, commented:

> The addition of Congressman Reuss was particularly important. He was the key. Not only is he Chairman of the Banking Committee, but he is hardly known as a rabble rouser. He is extremely well respected among Republicans as well as Democrats.[18]

With the assistance of Chairman Reuss, Harrington had little trouble persuading Ashley and Moorehead to join the coalition. Both men represented cities in economic difficulty, and both were from states that were designated as losers in the determination of federal spending.[19] With the aid of these three congressmen, on September 1, 1976, Harrington convened the first formal meeting of what would later be called the Northeast–Midwest Congressional Coalition. Approximately two dozen northeastern representatives attended the meeting, and Harrington's dream began to become reality.

THE OBJECTIVES ARE DEFINED

From the September 1976 meeting, the Coalition's membership grew to 213 by 1978, nearly half the membership of the House. During the Ninety-fifth Congress, a 31-member steering committee formally directed the operation of the coalition, and Representatives Frank Horton (R-N.Y.) and James Oberstar (D-Minn.) were elected vice-chairman and secretary-treasurer, respectively. From the inception of the coalition, however, it was Harrington, who was elected chairman, and John Moriarty, who was designated as executive director of the staff, who ran the coalition on a day-to-day basis.

The coalition's immediate goal as defined by Harrington and Moriarty was to "raise the consciousness" of the Congress and the nation to the regional plight of the Northeast and the inequities of the flow of federal funds, particularly of federal assistance programs. To attain this goal, Harrington decided to concentrate on relatively basic issues involving the direct flow of federal funds such as community development funds, the food stamp program, welfare and education spending, and other so-called soft expenditures. Since these programs involve immediate expenditures of monies determined by formulas, the coalition's staff, at that time consisting of three former Harrington aides, was given the task of examining the formulas and of determining whether or not a greater share of federal dollars could or should be redirected toward the Northeast.[20] To accomplish this task, the coalition's staff began to identify federal policy issues that had regional implications and held the interests of the coalition's members. Five such issues were identified early in 1977, and task forces made up of interested congressional members were formed to take political action on five regional policies: capital markets, military installations, energy, welfare, and housing and community development. The immediate goal of each task force was to develop a paper that defined the issue and explained the regional impact of available policy options. Each task force was also responsible for monitoring the legislative process and alerting the coalition's membership of any pending decisions of interest.

To aid in the preparation of these papers, the coalition's political staff, headed by John Moriarty, was augmented by the formation of the Northeast–Midwest Research Institute in March 1977. The institute was founded as a nonprofit organization whose operating expenses are underwritten by grants from private foundations and state governments. Like the New England Caucus' Economic Research Office, the Northeast–Midwest Research Institute, headed by Thomas Cochran (another former Harrington aide), was to provide the coalition's membership with economic analyses of current policy decisions and options.

According to Moriarty, the coalition's initial political objective was to establish its credibility by revising some of the granting procedures used by federal assistance programs. Once this credibility was established, the coalition would then attempt to influence the direction of so-called hard expenditures, including business tax incentives, urban and regional development corporations, and energy and military procurement policies. It was Harrington's and Moriarty's belief in 1976 that the only way the Northeast would ever fully recover from the recession was through providing the region with permanent, long-term job prospects. It was the hard expenditures that would provide such prospects: the type of jobs needed to stabilize the Northeast's deteriorating economy and to halt the relocation of Snowbelt firms in the Sunbelt. In an interview with *National Journal* Harrington commented:

> We'd swap them [the Sunbelt states] some of our welfare money for some of that hard money that stimulates investment. Whether it's a military base or other investment, that dollar spent in the first instance is a lot more effective in the long run than the dollar that keeps the guy off the streets.[21]

The coalition's first success, however, came not in the redesign of a federal granting formula but in the rediscovery in March 1977 of Defense Manpower Policy Number Four, an executive order issued by the Office of Emergency Preparedness in 1952 mandating that defense expenditures be directed to areas of the country suffering from economic distress. Exposing the fact that less than 0.2 of 1 percent of the $42 billion in defense procurements were made under DMP-4, the coalition received scattered publicity and was largely responsible for initiating hearings on the subject (see Chapter 5).[22]

Although Harrington found the initial success and publicity generated by DMP-4 extremely gratifying, he realized that his coalition's political strength had not yet been tested. He knew that the true test of its strength would be determined on the floor of the House in a direct confrontation with the Sunbelt forces. Yet, it might be years before Defense Manpower Policy Number Four was debated on the House floor. He had to look elsewhere for his first regional confrontation. It was at this time that the bill that would later become the Housing and Community Development Act of 1977 was about to be introduced.

The next chapter documents the coalition's efforts to alter the formula of the housing and community development bill (H.R. 6655). Later chapters deal with the coalition's efforts to alter formulas in the elementary and secondary education bill (enacted in 1978), implementation of Defense Manpower Policy Number Four, the formation and passage of the Carter urban program of 1977–78, and the crude oil equalization tax. These case studies are heavily descriptive as well as analytic. The descriptive aspect of the cases is employed to expose how the coalition and Sunbelt forces attempt to build regional coalitions across several substantive policy fields, as well as different policy types.[23] It will be argued in Chapter 9 that the coalition's skills in formulamanship (the ability to defend old or create new criteria in federal aid formulas) has altered not only the intergovernmental flow of funds, but the decision-making structures in the House of Representatives as well. It will also be argued that a further decentralization of power is a natural by-product of formulamanship and is contributing to a crippling of the House as a policymaking body.

CHAPTER TWO *H.R.* *6655:* *The*

Coalition's First Victory

In mid-September 1976, John Moriarty, Shelly Amdur, and Laurence Zabar set up a coalition office in House Annex Number Two, located a few blocks from the Capitol. With their aid, Michael Harrington began to map out the political strategy that would ultimately become a guide for dozens of other congressmen, many of whom at this time were only vaguely aware, if at all, of what the Northeast–Midwest Congressional Coalition was and what it intended to accomplish.

As Harrington and the staff discussed what to do, they realized that the federal government allocated its economic resources in four basic ways and that only one of these ways could be, relatively speaking, easily manipulated in order to alter the state-by-state distribution of federal funds. One system of allocation that was difficult to change was the way salaries were paid to federal employees. Since these funds were allocated according to where the work was done, changing the state-by-state distribution of these funds would require the massive relocation of federal jobs and workers. This would not be an efficient way to correct regional spending inequities on a short-term basis. Another major source of federal expenditures was in the form of direct payments made to individuals under such programs as social security and welfare. These expenditures were sent to the state where those individuals resided, and the federal government could hardly force the aid recipients to move to help correct what the coalition viewed as an inequitable flow of federal funds. A third source of federal expenditures viewed as being difficult to manipulate on a state-by-state basis was the procurement of such diverse things as paper, furniture, and weapon systems, through contracts with private industry. Harrington and his staff knew that it was possible to select a private contractor on a regional basis. It was no accident that most defense procurement contracts, for example, were awarded to southern-based companies. This flow of funds to the South was directly attributable to its disproportionate representation on the Senate and House Armed Services Committees. But many procurement contracts would not be easily manipulated on a state-by-state basis. For example, most aerospace procurement went to California and several other Sunbelt states because aerospace firms were located in those areas. Also, because the geographic and physical needs of the nation differ—water projects, for example, are needed in the West—many procurement funds cannot be targeted to the Northeast.

The fourth source of federal expenditures, which was viewed by Harrington and the coalition's staff as the easiest type of federal expenditure to manipulate on a state-by-state basis, was the federal grant.[1] In former times, federal grants accounted for only a tiny fraction of the federal government's expenditures, but in the previous two decades the total amount of federal aid provided to states and localities had risen dramatically. In 1955 federal aid amounted to only $3 billion. By 1964 this figure had risen to $10 billion, and by 1976 this figure had increased to $59 billion. Harrington reasoned that this amount of money could have a significant impact on the Snowbelt's economy. By 1981 federal aid to states and communities exceeded $90 billion (see Table 2.1).

Harrington knew that the New England–Great Lakes states, which already received more grant money on a per capita basis than any other region, could get an even larger share of such funds if

Table 2.1　Federal Aid to States and Localities 1955 through 1981

			(dollar amounts in billions)		
1955	$3.2	1964	$10.1	1973	$41.8
1956	3.7	1965	10.9	1974	43.4
1957	4.0	1966	13.0	1975	49.8
1958	4.9	1967	15.2	1976	59.1
1959	6.5	1968	18.6	1977	68.4
1960	7.0	1969	20.3	1978	77.9
1961	7.1	1970	24.0	1979	82.9
1962	7.9	1971	28.1	1980	89.8
1963	8.6	1972	34.4	1981	91.1 (est.)

SOURCE: Advisory Commission on Intergovernmental Relations, *Significant Features of Fiscal Federalism* (Washington, D.C.: U.S. Government Printing Office, October 1980), p. 161.

the formulas used to allocate the funds were changed.[2] Although not an easy task, altering federal formulas was certainly a better prospect than requiring the massive relocation of federal workers or forcing the relocation of millions of individuals receiving direct payments from the federal government.

Once the decision was made to concentrate the coalition's initial efforts on federal grant formulas, John Moriarty assigned Shelly Amdur the task of identifying grant programs that would be considered during the Ninety-fifth Congress and to conduct the research necessary to determine what changes could be made in various grant formulas that would result in an increase of funds for the Snowbelt. Amdur discovered that one of the largest federal grant programs, the housing and community development block grant (CDBG) program, was going to be reconsidered during the upcoming congressional session. Also, the bill was to be considered by the House Banking, Finance and Urban Affairs Committee. Both the chairman of the committee, Henry Reuss (D-Wis.), and the subcommittee of jurisdiction, Thomas Ashley (D-Ohio), were prominent coalition members. Harrington and Moriarty immediately realized that the CDBG program was a good place for the coalition to begin its efforts to redirect federal funds away from the Sunbelt.

FROM GRANTSMANSHIP TO FORMULAMANSHIP: NIXON AND FEDERAL AID

The Housing and Community Development Act of 1974, precursor of the Housing and Community Development Act of 1977, was a major part of President Nixon's effort to change the role of the federal bureaucracy regarding federal assistance programs. In a nationally televised speech on August 8, 1969, he called his new approach a "New Federalism" that represented an era in which:

> After a third of a century of power flowing from the people and the States to Washington, it is time for a New Federalism in which the power, funds and responsibility will flow from Washington to the States and to the people.[3]

The major means by which President Nixon planned to achieve this new era was to shift responsibility for federal assistance funds to the state and local levels by allocating the program's funds through general revenue sharing.

At the time of President Nixon's revenue-sharing proposal, nearly all federal assistance funds flowed through specific, single-purpose, categorical grants developed primarily during the Kennedy and Johnson administrations. To receive such grant funding, each state and community applied to the executive department that held jurisdiction over that grant. The executive department would then determine the merits of each state's or community's application and decide which would get what share of the funds, either according to its own criteria or in concert with criteria that had been established by the Congress in passing the program. The competitive process of applying for project grants has been called grantsmanship. The state and localities with superior grantsmanship skills (ability to disentangle federal red tape) generally received the greater share of the available aid. Since general revenue-sharing grants and other formula grants were distributed to the states and communities according to a formula based on predetermined criteria, such as population or per capita income, the interstate and intercommunity competition that became so prevalent under categorical grants system was supposedly eliminated, as was the judging role of the federal bureaucracy. In theory, the states and their localities would be free to spend the money as they wish.[4]

Daniel Elazar postulated in 1972 that the New Federalism was chimerical, that it did not create greater power for the states but replaced a noncentralized governmental system with a centralized one.[5] This case study, as well as the four that follow, substantiates Elazar's hypothesis. Although the increasing use of formula grants in the past decade has short-circuited the influence of grantsmanship over grants (75 percent of all federal aid was distributed by formulas in 1975), it has unleashed a whole new kind of conflict at the federal level.[6] In the past, states and localities primarily battled within the federal bureaucracy, and grantsmanship skills largely determined who got what. Now they do battle in the Congress through their representatives, and it is their representatives respective formula-manship skills that largely determine who gets what. The outcome of the battle is still determined by the central government.

THE 1974 NEEDS FORMULA: SETTING THE STAGE

The community development block grant program signed into law by President Nixon in 1974 consolidated ten categorical grants into a single, comprehensive grant that was to be distributed to cities and counties according to an "objective" needs formula. The needs formula, which determined who received what share of $8.3 billion that was to be spent over three years, was based on population (as determined by the Census Bureau), amount of housing overcrowding (defined as the number of housing units with an average of 1.01 or more persons per room), and poverty (which was weighted twice and determined by the Office of Management and Budget). Each city and county, however, was guaranteed until fiscal 1978, through a hold harmless clause, at least the same amount of funding received prior to the consolidation of the ten categorical grant programs. In this way, all three partners in the subgovernment triangle (subcommittee members, HUD officials, and clientele interest groups) were protected from any immediate losses. After fiscal 1977, however, when the program's authorization expired, the hold harmless clause would be phased out by thirds down to the formula level.[7]

THE CARTER ADMINISTRATION'S PROPOSAL

As fiscal 1978 approached and the housing and community development proposal was scheduled to be introduced by the new Carter administration, the Department of Housing and Urban Development received the report of an in-house study that concerned the implications of phasing out hold harmless and an outside study on the same subject that the department had funded and was conducted by the Brookings Institution.[8] Both studies indicated that if the 1974 needs formula were retained in its then current form, and hold harmless were phased out, the amount of aid provided recipients located in western and southern states would increase, while the aid provided recipients located in northeastern states would decline. Both studies concluded that the major factor causing this was that the designation of poverty, which was weighted twice in the needs formula, did not take into account a cost-of-living factor. Since the cost of attaining a comparable living style is generally higher in the northeastern and midwestern states than in the western or southern states, northeastern and midwestern residents tend to have higher per capita income levels than those in the South or West. Since poverty is determined by per capita income, the 1974 needs formula treated many Sunbelt residents as poverty-stricken, despite the fact that their living style was comparable with, or even better than, many northeastern residents who were not counted as being poverty-stricken by the formula. As the Brookings Institution study stated:

. . . It is in large measure because of the double weighting of poverty in the formula and the high level of poverty in the southern regions that they are so significantly advantaged in the CDBG formula, increasing their share from 29.2 to 36.8 percent of the total.

Conversely, for the two regions showing the greatest declines—New England and Middle Atlantic—their below average levels of overcrowding and poverty result in the reduction of their share from 32.6 percent to 22.1 percent of the CDBG total.[9]

The 1974 needs formula's use of population as a criterion of need was another factor that contributed to its favoring the Sunbelt. According to the Brookings Institution study, a given community's population change is a better indicator of economic need than a community's absolute level of population. The study argued that if population loss instead of the current population level were used in the eligibility formula, the older cities of the northeastern states, which were (and still are) losing population, would justifiably receive a larger portion of the program's funds.

Recognizing that the phasing out of hold harmless meant that their funding levels would decline, representatives of northeastern interest groups from the National League of Cities, the U.S. Conference of Mayors, and several other associations appealed to their subgovernment compatriots in the Department of Housing and Urban Development (HUD) either to include a new hold harmless provision in the housing and community development bill to be introduced or to revise the needs formula so that they would not lose any funds. At about this time, February 1977, the

Northeast–Midwest Congressional Coalition, through Amdur's efforts was seriously studying the effects of federal formulas on the economic well-being of the northeastern states. Amdur, then a research assistant for the coalition, recalls the manner in which the coalition prepared to address this issue:

We knew the community development bill was coming up and that we had to deal with it. It was the first issue to come up [on the legislative calendar] which we knew, from an urban point of view, was bad for our region. It was clear that the Nixon shift was away from urban centers and towards the suburbs, to growth areas.

. . . We tried to find out what was happening with it [the CDBG's formula] over at H.U.D., but they refused to give us any information.

It was about this time that we sent out letters to the members of the Coalition asking them if they would be interested in joining a Housing and Community Task Force. [Once formed] it was a small Task Force of eight members, but it was very active. I remember that before Secretary Harris introduced the Administration's bill we had already held several staff meetings with the staffs of the Task Force's members to try to figure out what the figures [of the formulas] would be.[10]

Before Secretary Harris introduced the administration's proposal, the members of the coalition's Housing and Community Task Force met twice in order to exchange their views on the current needs formula. From these meetings and many separate meetings between the task force cochairmen, Stanley Lundine (D-N.Y.) and Paul Tsongas (D-Mass.), and the coalition's founder, Michael Harrington, an informal consensus was reached that the coalition could not support the continuation of the current formula even with another hold harmless provision.[11] It was agreed that the coalition would seek a new definition of need that would redirect a greater share of the program's funds to the northeastern states. Since both Lundine and Tsongas were junior members of the Banking Committee, they would work from within the committee to achieve the coalition's goals, and Harrington would gather support for their efforts from the ranks of the coalition. What the coalition's new definition of need was to be, however, had not been decided upon by the time the secretary of housing and community development, Patricia Harris, announced the administration's proposal.

On February 24, 1977, Secretary Harris submitted the Administration's proposal before Thomas Ashley's Housing and Community

Development Subcommittee. The proposal not only increased the funding of the program from $8.3 billion to $10.95 billion over the next three years, thus increasing the total outlay so that urban areas in the northeastern states had a greater likelihood of retaining their current funding levels, but also revised the 1974 needs formula so that more economic aid was targeted to the northeastern states.

In order to improve the "equity" of the program, Secretary Harris proposed a dual formula to be used for cities and counties whose population exceeded 50,000 persons. The city or county would then have the option of selecting whichever formula gave it a greater allotment of funds. This new, dual formula retained the 1974 needs formula and added a second formula that provided aid according to the community's age of housing (weighted 50 percent), poverty (weighted 30 percent), and growth lag (weighted 20 percent). The "age of housing" factor referred to the number of existing housing units built prior to 1940 and represented the administration's concern for the physical deterioration of the infrastructure within the nation's older cities. "Growth lag" referred to the extent to which a city's population growth rate between 1960 and 1973 fell short of the average population growth rate for all metropolitan cities during this period.[12]

All active participants immediately recognized that this second formula represented an administration effort to aid the larger cities of the Snowbelt. These cities not only experience growth lag to a greater extent than cities located in other regions but also tend to have older housing stock. Eligibility requirements for smaller cities (those with populations below the 50,000 level), however, would continue to be allocated funds under the 1974 needs formula.

THE LUNDINE AMENDMENT: FORMULAMANSHIP
SKILLS IN ACTION

As hearings before Ashley's subcommittee began on the bill, Harrington, Lundine, and Tsongas knew that the new, second formula would provide added economic assistance to the Northeast, but did not know whose districts would receive the "bonus" money and what the total amount of added revenue would be. Since they individually lacked the resources to answer these questions and the administration had not provided the answers, Shelly Amdur was asked to undertake a study of the administration proposal's effect upon the Snowbelt. As she began her study, Amdur almost immediately recognized that the bill had a major drawback for the Snowbelt. As she put it:

We looked at the bill, read it, and realized that the small cities part had a lot of errors in it.

. . . They had left the small cities [under 50,000 persons] under the old formula which would have cost the small cities of the Northeast and Midwest millions of dollars.

. . . At one point we talked to H.U.D. about the new formula and the small cities part, but H.U.D. hadn't done their homework on it.[13]

As a result of Amdur's research, negotiations to modify the bill, led by Housing and Community Development Subcommittee Chairman Thomas Ashley and Stanley Lundine, were opened with Carter administration officials, principally HUD Assistant Secretary Robert Embry and Presidential Advisor Stuart Eizenstat. As these negotiations were being conducted, the Northeast–Midwest Congressional Coalition submitted to the Carter administration a five-point cities entitlement program that urged a revision of the administration's policy toward small cities. Given Ashley's position and hoping to avoid a policy setback so early in the administration, Eizenstat and Embry promised to support an amendment that would substantially increase the amount of aid provided to northeastern cities whose populations were under 50,000 persons by including them under a dual formula similar to the administration's dual formula for large cities.[14]

As soon as the Carter administration approved the small-cities dual formula approach, the coalition's Housing and Community Development Task Force sent letters to coalition members informing them of the administration's action and of the resulting improvement for their region of the administration's proposal, now designated H.R. 6655.

As Ashley scheduled the markup session on H.R. 6655 for March 29, 1977, Harrington, Lundine, and Tsongas personally contacted various members of the Housing and Community Development Subcommittee to urge their support both for the president's dual formula for large cities and for an amendment, to be introduced by Lundine, that would put small cities under a dual formula similar to the formula for large cities. Just before the scheduled vote on the small-cities dual formula was to take place, the coalition's task force sent the eighteen members of the twenty-five-member subcommittee who were from the Snowbelt a letter and memorandum explaining the reasons why they should support the dual formula for small cities.

On March 29, 1977, the House Banking Committee's Subcommittee on Housing and Community Development voted 16–6 in favor of Lundine's amendment to the administration's proposal. All 6 opposing votes were cast by representatives of the Sunbelt, and all 16 votes in favor of the amendment were cast by Snowbelt representatives.[15] (Since the chief author of the amendment was Stanley Lundine and he offered the amendment for consideration before the subcommittee, the amendment became known as the Lundine amendment.)

At the time of the subcommittee vote—the first legislative victory for the coalition—no one had exact figures indicating who would receive what amount of money as a result of the Lundine amendment's adoption. The coalition's efforts to inform the subcommittee members of the potential benefits of the amendment for their districts, however, coupled with the support of the Carter administration and of Subcommittee Chairman Thomas Ashley, convinced many of the subcommittee members that it would not only be safe but also politically expedient to vote for the amendment. For the most part, these northeastern representatives voted for the amendment because they believed that, since the administration's dual formula for large cities would benefit their districts, a similar formula for small cities would also send more money into their districts.

The adoption of the Lundine amendment by the House Banking Committee's Subcommittee on Housing and Community Development provides an excellent example of the effect that the coalition's information resources can have on congressional policy. The decisions congressmen make are often defined by the information with which they are provided, and in this particular case the only persons who possessed credible information about the effect of the proposed change in the 1974 needs formula were the members of the coalition's Housing and Community Task Force. In this connection, what Amdur said when questioned about the small cities part of the administration's proposal bears repeating: "at one point we talked to H.U.D. about the new formula and the small cities part, but H.U.D. hadn't done their homework on it."[16] Apparently, even the Carter administration was not certain about the new, dual formula's implications. This gave the coalition members a clear informational advantage over the congressional members of the Sunbelt, both on and off the Banking Committee, and over the Carter administration as well. This advantage, coupled with the efforts of Ashley, Lundine, and Tsongas within the Banking Committee, was instrumental in opening the way for the administration's and the subcommittee's acceptance of the Lundine amendment.

On April 28, 1977, by a vote of 30–3, the Snowbelt-dominated House Banking, Finance and Urban Affairs Committee (twenty-eight of the forty-seven members of the committee were members of the coalition) approved the housing and community development bill. The Banking Committee endorsed both the administration's dual formula for large cities and the coalition's dual formula for small cities.[17]

As the bill was being scheduled for floor debate in the House, the coalition's staff had already proved that the possession of superior information can have an important influence on congressional decisions. Mere possession of information, however, does not always assure favorable outcomes; information must be used skillfully and put in the right hands. Recognizing this fact, the coalition's staff used its informational advantage to attract additional political allies. By the time the bill reached the floor of the House, the coalition's staff had not only informed its members of the bill's progress and effect upon the flow of community development funds but had also contacted the members of the Northeastern Governors' Conference, who were already actively supporting the bill, and the mayors of several major Snowbelt cities in order to coordinate their efforts to pass the bill as reported by the House Banking Committee. The staff also arranged for a computer analysis of the effect of the formula changes upon each of the nation's congressional districts (providing the inspiration for describing the coalition's tactics as computer politics). The computer run indicated that fifty-six congressional districts outside the Snowbelt region would still be favorably affected by the new, dual formula. The coalition's staff sent each of the congressmen affected a copy of the computer printout, which indicated that they fared better under the new, dual formula than under the old, single formula. It was the coalition's hope that these representatives would vote along with the Snowbelt representatives and thus insure passage of the bill as written.

THE SUNBELT REACTS TO THE COALITION'S VICTORY

The adoption in committee of both the Carter administration's dual formula and the Lundine amendment proved too much for Sunbelt Congressmen Mark Hannaford and Jerry Patterson, both California Democrats and members of the House Banking Committee.[18] On May 4, 1977, they sent a "Dear Colleague" letter to representatives whose districts would "lose" funds under the new, dual formula.[19] (Since each applicant had a choice between the old and new formula, no one lost money in an absolute sense because more money was authorized for the new bill. The Snowbelt, however, stood to gain most of the newly authorized money.) Hannaford and Patterson charged in the letter that the new formula created "gross inequities" because it increased funds to cities with older housing stock regardless of the condition of that housing stock. As an example, they mentioned that "beautiful old San Francisco," a city that had relatively old yet well-kept housing, would receive more than twice as much per capita funding as Los Angeles, a city that had relatively new housing, yet actually warranted more aid than San Francisco because the housing had already begun to deteriorate. As a result of this inequity, Hannaford and Patterson stated that they would offer an amendment to the housing and community development bill that would strike the new, alternative formula so that all community development funds would be allocated according to the original formula.[20]

The next day, May 5, 1977, Michael Harrington, Frank Horton, and Stanley Lundine, unaware of Hannaford's and Patterson's letter, sent out their own "Dear Colleague" letter urging support for the housing and community development bill, including the Lundine amendment.[21] When the contents of the Hannaford and Patterson letter became known, the coalition's Housing and Community Development Task Force quickly sent a letter (May 9, 1977) to all coalition members informing them of the impending effort to amend the bill on the House floor and urging them to adopt the bill without amendment.[22]

Debate on the bill began on May 8, 1977. After three days of debate and the adoption of numerous minor amendments, the housing and community development bill (H.R. 6655) was passed on May 11, 1977, 369–20, but not before Hannaford and Patterson had challenged the new, dual formula. On May 10, 1977, Hannaford introduced an amendment to H.R. 6655 that would have deleted CDBG's small- and large-city's dual formula and reverted to the original 1974 formula. In presenting his amendment, Hannaford declared that the new formula forced southern and western taxpayers to subsidize the revitalization of northern cities such as Newark and Detroit while neglecting the needs of cities such as San Diego and Los Angeles.

> . . . I have a personal bias against the concept embodied in the new formula for it contains a conflict between relatively new cities and relatively old cities, and I was a mayor of a new city [Lakewood, Calif.] and most of the cities in my district and my state fall into that category.
> . . . There are great distortions in this new formula. For example, the community development entitlement for Los Angeles in 1977 was $17 per capita, and for Detroit it was $20 per capita, an acceptable inequity. Next year under the new formula, Los Angeles will improve slightly to just under $19 per capita, while the per capita allowance for Detroit jumps to $42.49, well over 2 to 1. This is an absolutely unacceptable inequity.
> . . . The new formula is heavily biased against the West. It is heavily biased against the suburbs.
> . . . I cannot accept that the suburbs in my district in Los Angeles and Orange County, California . . . , should be taxed to support the revitalization of Detroit or Newark.[23]

In presenting his opposition to the new, dual formula, Patterson was particularly critical of its use of the age of housing as a criterion of a city's need.

> The real issue is: do we want to address poverty or do we want to address old houses? . . . Poor people live throughout the United States. They are not entirely contained within older cities.[24]

As debate on the amendment continued on the floor of the House, William Alexander (D-Ark.), articulated the thoughts of many in the Sunbelt by attacking the new, dual formula in a broader sense.

In record numbers over the past few years Americans have shown a preference to live in the South and the West. Certainly we should not penalize them for this choice by letting their cities deteriorate to accommodate other regions of the country.[25]

Despite Hannaford's and Patterson's efforts and the fact that this was the first test of the coalition's strength on the House floor, the Hannaford amendment was defeated 149–261. The vote itself was split along regional lines. The representatives of the then sixteen coalition states voted 5–189 to defeat the Hannaford amendment, while the representatives of the fourteen Sunbelt states voted in its favor 119–27. The map shown in Figure 2.1 graphically displays the regional alignment evidenced by this vote.

The coalition's activities were clearly one of the factors behind this regional alignment. But before considering the coalition's influence, let us look at the influences working against a regional alignment. One reason for the twenty-seven Sunbelt defectors was that the Carter administration opposed the Hannaford amendment because it would have dismantled its dual formula. It is no accident that Georgia representatives, the president's home state, voted 4–6 to support his program despite the fact that supporting the amendment would have helped their districts. In fact, the administration lobbied among Democrats of all regions asking them to oppose the Hannaford amendment. This effort, of course, also helped the Northeast–Midwest Congressional Coalition in its efforts to persuade Democrats from the coalition states to vote against the amendment.

One factor that helps account for the large number of western states that supported the coalition's position was that fifty-six congressional districts outside the Northeast would benefit by the administration's dual formula. Hannaford's amendment would have resulted in a loss of those benefits. Representatives of such districts were thus inclined not only to oppose the amendment but also to seek their friends' help in opposing it. The fact that three "nona-

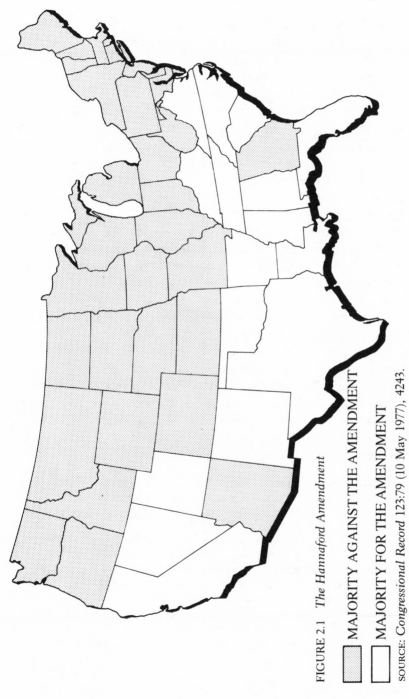

FIGURE 2.1   *The Hannaford Amendment*

▨ MAJORITY AGAINST THE AMENDMENT

☐ MAJORITY FOR THE AMENDMENT

SOURCE: *Congressional Record* 123:79 (10 May 1977), 4243.

ligned" states (Kansas, Washington, and West Virginia) voted unanimously against the Hannaford amendment despite the fact that only one of the congressional districts in each state was significantly benefited by the administration's dual formula indicates that within-state logrolling probably took place.

Party influence is one factor that could possibly rule out the regional factor in explaining the defeat of the Hannaford amendment, but the pattern of the voting indicates that both Republicans and Democrats opposed the amendment, 45–89 and 104–172, respectively. Closer examination of the vote reveals that the parties themselves were split along regional lines. Republicans from the coalition states opposed the Hannaford amendment, 3–68, but those in the remaining states supported the amendment, 42–21. Democrats from the sixteen coalition states also strongly opposed the amendment, 2–121, whereas Democrats from the remaining states supported it, 102–51.[26]

Thus, it is clear that opposition to the Hannaford amendment was rooted in regional considerations rather than in party affiliation or even ideology. But what role did the coalition play in influencing its members' voting behavior? Put another way, was this regional response solely the result of the coalition's activities, or were other forces at work that supplemented or even supplanted the coalition's efforts? John Moriarty, then executive director of the Northeast–Midwest Congressional Coalition, was convinced that the House regional response to the Hannaford amendment was tied to the coalition's efforts:

The Coalition . . . successfully turned back an effort by Southern Congressmen to revert back to the old, less desirable formula. As a result [of the Lundine amendment], small cities in the Northeast and Midwest (which are afflicted with a greater degree of urban decay) will receive roughly 25 percent more in Community Development funds than would otherwise be the case . . . the Coalition formula victory at the subcommittee level [Lundine] and on the floor of the House leaves little doubt of the potential of this new regional organization. In the crucial floor vote, the Coalition carried all but five of its members.[27]

We shall return to this question shortly.

The housing and community development bill, as passed by the

House, would have extended the community development block grant program for three years and authorized $12.45 billion to fund it. Besides continuing funding for the ten programs within the block grant, the House bill also created a new program, the urban development action grant (UDAG) program, which was authorized to spend $400 million annually on problems specifically related to large metropolitan areas.[28]

COMPLICATIONS IN THE SENATE: ANOTHER FORMULA IS ADDED

While Moriarty and other members of the Northeast–Midwest Congressional Coalition were celebrating their first major legislative victory, the bill moved over to the Senate's Banking, Housing and Urban Affairs Committee, chaired by William Proxmire (D-Wis.), where the controversial dual formula was expanded by the addition of yet another formula. This third formula was almost identical to the formula that had brought on the challenge from Congressmen Hannaford and Patterson, but instead of counting the absolute number of pre-1940 housing stock in a metropolitan area, it measured the proportion of pre-1940 housing stock in a metropolitan area and compared that with the pre-1940 housing stock in all metropolitan areas. The effect of the change, known as the impaction adjustment amendment, which was pushed by Senators Harrison Williams (D-N.J.) and Edward Brooke (R-Mass.), was to shift an even larger portion of the available funds to the Snowbelt. To pay for the added revenues that would be given to older, mostly northeastern cities, the Senate version of the bill deleted the funds slated for the urban development action grant program and used the money to fund the impaction adjustment amendment, which was to be phased in during the three-year life of the bill.[29]

The Senate version of the housing and community development bill passed quite easily, on June 7, 1977, 79–9, largely because of the lack of dissent within the Senate Banking Committee, which like the House Banking Committee was dominated by representatives from the Northeast.

ASHLEY KEEPS HIS WORD DESPITE THE CONSEQUENCES

Despite the lopsided votes in favor of the bill in both the House and the Senate, the housing and community development bill languished in conference for nearly three months because of Housing and Community Development Subcommittee Chairman Thomas Ashley's stubborn resistance to the Senate's impaction adjustment amendment.

The UDAG program (which targeted aid to large metropolitan centers) had been included in the House version of the bill to appease the House Banking Committee's representatives of large urban areas, particularly those from New York. While the Senate's impaction adjustment amendment would not only accomplish the same objective but would also direct even greater sums to these areas, Subcommittee Chairman Ashley was caught in a bind. In order to get the UDAG program adopted within his subcommittee without undue friction, Ashley had made a personal commitment to his subcommittee's Sunbelt representatives that UDAG would be the absolute extent of their "losses" relative to the housing and community development bill. As a result, Ashley, who had no idea at the time that the Senate would adopt a formula that would direct even more aid to the northeastern metropolitan centers, could not support the Senate's three formulas without going back on his word to these representatives.[30] As Paul Tsongas commented, in retrospect:

> They had come over to the Northeast's position in committee and to push them even further would have been a mistake.
>
> Ashley had made commitments and you can't turn your back on people, especially after they had given in to you. I would have done exactly the same thing.[31]

Mark Hannaford, who agreed that Ashley's honor was at stake, recalls that Ashley was made aware of the Sunbelt's resistance to the House version of the housing and community development bill by the vote he initiated on the floor of the House. An acceptance of the Senate's impaction adjustment amendment, Hannaford insisted, would have caused an even more bitter floor fight over the conference report, a fight Ashley would naturally want to avoid.[32]

Ashley's decision to oppose the Senate amendment despite the short-term benefits that it would provide his district highlights the importance he placed on his position within the congressional committee structure and the power associated with it. His opposition to the amendment also serves to illuminate the enhanced role that Michael Harrington had assumed during the Ninety-fifth Congress. As chairman of the Northeast–Midwest Congressional Coalition, Harrington—initially with little institutional power owing to his junior status and, as mentioned earlier, considered a virtual outcast by most of his colleagues—had become a major spokesman for the Northeast and the Midwest on matters concerning federal assistance programs. As such, Harrington's stature in the House was enhanced to the point where he was consulted on issues far beyond the jurisdictional limits of his assigned committees (e.g., International Relations and Governmental Affairs). During the formation of H.R. 6655 Harrington, who was not a member of the Banking, Finance and Urban Affairs Committee, was in continual contact both with Carter administration officials and with Subcommittee Chairman Thomas Ashley. He was also actively involved with the coalition's Task Force on Housing and Community Development, providing advice and guidance in its attempt to revise the formula of the housing and community development bill. When the bill eventually became stuck in conference because of Ashley's opposition to the impaction adjustment amendment, HUD officials, who feared that existing authorizations would expire while debate continued,[33] approached Harrington and asked him to speak with Ashley to expedite a compromise with the Senate conferees. These officials of the executive branch would never have taken such action prior to the formation of the coalition. Harrington had had virtually nothing to do with the formation of housing policy before the coalition had come into existence. Now Harrington and Tsongas, both Massachusetts Democrats, approached House Speaker Thomas O'Neill, also a Massachusetts Democrat and known to personally support the impaction concept, and asked him to talk to Ashley on behalf of the Senate version of the bill. The Speaker contacted Ashley, not because he was technically a member of the coalition or felt a need to do so on regional grounds, but, according to several of his aides, because the Speaker was a personal friend of both Harrington and Tsongas and because they were both Democrats from his state. The Speaker's effort, however, failed to persuade Ashley to accept a compromise that included the impaction adjustment amendment.

Harrington and Tsongas, refusing to give up, then approached Ashley with a compromise that had been researched by the Northeast–Midwest Research Institute's staff. Although Ashley also rejected the coalition's compromise, the sequence of events—the fact that HUD officials approached Harrington for help, his ability to contact and enlist the Speaker's support, and his running interference for the bill throughout its development—indicates that Michael Harrington, capitalizing on the coalition's informational support, had achieved a stature in the House somewhat akin to a committee chairman's. In consequence, Harrington was able to provide the interests of the Snowbelt with a degree of political clout not available through the traditional committee structure and otherwise not evident before the formation of the Northeast–Midwest Congressional Coalition. As Tsongas stated:

> John Moriarty is a great guy and is very intelligent, but Michael Harrington is the real political brains behind the organization. The Coalition's staff, itself, serves an informational function. Harrington provides the rest.[34]

It was this combination of informational advantage and Harrington's political leadership that provided the Snowbelt representatives an organizational advantage over the Sunbelt concerning the distribution of community development funds.

Despite Harrington's efforts, and two compromise gestures offered by Senate conferees, the Senate conferees were forced to eliminate their impaction adjustment amendment from the bill. In return, they received a guarantee from Ashley that in the distribution of the UDAG funds (approximately $400 million) Secretary Harris would take into full consideration, as primary criteria for determining need, the factors of the Senate's third formula: impaction, poverty, and growth lag.[35]

The conference report was passed by the Senate on October 1, 1977, 54–19, and by the House on October 4, 1977, 384–26.[36] The only major opposition to the report came in the Senate where southern Republicans viewed the bill as being discriminatory against their region. In an interview with *Congressional Quarterly*, their spokesman, Senator Jesse Helms of North Carolina, stressed a point that is shared by many in the Sunbelt: that the Northeast has caused its own fiscal problems by providing excessive governmental assistance to the poor and unemployed and neglecting the needs of its business community.

> I see no reason why the rest of the country should maintain a chronic bailout of the Northeast because the political leaders of that area refuse to put their house in order. In fact, the greatest disfavor we can do the Northeast is to be overly generous with federal funds; this will merely postpone the day of reckoning.[37]

The Housing and Community Development Act of 1977 extended the CDBG program for three years and increased its authorization during that period to $12.4 billion. President Carter signed the bill into law on October 12, 1977.[38]

CONCLUSION: MANY QUESTIONS ARE LEFT UNANSWERED

In terms of federal assistance, the housing and community development bill, with the coalition's Lundine amendment included along with the dual formula of Secretary Harris (which had been successfully defended) increased the Snowbelt's share of funds by approximately $750 million. Although this result was a far cry from reversing the Snowbelt's $29.4 billion discrepancy between federal taxes collected and monies allocated, the coalition had proved that computer politics (the use of information to gather support for a given policy) could disrupt a subcommittee's standard operating procedures. Under normal circumstances, Hannaford and Patterson would not have had reason to appeal the Housing and Community Development Subcommittee's decision concerning the allocation of CDBG funds to the House floor. The coalition's use of computer politics successfully overrode the Northeastern representatives' natural tendency to logroll with their Sunbelt colleagues on the subcommittee. The coalition had also proved that it could overcome party and personal differences among its members that usually prevented the Northeastern states from voting as a bloc on the House floor. The defeat of the Hannaford amendment, however, did leave several questions unanswered concerning the coalition's real political strength. It was not the coalition, for example, that initiated the 1977 change in the 1974 needs formula. The Carter administration's dual formula was designed to accommodate the pressures asserted by an alliance of northern interest groups, suggesting the possibility that the coalition may have won on this particular issue because allied clientele interest groups—the U.S. Conference of Mayors, the National Association of Housing and Redevelopment Officials, and the National League of Cities—were already aware of, and prepared to fight for, the dual formula. In this regard, during the debate preceding the vote on the Hannaford amendment, Ashley indicated on the House floor that "every major interest group that is concerned with our cities. . . . support the bill as it has been presented to the Members of this House and they strenuously object to the adoption of the amendment that is under consideration."[39] The fact that the bill was also supported by both President Carter and the House leadership, of course, naturally aided the bill's chance for passage, as did the fact that the bill allocated extra funds to fifty-six congressional districts located outside the Snowbelt.

This single case study does not prove that the coalition's existence strongly and directly influenced its members' vote on the Hannaford amendment. There were many intervening variables (northern interest groups, House leadership, Carter administration, and Banking Committee support for the bill). But the activities of Lundine, Tsongas, and Harrington on behalf of the Lundine amendment and the president's dual formula do indicate that the coalition's general membership was provided, either personally or through "Dear Colleague" letters, with relevant political information that would otherwise have been denied them because they were not members of the House Banking Committee. Yet it is difficult to gauge what effect this information had on these members' decision to oppose the Hannaford amendment as a regional bloc since there would certainly have been a general recognition of the defects of the amendment vis-à-vis their districts even without the coalition's information. The fact that only 5 of 194 coalition members voting supported the Hannaford amendment, however, does suggest that at the very least, this information served to reinforce their presumably initial attitudes against the amendment. Furthermore, interviews with several coalition members indicate that the congressional members of the coalition who were not directly involved with the Housing and Community Development Task Force used the coalition's information resources on this issue as a voting cue. That is, they used it as a means of supporting their initial reactions to the bill with factual data to enable them to arrive at a reasoned voting decision. It is important to note once again that it was Shelly Amdur, not HUD or the Banking Committee's staff, who first realized that the administration's proposal adversely affected the small cities of the Northeast. It was this kind of political sensitivity to the needs of the coalition membership that initially caused the membership to use the coalition's informational resources as a voting cue and (as will be shown in other case studies) that reinforced the membership's confidence in the coalition's information as a voting cue.

The coalition's first legislative victory also served to publicize and extend the regional debate over federal assistance. Shortly after the passage of the Housing and Community Development Act of 1977, for example, *U.S. News & World Report* published an article concerning the coalition entitled "The Porkbarrel War Between the States."[40]

Given the series of articles published in the *National Journal* and other prestigious publications, it was clear that the coalition had successfully achieved its initial objective of publicizing its cause. As Paul Tsongas later stated in an interview: "The existence of the . . . Coalition has served to raise the consciousness of all decision-makers."[41]

The coalition's victory was not without drawbacks, however. The publicity generated by the victory tended to accentuate the conflict between the two regions. For example, the article in *U.S. News & World Report* began as follows:

More than a century after the great conflict between the Union and the Confederacy, the North and the South again are locked in a battle.
This war is taking place in Congress, fought with press releases and computer printouts, and accompanied by furious legislative maneuvering.[42]

This publicity not only raised the awareness of the Congress and the nation on the plight of the Northeast; it also increased the political stakes involved in the battle over the flow of federal assistance funds, thus presenting the coalition with a greater difficulty. Now Sunbelt representatives had to measure the regional debate not only in terms of dollars and cents but, as a public issue, in terms of electoral significance as well. In other words, Sunbelt congressmen were suddenly faced with the possible charge from their constituents that they were not adequately defending "their" federal funds.

Several Sunbelt representatives, led by California's Mark Hannaford and upset at the adoption of the Lundine amendment and the administration's dual formula, announced shortly after the House vote on H.R. 6655 that they would attempt to organize the House Sunbelt representatives along the same lines as the coalition's. They even turned to the Southern Growth Policies Board, an interstate research agency that was, in 1977, chaired by Governor George Busbee of Georgia and supported by the governments of thirteen southern states, to become an aggressive political information source, one to match the efforts of the Northeast–Midwest Research Institute. These congressmen ran into several difficulties in forming their Sunbelt coalition, however. Many Sunbelt representatives still preferred to maintain the low-profile, informal organizational approach to congressional legislation that had served their interests so well in the past, owing to their comparatively senior status on the important committees of the Congress. At that time, many did not see a need to alter their congressional behavior just because northeastern representatives had won one battle.

Harrington, however, perceiving that the publicity surrounding the coalition was helping to change the wait-and-see attitude of some of these southern and western representatives, began a campaign to soften the tone of the press coverage of the fight over federal assistance funds. The opening paragraph of a letter signed by Harrington and Frank Horton (R-N.Y.), cochairman of the coalition, that appeared in the New York Times on July 1, 1977, serves to illustrate this point.

There has been an increasing national awareness of regionalism—particularly as it has emerged in the so-called sunbelt-snowbelt controversy. As co-chairmen of the largest regional group in Congress—the Northeast–Midwest Economic Advancement Coalition—we are concerned about the direction and effect of that discussion. Unfortunately, many of the Coalition's recent actions have been interpreted by much of the press, and therefore perceived by the public, as a renewed War Between the States. Such attitudes can only be counterproductive and must be dispelled.[43]

In an effort to dispel these attitudes, nearly every piece of correspondence put out by the coalition in 1977 included a paragraph that attempted to discredit the notion that it was instigating sectional warfare. For example, in a letter to White House delegates to the National Conference on Balanced Growth, dated January 23, 1978, the coalition leaders wrote:

> . . . At the outset, we should say something about the Coalition. We are not in the business of fostering sectional warfare. No member of the Coalition has ever suggested that the economic problems of the South have been eradicated. Nor would they. The Coalition simply seeks to direct the Federal government's attention and assistance to the present areas of greatest need.[44]

Despite these efforts to blunt the combative tone of the press, the coalition's first legislative victory and the publicity it generated did cause the Sunbelt forces to take some initial countering organizational moves. For example, the Southern Growth Policies Board began to conduct some economic analyses of its own concerning the flow of federal dollars. When it addressed the question of which region deserved to receive more federal funds—the Snowbelt or the Sunbelt—its economic analyses indicated that the South, not the Northeast, was in greatest need. As a result, the Southern Growth Policies Board's analyses began to be used by Sunbelt legislators to counter the analyses conducted by the Northeast–Midwest Congressional Coalition's information resources. Thus, the Sunbelt/Snowbelt controversy—the economic and political debate over which region deserved a greater portion of federal economic assistance—was born. Ironically, the initial battleground of this sectional conflict, as this case study has indicated, was the federal needs formula of a federal assistance program, a needs formula that was created to take the federal government out of this area of controversy. Although state and local governments may now be less concerned about the influence of grantsmanship skills on their federal assistance funds, they have to be increasingly concerned about the determination of the formulas themselves.

CHAPTER THREE *The Sunbelt/Snowbelt*

Controversy: The Economic Debate and

Its Political Consequences

The object of this chapter is to describe the efforts undertaken by Democratic Representative Mark Hannaford of California to organize the representatives of the South and the West into a formal regional caucus and to determine why his efforts were not successful. I will argue that Hannaford's efforts met with difficulty because most of the Sunbelt representatives had become accustomed to a certain style of politics that had provided the Sunbelt with more than its share of the federal largesse for a generation. This style of politics—low-keyed and informal and based on logrolling among committees—was in direct contrast to the combative style of politics Hannaford proposed. In the eyes of many Sunbelt representatives, Hannaford's proposal to form a caucus was a counterproductive overreaction to the Northeast's housing and community development bill victory. They did not see, as Hannaford did, the need to change an older generation's style of politics just because the Northeast had scored a victory in a policy area in which northeastern forces had always fared well. They were still confident of their individual abilities to obtain a sufficient portion of federal funds to satisfy their own political needs through the traditional practice of logrolling. They remained firm in their conviction that it was not in their interest to abandon the norms of committee specialization and reciprocity.

This chapter also provides an outline of the role assumed by the Southern Growth Policies Board, a southern-state-supported research agency, in the Sunbelt/Snowbelt controversy. The board conducted its own economic analysis of the nation's economy and found that—contrary to the claims of the Northeast–Midwest Congressional Coalition, the *National Journal,* and several economic forecasting agencies—whereas the rate of southern economic growth had exceeded the growth rate in the northeastern states, the actual level of economic attainment in the South remained far below that of the Northeast. This, the board researchers believed, indicated that the flow of federal funds was not inequitable, as the northeasterners claimed, but was actually consistent with the liberal philosophy of providing governmental assistance to those areas in greatest economic need.

THE SUNBELT'S RESPONSE TO THE COALITION: HANNAFORD'S EFFORTS ARE REJECTED IN THE HOUSE

Mark Hannaford has been described as a bouncy, bantam-sized fighter,[1] not the type of person who was going to take the coalition's challenge to the Sunbelt's share of federal funds lying down. He had taken the housing and community development fight to the floor of the House and lost; but, if the coalition was going to continue to press for a larger share of federal funds, he was prepared to take whatever steps he believed necessary to stop it. As Hannaford said in an interview:

The Snowbelt region is just not being screwed as they say they are. I will admit that the circumstances of their older cities is a bit more dire than the Sunbelt cities, their problems may run deeper than ours, but I don't want to be screwed blue either and that is exactly what they [the Northeast–Midwest Congressional Coalition] are trying to do.[2]

Shortly after the Sunbelt's defeat on the formula revisions of the housing and community development bill of 1977, Hannaford decided to counter the coalition's organizational activities by organizing the congressional members of the Sunbelt along the same lines as Harrington had done in forming his coalition for the Northeast. After talking with several dozen of his Sunbelt colleagues, however, he found that only his closest friends were interested in joining his regional caucus. Most of the other Sunbelt legislators indicated that they did not believe they needed a formal caucus to protect their economic interests. While the northeastern legislators had won on the housing and community development issue, the North's victory had not cost the southerners in an absolute sense, since the program's funds were expanded. Besides, most Sunbelt legislators told Hannaford, the North had always done well in the determination of federal grant allocations, especially housing and community development funds. In their view, Hannaford, as a member of the Housing and Community Development Subcommittee, was too close to this single issue to realize that the Sunbelt was still doing quite well in the overall determination of federal resource allocations without a caucus. Caucus politics, they believed, was for those who wanted to circumvent the institutional power structure, not for those who were well situated within that power structure. While Hannaford lacked a committee or subcommittee chairmanship, most Sunbelt legislators did hold at least one subcommittee chairmanship. As already indicated, the coalition's initial attempt at redirecting federal resources dealt with a distributive domestic policy whose politics was dominated by actors at the subgovernment level, a level that was dominated on this specific issue by northeastern legislators. These Sunbelt representatives knew, however, that the Sunbelt was well represented in policy areas outside the urban area. In their view, the coalition had yet to prove that it could be a real threat to their dominance in these other areas. Until it proved to be a threat in areas such as defense-related expenditures, for example, the Sunbelt representatives, as a group, took the attitude that when you are dealt a strong hand in a game of poker—or politics—it is foolish to turn in the strong hand (logrolling politics) and pick up a new, untested one (caucus politics).

Another reason the congressional members of the Sunbelt were hesitant to formally organize into a regional caucus was that many felt that forming a Sunbelt caucus would be a form of "grandstanding"—an unacceptable act done simply to attract media attention to the organization's members and leaders and not to the problem at hand—the North's assault on the distribution of federal assistance funds. The fact that Hannaford was from a very marginal district did little to lessen this suspicion.

Aside from these general reservations concerning the formation of a caucus, many Sunbelt legislators did not see how such a caucus could work because, unlike the Northeast and Midwest, the Sunbelt did not possess a unifying theme (such as those unifying the Northeast—the recession and the adverse flow of federal funds) that could bind together the region's diverse ideological perspectives. As Arizona Democrat Morris Udall stated:

> They have all the issues. Their cities are decaying and they feel they are screwed on federal formulas. That's the kind of thing that can bring a Jacob Javits and a James Buckley together.[3]

Hannaford's home state of California exemplifies the difficulty of organizing the Sunbelt. In an economic sense, the core region of the American economy—as characterized by a high capacity for generating innovative change at high levels of development—has been the manufacturing belt of the Northeast and Midwest. Since World War II, however, a second, comparable core region has grown in southern and parts of northern California. Whereas California as a whole has grown and, in this respect, shares with many parts of the South the pains and fruits of this growth, other areas of California—such as the Los Angeles area that serves as a core region—share with the Northeast and Midwest the problems associated with environmental degradation and the management of a highly complex metropolitan society.[4] As a result, although California in the aggregate can be categorized as a growth state fully attuned to the expected ideals of a Sunbelt, growth-oriented coalition, because of the varying economic conditions within the state, any legislative policy espoused by such an organization would encounter much difficulty in attaining solid support in the state.

Once Hannaford recognized the futility of forming a Sunbelt caucus, he decided to drop the idea. Instead, he attempted to put together an informal communications network among his Sunbelt colleagues that would at least monitor the coalition's activities. At the same time, Hannaford decided to spend less time on the regional issue and more time on his own political future. As he remarked in an interview, with the wisdom of hindsight, "my constituents don't really understand what this is all about."[5]

Being from a marginal district, Hannaford believed that he could not enjoy the luxury of spending the time that would obviously be necessary to form a Sunbelt caucus. Thus, he would concentrate his efforts on constituent service in a more direct sense, through casework. Also, Hannaford knew that he was up for selection to the

Appropriations Committee, a post he had long coveted not only as a means of enhancing his position within the Congress but as a way of making his political presence in his district more secure. As Hannaford stated:

I, quite honestly, withheld my assault for political reasons. Frankly, I was expecting to be appointed to the Appropriations Committee this Congress. To get on the Committee you have got to avoid, at least, the opposition of the Leadership.

The Leadership, as you know, is composed of people, like many other things around here, who have a bias towards the Snowbelt.[6] I did not want to make waves of a sectional kind; if I did, then I probably would have lost the Appropriations appointment.[7]

Unfortunately for Hannaford, he never had the opportunity to be considered for the Appropriations Committee position because he was defeated for reelection in 1978 by Republican Daniel Lungren. According to Hannaford, his efforts to form the Sunbelt caucus were never discussed during the campaign and had little effect on the outcome of the election, though some of his financial backers approved of his efforts. As a result of his defeat, Sunbelt legislators lost the leading advocate of a Sunbelt caucus, and the northeastern representatives' unorthodox caucus style of politics thus remained set against the Sunbelt legislators' more traditional committee bargaining style of politics.

THE SUNBELT'S RESPONSE TO THE COALITION: THE STATES HEED GOVERNOR BUSBEE'S WARNINGS

The Coalition's efforts to redirect the flow of federal funds affect not only the political fortunes of congressmen but those of the various states' political leaders as well. It is the states and localities, after all, where the federal funds end up. If the amount of money that comes into a state in the form of a federal grant declines, local and state politicians are forced either to increase state and local taxes or to reduce services, neither of which is politically popular. If the federal government cuts back on the amount of federal contracts awarded in a given state or locality, then unemployment will likely increase in that state or locality, which is certain to be viewed as a political liability. For these reasons, as one would expect, state and local leaders from the Sunbelt opposed the efforts of the North-east–Midwest Congressional Coalition to redirect federal funds away from their region. At first, though, Sunbelt politicians at the state and local levels did not take the coalition's efforts seriously. Governor Reuben Askew of Florida indicated in the introduction to the Southern Growth Policies Board's publication, *The Economics of Southern Growth*, published shortly after the formation of the Northeast–Midwest Congressional Coalition, that the coalition was nothing more than a "paper" organization and had little real political clout with regard to the dispersal of federal funds.

The situation in the Northeast is still in flux. But a broad-ranging regional approach by the states seems to be emerging. As of early 1977, several groups have been formed in the Northeast. These include the Coalition of Northeastern Governors (CONEG), the Coalition of State Legislators, and a "paper" organization in the Congress—the Northeast–Midwest Economic Advancement Coalition which was created in 1976 to mobilize political resources to reverse economic decline in the Northeast.[8]

The coalition's success in gaining national media attention for its cause through its efforts to redirect housing and community development funds quickly convinced state and local Sunbelt leaders that the coalition was much more than a paper organization and that it warranted a response. Like their political compatriots in the Congress, however, state and local politicians of the South and West experienced difficulties in coordinating their response to the coalition's efforts, which they knew were being funded, at least in part, by various state governments of the Northeast—which were underwriting the expenses of the Northeast–Midwest Research Institute.

These difficulties were caused by a number of interrelated factors. Because categorical grants were relied upon as the main method of directing the flow of federal funds during the 1960s, state and local political leaders of the South and West had little reason to join forces to secure federal funds. They were forced to compete head to head for federal funds. Naturally, this background of political competition was not a help in the formation of political alliances. Although each region had established its own regional Governors' conference to facilitate regional economic cooperation within the

South and West, respectively, neither group devoted much attention to fostering cooperation between the regions. The only time the state political leaders of the South and West met on a regular basis was at the annual National Governors' Conference. Also, in the past, western and southern politicians had rarely communicated with one another, since there had been little incentive for them to do so.

After the coalition had emerged as a political threat, one might think that lines of communication would have been established among the local and state leaders of the South and West, but such was not the case. Each region reacted to the coalition's efforts separately and differently. Why this occurred has a lot to do with the differing economic problems faced by the West and the South. Excluding California, the west is just beginning to grow economically, whereas most of the South and the noncore regions of California are in the midst of growth, and the core regions of California are beginning to experience decline. Thus, the Sunbelt is not nearly as economically homogeneous as the Snowbelt, which in an economic sense is almost entirely mature. As a result, its political leaders at the federal, state, and local levels share a common concern for their region's economic future to a greater degree than the Sunbelt politicians. Many rural western states like Wyoming, for example, have very little in common with the more industrialized Sunbelt states on the issue of the determination of federal funds. They receive very few of these funds on a percentage basis because of their relatively low state populations.

The western states reacted to the coalition's housing and community development bill victory in August 1977 when the Western Governors' Conference voted to merge a number of western state organizations into a regional group called Westpo (Western Policy Office). Westpo's primary function was to further promote regional cooperation within the western states so that they would be better able to manage their region's growth problems. Its secondary function, reflecting the West's lesser concern with federal assistance programs, was to monitor federal legislation's effect on the western region.[9] When the Southern Governors' Conference took place, on the other hand, a regional group was already in place to promote regional cooperation in the management of growth problems, the

Southern Growth Policies Board, which was formed in 1970 and was based in Research Triangle Park, North Carolina. In response to the coalition's housing and community development victory, Governor George Busbee (D-Ga.), then chairman of the Southern Growth Policies Board, called upon southern states to increase the amount of money provided to the board ($258,000 in 1976) so that it could expand its senior research staff of four and open a Washington office dedicated to studying the impact of federal legislation and formulas on the flow of federal assistance dollars to the South. As Governor Busbee made the request for additional monetary support, he stated:

We in the South are going to be eaten alive if we don't wake up and react.
. . . [Addressing the other Governors] you can pay the Southern Growth Policies Board now, or the North later. [10]

Additional funds were generated from four southern states (Georgia, North Carolina, Oklahoma, and Florida), and on August 1, 1977, the board opened a Washington office for the first time. It was staffed by three permanent researchers, a secretary, and a scholar in residence who was selected to serve in the Washington office on a yearly basis from among the South's leading universities. [11] The Washington office complemented the research efforts of the four permanent researchers (and support staff) located at the board's headquarters. Research in the North Carolina office would continue to focus on attaining mutual intraregional economic cooperation among the southern states; research at the Washington office would focus on preventing the federal government from hindering the South's continued economic growth. According to Dr. Bernard Weinstein, scholar in residence at the board's Washington office in 1978:

The Southern Growth Policies Board had been lethargic in dealing with federal policy until 1977 because the Board was doing what it was set up to do, dealing with the management of growth and planning for the continuation of growth in the South.
. . . The establishment of the Washington office was a big change in the Board's modus operandi. Now we have Dave Peterson who can play the formula game as well as, or even better than, anyone working for the Northeast. The North, however, had a tremendous jump and we are still

basically a research and information disseminating organization. We are not even allowed to lobby under our IRS classification.[12]

While the establishment of the board's Washington office increased the political research capabilities of the South as well as of the Sunbelt as a whole, as Weinstein indicated, the Northeast–Midwest Congressional Coalition's combination of its political research capabilities with its caucus function made its political organizational capabilities far superior to those of the Southern Growth Policies Board or of Westpo. The coalition had not only assembled a competent research staff but had also set up an informal, but effective congressional communications network through its task forces and through issuance of its "Dear Colleague" letters. The board, in contrast, because of its IRS classification, was not even allowed to call a meeting of southern congressmen in order to present a case either for or against any policy action. Nor was the board allowed to send any of its issue papers directly to any congressional member or to testify before any committee holding hearings on an issue. Instead, it was forced to send its issue papers to the governors of the South, who as board members were entitled to copies and who were, in turn, free to send the issue papers to anyone they pleased. As a result, researchers at the board's Washington office were never certain who would receive their work or when. Consequently, the board's efforts at influencing the direction of federal policy decisions were obviously curtailed, and one could sense an air of jealous frustration when speaking to its staff about the coalition's access to its congressional membership.

THE SUNBELT/SNOWBELT CONTROVERSY: THE BATTLE IS JOINED

While the Sunbelt's organizational abilities, in a formal caucus or lobbying sense, were not particularly heightened by the establishment of Westpo or of the Southern Growth Policies Board's Washington office, the board did provide an immeasurable assistance to the Sunbelt's political cause. Its Washington office, in conjunction with the North Carolina office, did this by attacking the legitimacy of the North's claim that the Snowbelt had replaced the

Sunbelt as the nation's most economically depressed area and therefore was deserving of more federal funds. The first step taken by the board in this regard actually originated from the board's North Carolina office shortly after the Washington office was established. David Gillespie, director of the board's intergovernmental affairs, sent a written reply to the *National Journal* concerning its two articles (June 26, 1976, and July 2, 1977) indicating that a massive flow of federal funds existed from the Northeast and Midwest to the South and West. His letter was subsequently printed, in part, in the *National Journal* on August 27, 1977. Gillespie indicated that the statistical data the *National Journal* used were highly questionable. He pointed out that the authors of the two articles could not decide how to allocate payments on the federal debt to each of the states so they omitted them; that the authors admitted that they had problems in determining where the money paid to defense contractors actually went, since much of the work specified in the contracts awarded was done by subcontractors; and that, as conceded by the authors, the Community Services Administration and the Treasury Department were unable to reconcile their own figures on the distribution of funds.[13]

With this reply to the *National Journal*, the Southern Growth Policies Board had taken its first step into the Sunbelt/Snowbelt controversy. The political debate that had already begun was carried on in the halls of the Congress between the representatives of the Northeast and the rest of the nation (primarily the southerners who had more at stake than the western representatives), but the economic debate that served as the intellectual underpinning of the political debate was destined to be conducted between the Southern Growth Policies Board and the staff of the Northeast–Midwest Congressional Coalition and its Research Institute. The political debate would determine regional winners and losers. The economic debate would attempt to ascertain which region actually held a greater "right" to the federal funds rather than which had the greater political strength to get them.

The first major step for the Southern Growth Policies Board in this economic debate was the publication of *The Economics of Southern Growth*.[14] While this series of economic studies of the current status of southern growth was begun before the North-

east–Midwest Congressional Coalition's formation and was meant
to ascertain exactly what economic problems faced the South on
an intraregional basis, the coalition's activities and the publication
of the two *National Journal* articles convinced the board's leaders
that it had to address its economic problems not only with intraregional solutions in mind but with interregional ones as well. For
this reason, as the concluding chapter in this series of economic
reports, E. Blaine Liner, executive director of the Southern Growth
Policies Board, included a study conducted by two visiting economists at the Commerce Department's Economic Development Administration, D. L. Jusenius and L. C. Ledebur. This study, entitled
"A Myth in the Making," was widely reprinted. It compared the
data on economic growth rates in the southern states with the economic status of the northeastern states.[15] They conceded that most
of what the *National Journal* and the Northeast–Midwest Congressional Coalition were saying about the South's economic growth
was true. They also argued, however, that while the South's rate
of economic growth had exceeded the economic growth rate of the
Northeast, the South still fell far below the Northeast's level of
economic attainment. Since the implicit and often explicit goal of
public policy, they argued, is to attempt to redress the imbalance
in the distribution of economic welfare among the regions, the
South should continue to receive a greater portion of federal economic assistance than the Northeast.[16]

Jusenius and Ledebur examined seven indexes of economic well-
being before concluding that the South's economy was still weaker
than that of the Northeast: population, per capita income, distribution of income, poverty, personal wealth, unemployment, and
employment. In each case, the South's economic outlook had improved compared with the Northeast's during the previous two decades but still fell short of the level of economic attainment in the
Northeast. Per capita income, for example—the most often used
determinant of need in federal assistance allocation formulas—indicated that in 1975 the South was in a weaker economic condition
than the Northeast. Every state in the South fell below the national
average per capita income level in 1975; only two Northeastern
states, Wisconsin and Indiana, were below the average.[17] Even after
adjusting the per capita income figures by a cost-of-living differ-

ential, which northerners argued made this index a more accurate determinant of economic need, Jusenius and Ledebur found that the northeastern states still fared much better than the southern states. In the Northeast, only four states fell below the national average per capita income level when adjusted for cost-of-living differentials: Wisconsin, Indiana, Massachusetts, and Rhode Island. In the South, in contrast, only three states rose above the national per capita income level after adjusting for cost-of-living differentials: Texas, Florida, and Virginia. The authors concluded, therefore, that:

adjusting per capita income figures for cost-of-living differentials does not change significantly the overall picture of relative regional well-being. Adjusted per capita incomes in the North are generally higher than those in the South.[18]

Jusenius' and Ledebur's analyses of the other economic indexes also indicated that the South was still in a weaker economic state than the Northeast. They argued that the South had a more unequal distribution of income than the Northeast, contained the nation's highest levels of poverty, had only 22.6 percent of those Americans who enjoyed assets of $60,000 or more (48.5 percent resided in the Northeast), and had an unemployment rate only 1 percentage point lower than the Northeast during the recession (despite the fact that the Northeast's economy was supposedly harder hit by the recession because of its manufacturing-dominated economy).[19]

As a by-product of the rapid economic growth of the South, Jusenius and Ledebur conceded that the northeasterners were correct in claiming that the South's population growth rate was much higher than the Northeast's between 1970 and 1975. However, Jusenius and Ledebur argued that while nearly half of that increase was the result of northern migration into the South, Florida alone accounted for nearly 30 percent of the South's population increase.[20] And whereas this was the first time in American history that more people moved from the Northeast to the South rather than the reverse,[21] this net immigration southward was potentially a short-term response to the recent cyclical downturn in the economy of the industrialized Northeast rather than a long-term trend that would continue in the future.[22] Also, although northerners were moving into the South, this did not indicate that the South was draining people and jobs from the North. The idea that the South was luring northern businesses to the South and that this was the cause of the southern migration and of the higher unemployment levels in the Northeast was a myth. More than 50 percent of the employment losses in the Northeast during the recessionary period were attributable to the death of firms located in the Snowbelt, whereas during this period only 1.5 percent of the Snowbelt's unemployment was attributable to the outmigration of firms.[23] Sixty-four percent of the employment growth in the South, on the other hand, was caused by the expansion of existing firms in the South; only 1.66 percent resulted from the immigration of northeastern firms.[24]

ECONOMIC REALITIES: LET THE SNOWBELT DIE?

Many Sunbelt economists argue that by focusing only on federal expenditures the Snowbelt has really masked a much larger and more complex economic issue. Many federal policies—such as tariffs, labor laws, banking, transportation, and energy regulations— affect interregional economic prosperity. Also, even larger economic forces are at work that must be considered. As Bernard Weinstein, 1978 scholar in residence at the Southern Growth Policies Board's Washington office, explained:

> You have to look at the entire international economic system to really understand why this Sunbelt/Snowbelt controversy has come about. We have, through federal policy, created an open economy where we must compete not only on an interstate level, but an international level as well. The industrial base of the North is so inefficient, and now that they must compete with other industries in other regions of the country and abroad, they simply cannot handle it.
> . . . The Northeast, having industrialized first, is dominated by site-specific industries, particularly industries producing durable goods. In this sense, the industrial base of the Northeast has become obsolete. For example, New York's growth industries are in communications, advertising, finance, and the arts. Its population, however, is for the most part poor and unskilled, totally unsuited for these growth industries. Since New York's industrial base in durable goods can no longer compete in the free market system, New York really does not have an economic base to support

its population and no one can develop this economic base for them without a huge expenditure of federal funds.

New York is not alone in the Northeast. . . . I think of places like Newark [N.J.], Buffalo, parts of Cleveland. There are a lot of people living there, but there is no economic base to support them. Although given the current state of politics it is probably not feasible, it would be a whole lot easier and cost efficient in the long run to find jobs for the people of these areas elsewhere than to bring jobs into those areas.[25]

These sentiments were echoed by the 1980 *Report of the President's Commission for a National Agenda for the Eighties.*[26] The report indicated that the relative decline of the older cities of the Northeast was part of a larger and irreversible economic dynamic. The report went on to argue that the primary responsibility of the federal government was to assist people directly, not indirectly by assisting places (or regions). The best means of assisting people, it was argued, was to create policies that would help people in their efforts to migrate to where jobs were (the Sunbelt) rather than to fruitlessly attempt to bring jobs to the economically unattractive Northeast. In reference to the older cities of the Northeast, the report noted:

faced with declining population and economic vitality [older cities of the Northeast] stand as "withering monuments to the industrial age."[27]

THE WASHINGTON OFFICE: FIGHTING FIRE WITH FIRE

The Jusenius and Ledebur article established in print the Southern Growth Policies Board's opposition to the Snowbelt's claims of economic calamity. The President's Commission for a National Agenda for the Eighties agreed, indicating in 1980 that:

. . . With regard to the . . . Sunbelt/Snowbelt sectional competition, the North remains dominant on all measures of economic performance and has lost ground to the South in relative terms only.[28]

The function of the board's Washington office was to alert southern political leaders of the economic shortcomings of the coalition's arguments and to aid, in any feasible way, in preventing the coalition from achieving its goal of redirecting federal funds to the

Snowbelt. In this regard, Dr. David Peterson, an economic consultant, was hired to monitor the legislative process and keep the board's member states informed of any changes in federal grant formulas that would penalize the South. Peterson soon discovered that the Northeast–Midwest Congressional Coalition was supporting changes in the allocation of funds to be distributed under Title 1 of the Elementary and Secondary Education Act of 1978. Governor George Busbee, board chairman, subsequently met with several of the South's congressional leaders on the subject, including Carl D. Perkins (D-Ky.), chairman of the House Education and Labor Committee. Representative Perkins was reportedly very receptive to the governor's request to oppose any changes that would hurt the South as a region, setting the stage for the first confrontation between the coalition's computer politics and the Sunbelt's more traditional logrolling politics.

CONCLUSION: "REAL" NEED, A STATISTICIAN'S NIGHTMARE

Jusenius' and Ledebur's article, as already mentioned, marked a turning point in the Sunbelt/Snowbelt controversy. The Northeast–Midwest Congressional Coalition would have to face not only a political challenge to their efforts but an intellectual challenge as well. In this regard, it is interesting to note that both the coalition's and the board's economists examined the same set of economic statistics, yet came to very different conclusions concerning the relative economic strength of their respective regions and their "right" to federal assistance funds. The northern economists examined the economic data from the perspective of the prevention of further decline, whereas the Board's economists examined the economic data from the perspective of the protection of ongoing growth (evident even in the board's name). These divergent perspectives account for the different indexes used by the two sides in their examination of their region's relative economic well-being. The southern economists and representatives accentuate the fact that its per capita income level is still well below the national average and that the Northeast's is still well above the national average.

Northern economists and representatives, for their part, stress the fact that when one takes into consideration a cost-of-living differential, the "real" adjusted per capita income level of the Northeast drops below the national average and the South's and the West's rise above the national average.[29]

The importance of this debate over economic strength and over which economic indexes are better indications of need lies in the fact that the formulas used to allocate federal funds in the various grant programs were constructed to provide an objective criterion of need—so that federal assistance funds would go only to those areas of greatest economic need. The coalition, however, was arguing that the current formulas' use of per capita income as a measure of economic health—40 percent of all grant dollars were allocated to state and local governments according to the per capita measure in 1977—was inadequate because it did not take into consideration geographic variations in cost of living. They argued that because per capita income does not measure real purchasing power, it does not measure real economic need. The Sunbelt argued, conversely, that per capita income was an adequate measure of economic need. Politically, the resolution of this argument has great consequences. As Table 3.1 indicates, Massachusetts, like most other coalition states, would receive a greater amount of federal funds if cost-of-living differentials were used in the determination of economic need while most other states would receive less (1 represents the least economic need, 50 the most economic need). It is amusing that, whereas northern advocates found that cost-of-living differentials cause the per capita income measure of economic well-being to indicate that the South was economically better off than the Northeast, Jusenius and Ledebur also examined the results of adjusting per capita income for cost-of-living differentials, yet still found that the South was the less well off region. The reason for this difference was that Jusenius and Ledebur adjusted per capita income only for cost-of-living differences, whereas the Northeast–Midwest Congressional Coalition's economists also adjusted per capita income by state and local taxes as well as by federal transfer of payments. Both sets of economists examined the same statistical data, yet came up with different conclusions about which region was better or worse off because they began their studies with

Table 3.1   Comparison of Per Capita Income, By State

	Column I			Column II	
	Rank	Unadjusted Per Capita Income—1975		Rank	Adjusted Per Capita Income Minus Taxes & Transfer Payments & Cost-of-Living—1975
United States	—	$5903	United States	—	$3008
Alaska	1	9535	Alaska	1	4569
Connecticut	2	6965	Wyoming	2	3886
Illinois	3	6792	Delaware	3	3834
Delaware	4	6745	Nevada	4	3604
New Jersey	5	6716	Nebraska	5	3585
Nevada	6	6673	Texas	6	3568
Hawaii	7	6658	Illinois	7	3563
California	8	6596	Colorado	8	3536
New York	9	6564	Iowa	9	3504
Maryland	10	6459	North Dakota	10	3498
Washington	11	6284	Connecticut	11	3493
Michigan	12	6169	Kansas	12	3459
Nebraska	13	6106	Washington	13	3419
Wyoming	14	6079	Maryland	14	3336

15	Iowa	6076
16	Massachusetts	6066
17	Kansas	6046
18	Colorado	5998
19	Pennsylvania	5941
20	Rhode Island	5888
21	Ohio	5832
22	Minnesota	5817
23	Virginia	5786
24	North Dakota	5781
25	Oregon	5752
26	Wisconsin	5674
27	Indiana	5656
28	Florida	5640
29	Texas	5635
30	Missouri	5490
31	Montana	5433
32	New Hampshire	5375
33	Arizona	5316
34	Oklahoma	5259
35	Idaho	5177
36	Georgia	5072
37	Vermont	4962
38	West Virginia	4946
39	Utah	4938
40	South Dakota	4924
41	North Carolina	4922

15	Virginia	3320
16	California	3215
17	Ohio	3209
18	Montana	3188
19	Idaho	3175
20	New Jersey	3162
21	Michigan	3137
22	Oklahoma	3124
23	Indiana	3070
24	Florida	3044
25	Oregon	3038
26	Missouri	2969
27	Georgia	2965
28	Minnesota	2959
29	Pennsylvania	2952
30	North Carolina	2929
31	Hawaii	2913
32	Tennessee	2895
33	Louisiana	2863
34	Wisconsin	2853
35	Utah	2842
36	South Dakota	2821
37	Kentucky	2812
38	Arkansas	2757
39	New York	2756
40	South Carolina	2739
41	Alabama	2728

Table 3.1　(Continued)

	Column I		Column II	
	Unadjusted Per Capita Income—1975		Adjusted Per Capita Income Minus Taxes & Transfer Payments & Cost-of-Living—1975	
	Rank		Rank	
Tennessee	42	4909	West Virginia	42	2717
Louisiana	43	4895	New Mexico	43	2678
Kentucky	44	4886	Arizona	44	2662
Maine	45	4785	New Hampshire	45	2653
New Mexico	46	4768	Mississippi	46	2600
Alabama	47	4648	Rhode Island	47	2591
Arkansas	48	4617	Massachusetts	48	2395
South Carolina	49	4615	Vermont	49	2297
Mississippi	50	4079	Maine	50	2231

SOURCE: Bureau of Economic Analysis, Department of Commerce, Survey of Current Business, May 1977, pp. 16–18.

different assumptions concerning what constituted the cost-of-living differential. Since the southern economists viewed the cost-of-living differential from the perspective of the protection of ongoing growth, they were more conservative in their definition of what constituted the differential. Northern economists, as individuals interested in preventing further decline, were more liberal in their definition of the cost-of-living differential. Southerners get very upset when northerners include state and local taxes as part of the cost-of-living differential. They insist that these kinds of adjustments, if taken into account, would result in the federal government's subsidizing of state and local government services in high-income, high-tax states and that it would avoid addressing the real issue of the role played by "overdeveloped" northern public sectors that inhibit business growth.[30]

While this intellectual debate about which economic index actually constituted an "objective" criterion of "real" need continued during 1977, the political debate over the distribution of federal funds resumed in the Congress in 1978 when the Elementary and Secondary Education Act of 1974 was considered for renewal. This would be the first time that the coalition's efforts to revise a federal allocation formula would be in direct opposition to the wishes of a committee chairman. Thus, the resolution of this conflict would provide a better indication of the coalition's political strength than the housing and community development issue had.

CHAPTER FOUR *The Elementary and*

Secondary Education Act of 1978:

Caucus versus Committee Politics

Following the Northeast–Midwest Congressional Coalition's housing and community development victory, the core, activist membership of the coalition—those who participate in coalition activities, either by contributing clerk-hire fees or by joining one of its
task forces—began to expand. From the initial group of about 25
in September, 1976, 60 of the 203 coalition members had joined at
least one of its seven task forces that were in existence in January
1978. Also, 50 of these activists provided a portion of their clerk-
hire fees to support the coalition's operating expenses. While most
of the Northeast's congressional delegation remained spectators—
members who appreciate the politically useful information provided
by the coalition but are not significantly motivated to join one of
its task forces or to provide a portion of their staff budgets to support
its activities—the coalition had attracted a sizable following who
were willing to donate some of their most valued resources, time
and money, to the cause.

Although the sixty activists defy most attempts at categorization,
they were somewhat less senior than other northeastern congressmen[1] and thus held fewer committee positions of power than their
northeastern colleagues; therefore, they had less of a stake in the
traditional committee bargaining style of politics. For example, only
fifteen of the fifty-nine coalition members who held committee
or subcommittee chairmanships during the Ninety-fifth Congress
joined any of the coalition's task forces. Eight of the chairmen
joined task forces that had nothing to do with their subcommittee's
jurisdiction. This fact indicates that they became active in the coalition's efforts out of the altruistic belief in the coalition's cause
and/or in order to obtain political clout in areas in which they were

prevented from having such clout by the jurisdictional limitations of the committee structure. It also indicates that they may actually have wished to put some distance between the coalition's combative style of politics and their own personal, logrolling relationships in their own subcommittees. Generally speaking, the other forty-five activists were the have-nots of the congressional power structure. Many believed in the regional cause of the coalition, but many were also looking for a means of having an impact upon legislation their junior status prevented them from having, both within their own committee's jurisdiction and within the substantive policy areas of other committees.

It is also interesting to note that although the coalition's activists had less seniority than other northeastern representatives, they did not differ significantly from them in terms of electoral marginality (vulnerability to defeat).[2] Most of the activists, like most of the spectators, held safe seats. For the most part, those from very marginal districts viewed other activities with a higher priority. As Mark Hannaford and Michael Harrington discovered, participation in caucus activities may enhance one's power position within the Congress, but it does not necessarily enhance one's electoral position. For one thing, caucus activities consume energies that otherwise might be devoted to casework; for another, joining a caucus allows for few electoral advantages in that individual credit for a caucus-won formula change is much more difficult to identify in the electorate's eyes than some more visible physical edifice that can be obtained by bargaining, that is, logrolling, within the committee structure. This is not to say that there are no electoral rewards associated with caucus activities. Several active coalition members regularly highlight their coalition activities in their newsletters to constituents. What matters is that most constituents are neither aware of, nor even care about, how a congressman achieves results; they are interested only in results. Most of the coalition's activists, however, were not in a position to use logrolling as a means to attain a sufficient portion of the federal largesse for their districts to satisfy their political (or personal) desires. Caucus activity, for these members, provided a means of fulfilling what Richard Fenno has noted is one of their basic desires: to develop what they view as good public policy.[3] If their name made the papers because of their association with the coalition, that was fine, but that is not why they joined the coalition.

As the core, activist group enlarged, coalition leaders Harrington and Moriarty discovered that they had a much easier time finding individuals willing to participate in their task forces. The Housing and Community Development Task Force for example, was primarily a two-man show (Tsongas and Lundine). As the coalition prepared to address itself to the next major grant program to be considered on the Hill, the elementary and secondary education bill, sixteen coalition members volunteered to join the coalition's Education Task Force.[4] This was one of the first indications that the coalition was beginning to convince the representatives of the Northeast–Midwest region that issues that were normally considered noncontroversial (or distributive) because there were no losers were actually redistributive when viewed from the geographic perspective.

1974, PRECURSOR OF 1978

The Elementary and Secondary Education Act, as enacted in 1965, was created to provide compensatory education for the disadvantaged and to provide federal aid to the handicapped. The act also assimilated the impact aid program that had been in existence since 1940. The impact aid program provides federal economic assistance to school districts that have large numbers of children whose parents work and/or live on nontaxable federal property.

The bulk of the funds of the Elementary and Secondary Education Act were under Title 1, Educational Aid to the Disadvantaged. These monies were distributed to the various counties of the United States through a formula that was computed according to an estimate of the number of eligible children multiplied by a payment rate per child. The number of eligible children was determined by the number of children aged five to seventeen (inclusive) whose families' income was beneath the poverty line as determined by the Census Bureau ($2,000 in 1960); the total number of children in families with Aid to Families with Dependent Children (AFDC) payments of $2,000 or more; and the number of institutionalized, neglected, delinquent and foster children supported by public funds. The payment rate was set at 50 percent of the average state or national expenditure per pupil, whichever was greater. Poverty was used as the essential criterion for determining funding because of the prevailing belief that children in poverty-stricken (or AFDC-supported) families were in greater need of remedial education than other children.

Since the AFDC program was relatively small in the early 1960s and the median income of the southern states was lower than that of the northern states, the formula favored southern counties over northern counties. By the late 1960s, however, the program grew in terms of both numbers and payment rates. Because most AFDC recipients were concentrated in the metropolitan centers of the Northeast, the number of AFDC Title 1 eligible children grew in the Northeast. Between 1966 and 1974, when the act was to be reconsidered, the number of children eligible under the AFDC portion of the formula had grown from 10.5 percent of the total Title 1 eligible population to 53.4 percent.[5] As a result, Title 1 funds shifted away from southern counties and toward the Northeast.

Despite the fact that most of the members of the House Education and Labor Committee were from the Northeast (twenty-three of thirty-seven members), the committee voted 31–4 on February 4, 1974, to revise the formula to increase the South's share of Title 1 funds. Pushed by the chairman of the committee, Carl Perkins (D-Ky.), the committee reduced to two thirds the number of children counted as eligible from those families whose AFDC payments brought their incomes above the poverty level.[6]

As one might suspect, the 31–4 vote accepting this revision masks the real fight that occurred within the committee.[7] Six northeastern congressmen who voted for the revision on the final committee vote did so only to give the committee's final decision an air of unanimity (a common practice on the Hill to promote harmony within the committee and to facilitate logrolling between committees by making the decisions reached seem to be noncontroversial). During the markup session, however, these six northeastern congressmen and the four who refused to vote for the formula revision on the final vote charged that the formula change favored rural at the expense of urbanized states because the revision unjustly excluded a cost-of-living criteria in defining poverty.[8] Despite their protests, the revisions were easily adopted because Perkins, as committee chairman, was able to use his position to convince many northeastern congressmen to support his position through quid pro quos.

The elementary and secondary education bill, with its revised formula, was adopted by the House on March 27, 1974, 380–26.[9] The previous day, however, Peter Peyser (D-N.Y.), a member of the Education and Labor Committee, introduced two amendments that would have increased Title 1 funds for New York and several other northeastern states. In deference to the Education and Labor Committee's solid 31–4 vote, plus the feeling of many members that the amendments would benefit only New York (i.e., without the coalition there was no reliable evidence to prove this not to be the case), Peyser's amendments failed, 87–326 and 17–73 on a standing vote.[10]

With action on the bill completed on the House side, the Senate Labor and Public Welfare Committee, chaired by Harrison Williams, Jr. (D-N.J.), reported its version of the bill for Senate floor action. The Senate bill, unlike the House bill, retained the 1965 formula for distributing Title 1 funds, including the full count of AFDC children. The committee reasoned that:

. . . High welfare payments to a great extent reflect high costs of living in certain regions of the country or within certain states, [like the chairman's state of New Jersey] rather than any ability to pay.[11]

When the bill reached the Senate floor, however, John McClellan (D-Ark.) offered an amendment to the bill that would have substituted the House version of the bill for the Senate's. The Senate adopted the McClellan amendment, 56–36. Thirty-two of the 36 opposing votes were cast by Snowbelt senators.[12]

On May 20, 1974, the Senate adopted its version of the Elementary and Secondary Education bill, 81–5.[13] Conference action on the bill, despite its identical wording concerning Title 1 funds, was delayed because of the inability of the conferees to resolve their differences over the two bill's differing provisions concerning busing. Once this problem was resolved, the House and the Senate adopted the conference report, 323–83 and 81–15, respectively, and President Ford signed the $25.2 billion, four-year extension of the Elementary and Secondary Education Act on August 21, 1974.[14]

THE SUNBELT AND SNOWBELT FORCES PREPARE FOR BATTLE

As mandated by the Elementary and Secondary Education Act of 1974, the National Institute of Education studied the regional distribution of Title 1 funds for fiscal 1977. The study indicated that the Northeast states received 22.9 percent of the program's funds, the North Central states 22.2 percent, the states of the South 39.9 percent, and the states of the West 14.9 percent. The study noted, however, that if AFDC-eligible children had not been included in the formula, the regional distribution would have been more heavily skewed toward the South. The study indicated that approximately 75 percent of AFDC children lived in five states: New York, Michigan, California, Illinois, and Pennsylvania.[15]

Because of the enactment of the formula revisions in the Housing and Community Development Act, David Peterson, the Southern Growth Policies Board's Washington-based consultant, began to examine the Elementary and Secondary Education Act. He was aware of the National Institute of Education's study and knew that the representatives of the five states with high concentrations of AFDC-eligible children would be interested in revising the current program's counting of only two thirds of AFDC-eligible children.

On December 13, 1977, the board released a position paper prepared by Peterson concerning the Elementary and Secondary Education Act, the board's first position paper of the Ninety-fifth Congress. The paper outlined the negative impact that several changes in the program's needs formula would have on the South's share of Title 1's funds.[16] The paper was sent to each of the board's member states' governors who, in turn, sent the paper to their respective federal liaison offices in Washington and to their state senators and representatives.

On February 28, 1978, in a message to the Congress, President Carter introduced his elementary and secondary education proposal. While the Carter administration sought a $644 million increase in Title 1 funds over the fiscal 1978 level of $1.7 billion, the Appropriations Committee had traditionally allocated only one half of the authorization level sought. Because the national inflation rate exceeded 10 percent, the Carter administration was actually offering a very minimal increase in Title 1 expenditures. Since it was known that the chairman of the House Education and Labor Committee opposed any changes in the formula and the National Education Association did not indicate any desire to see the formula changed, the Carter administration did not propose any changes in Title 1's formula.

The Northeast–Midwest Congressional Coalition, however, was not pleased with the regional distribution of Title 1's funds. On March 6, 1978, Dr. John Martin, a Congressional Science Fellow serving a postdoctoral fellowship in the office of representative James Jeffords (R-Vt.), a member new to the House Committee on Education and Labor, released a study of the Elementary and Secondary Act that had been undertaken at Jefford's and Thomas Cochran's request. Jeffords would later become chairman of the Northeast–Midwest Congressional Coalition's Education Task Force, and Thomas Cochran was the director of the Northeast–Midwest Research Institute. Although Martin was unaware of the Southern Growth Policies Board's paper, his study also examined the policy effects of several proposed changes, including the ones examined by Peterson. In stark contrast to the conclusions of Peterson's paper, Martin's study advocated nearly all the proposed changes in the program's formulas that the board's paper rejected, thus setting the stage for another regional battle over the distribution of federal assistance funds.

Reviewing the effect of the formula revisions adopted in 1974, John Martin's report for the coalition concluded:

> The 1974 ESEA Title 1 formula for grants to school systems relies on 1970 Census data, an inaccurate concept of poverty, and a deliberately incomplete count of AFDC recipients to determine the number of children eligible for services. Because these factors are used, the formula does not direct funds to many areas of great need, including the industrialized states of the Northeast and Midwest.
>
> . . . The questions which have been raised about continued reliance on the current formulas are serious; direct Congressional investigation and consideration of alternatives is now necessary. By subjecting all available alternatives to the light of Congressional debate and attention, an equitable formula can be constructed. Such an alternative might take into consideration any of these alternatives:
>
> · update the population estimate
> · define poverty to account for cost-of-living differences

· use full AFDC-eligibility count
· increase the ceiling on the cost factor
· concentrate funds in areas of great need
· remove the poverty basis of the program entirely.[17]

The board's paper authored by David Peterson, however, contended that many of these alternatives were not desirable. For example, Peterson argued that updating the present population estimate of poverty according to the 1975 Survey of Income and Education (SIE) produced by the Census Bureau would cost the seventeen southern states $104 million in Title 1 funds.[18] Also, the paper claimed that:

the timing of this survey [SIE] corresponded with the 1975 recession in the Northeast, and some contend that it exaggerates the poverty level situation in the Northern industrial states.

Some have also argued that in the future, this problem [of outdated data] will be solved as the census will be every five years. They contend that since the next census is only a couple of years away, the allocation process should not be adjusted on the basis of an unsound survey.[19]

The board's paper also argued against implementation of the full count of AFDC children:

Such a change would have the effect of redistributing funds to states already wealthy enough to afford AFDC payments greater than the poverty level. In effect, more federal funds would flow to the wealthier states, not those less able to overcome educational deprivation. This change would result in a reduction of $200 million in the South.[20]

The board's paper also objected to the proposal to increase the ceiling on the cost factor of 120 percent of the national average cost of educating each pupil because the effect of the change would reduce funding levels in the South where "high concentrations of educationally-deprived children create a climate of social and educational failure which requires even more intensive compensatory or remedial efforts [than in the North]."[21]

THE COALITION FORMS A TASK FORCE

Following the announcement of the Carter administration's proposal, which did not change the program's formula, the Northeast–Midwest Congressional Coalition, sensing a prime regional issue, organized to regain the ground the Northeast had lost in 1974. The first step in this direction was identifying the regional implications of the issue. Martin's report had accomplished this. The next step was informing the membership and the public of the "problem." To do this, the coalition distributed Martin's study to its members and to the press. As this was being done, Thomas Cochran, director of the Northeast–Midwest Research Institute; John Moriarty; and John Martin met to decide on the best course of action to take to act upon the findings in Martin's report. According to Martin:

> We decided to follow the basic approach which had been made by the coalition in the past. We decided to form a Task Force of interested members of the coalition whose focus would be this issue of ESEA Title 1 formulas.
>
> We did not have a specific formula alternative at that time, but a series of alternatives to choose from.
>
> [To start the task force] we sent press releases, memos and copies of my paper to the various offices of the members of the coalition."[22]

Since Jeffords had allowed Martin to work almost exclusively on the study for the coalition and he had a great interest in the legislation as a member new to the Education and Labor Committee, he was a natural choice for chairmanship of the task force. Jeffords, for his part, had little to lose by accepting the chairman's post. As a junior, minority member of the committee, he had relatively little power within the committee to influence the direction of its policy decisions.

The coalition ran into some difficulty when it looked for a cochairman for the task force however. Since Jeffords was a Republican from the Northeast, the coalition hoped to find a Democrat from the Midwest to cochair the task force. Paul Simon (D-Ill.), who was also new to the Education and Labor Committee, was asked to be cochairman, but after talking to several other members of the committee refused the post and eventually even refused membership on the task force. Dale Kildee (D-Mich.), another member new to the Education and Labor Committee, was then asked to be cochairman. He accepted the post because of Michigan's potential gain if the AFDC eligibility count were to be fully restored.

According to several aides, however, he did not take the position with great enthusiasm, since other Education and Labor Committee members had warned him that accepting the cochairman's post would be viewed within the committee as an infringement of its normal operating procedures. As a freshman representative, Kildee was being pressured to follow the norm of apprenticeship, to keep quiet and not make any disturbances. By taking the cochairman's post, he was potentially setting himself up for a direct confrontation with the committee's chairman—an act, he was warned, that could come back to haunt him in future years on the committee. When asked about this cochairman problem, Martin commented:

> The point was that nobody wanted to fool with this formula. There was a huge fight in 1974 over it and no one wanted to go ahead and do it again. The conventional wisdom was to leave it alone and, as it happened, the conventional wisdom became a self-fulfilling prophecy, until we came along.[23]

At this time (mid-March 1978) a meeting was held with the staff members of the sixteen coalition members who had joined the Education Task Force. Since half of these congressional volunteers were not members of the Education and Labor Committee and only three of the eight volunteers who were members of the committee were not new to the committee, the purpose of this meeting was to explain the regional implications of Title 1's formula. In this way, everyone would be familiar with the issue when it came up for legislative action. At this meeting, Roberta Stanley, an aide to William Ford (D-Mich.), approached Martin to indicate that Ford had read his study and was very interested in taking a leading role in the task force. Ford was one of the four members of the committee who had refused to vote for the committee's bill in 1974. Since that vote, however, the committee's composition had changed. Twenty of the thirty-seven members of the 1974 committee had left; thirteen of the twenty were from the Northeast, and seven were from the Sunbelt. Of their twenty replacements, fourteen were from the Northeast and six from the Sunbelt. Although this turnover meant a gain of only one seat for the Northeast, it did create a bloc of 20 representatives that the committee's chairman had not had time to get to know, so that he had no basis, in terms either of personal ties or of past favors, upon which he could persuade these members to vote according to his wishes.

Ford did not need the coalition to tell him (or his aides) about the regional implications of the program's formula. He needed a vehicle to help organize opposition to the southern bias of the committee's chairman. In 1974, the northeastern representatives on the committee never organized to oppose the committee's leadership. Ford was convinced that that was why they lost the formula fight in 1974. This year, however, with the aid of the coalition and these new members of the committee, Ford hoped that a unified stand against the chairman could be made early in the committee's deliberations, forcing Perkins to compromise, and accept revisions in the formula that were more favorable to the Northeast. Since Kildee remained lukewarm toward his role as cochairman, Ford took his place without any animosity resulting from the change.

Just as the coalition had resolved its problem of finding a co-chairman for its Education Task Force, the southern forces became aware of these efforts and organized to meet the challenge. Unlike the Snowbelt, which has a formal organization through which to focus its activities concerning legislation, the Sunbelt has an informal, loose alliance of autonomous political actors that attempts to influence legislation. On this issue, the Sunbelt's interests were represented by the governors, congressmen, and locally elected officials of the South, plus the public departments of education of the South. It should be noted that representatives of the western states were not actively involved in this issue. Except for California, the western states had little at stake on the issue. As a sparsely populated region, the West (including California) received only 14 percent of the program's funds. Only California, with its high concentration of AFDC-eligible children, had a real stake in any revisions made in the program's formula; and, of course, California stood in opposition to the South's position.

Although at that time the South had no central office in which to coordinate activities and no official body through which to exchange views, the region did have the Southern Growth Policies Board as an information resource, and it also had Peterson's paper. At this time (early April 1978), the board had not yet officially opened or fully staffed its Washington office, but Peterson was working out of the future site of that office, Suite 116 in the Hall of the States Building (the same building that houses several of the southern and northern states' federal liaison offices).

Because of Peterson's proximity to the liaison offices of several southern states, it was easy for him to communicate with them and to provide them with general information and statistical data concerning the effects the proposed formula revisions would have on their respective departments of education. His efforts to open lines of communication with the various southern interests were facilitated by the fact that by this time the board had distributed Peterson's position paper to the thirteen governors of the South who had had the paper distributed to the representatives and senators of the region as well as to their own federal liaison offices.

Ann Elmore, federal liaison representative for North Carolina, who was to become an active participant on behalf of the North Carolina Department of Public Instruction and of the South generally concerning the bill's formula revisions, commented on the manner in which the southern forces organized in opposition to the Northeast–Midwest Congressional Coalition:

> Someone got a copy of a memo and a study prepared for the North that they were going to use the SIE data in the formula.
>
> We knew that they wanted to change the formula and were looking at Title 1, so we prepared ourselves. We don't have a formal organization like the Northeast, but we do have an informal organization among ourselves.
>
> Each of the Southern states had its own office which communicates with their respective delegations. The state delegation of Alabama, for example, does not want to hear from me, but from their own people. Since I am from North Carolina, I worked closely with the North Carolina delegation and Ike Andrews [D-NC] who is a member of the House Education and Labor Committee, and his staff. I was, however, in contact with the Alabama person who was working with Representative Buchanan [D-AL] who is also on the Committee.
>
> [In early May] we [representatives of the Southern liaison offices] met in Atlanta during the annual meeting of the chief state school officers right before the Committee markup. At the meeting, we let all the delegates know the effect of the formula changes. Since we have only a few members on the Committee, we contacted all the states, even outside the South, who would lose funds if SIE were used instead of the census figures.
>
> Dave [Dr. Peterson] was very helpful throughout this period by providing us with information and statistical data.[24]

THE UNRAVELING OF THE COALITION: THE FAILURE TO REACH CONSENSUS

As the elementary and secondary education bill's scheduled markup session approached, the coalition held a meeting to coordinate its legislative actions. This meeting was not among aides, as in the past, but was the first (and last) formal meeting of the congressional members of the Education Task Force. The goal of the meeting was to identify which specific alternative formula to support from among the several alternatives available, to create a uniform political strategy to get that chosen alternative into the bill, and to present a united political front from the outset. Members of the meeting, however, were not able to decide upon which specific alternative to support. Jeffords supported the use of the Survey of Income and Education as a replacement of the Census Bureau's survey of poverty as the best alternative, while Ford advocated the reinstatement of the full AFDC count as the best alternative formula revision. (Michigan was one of the five states with high concentrations of AFDC-eligible children.) This difference of opinion might have been reconciled between the two men, but the eight members of the Education Task Force from New York believed that neither of these alternatives would best represent the interests of New York. They supported the Carter administration's proposal that advocated the use of the current formula along with a special concentration program that targeted aid to large, metropolitan centers.

Another problem arose at this meeting that required immediate attention. Apparently, several task force members who were also members of the Education and Labor Committee had serious reservations about the reliability of the coalition's data base and insisted on having more extensive data if they were going to fight for any revisions during the upcoming markup session. Reflecting on the results of the meeting, Martin stated:

> The result of the meeting was inconclusive as we still had no legislative strategy.
> Our fatal flaw was that we thought the Task Force would get together and decide upon a formula revision. The problem was that we couldn't get them together and when we finally did, the Task Force couldn't focus well.[25]

Following the failure of the task force to decide upon a political strategy, several coalition leaders met to see if they could come up with a strategy. This meeting was attended by John Moriarty, director of the coalition; Tom Cochran, director of the Research Institute; John Martin; Roberta Stanley; Chris Cross, legislative assistant to Albert Quie (R-Minn.) (who was the ranking Republican member of the House Education and Labor Committee and is now the governor of Minnesota); and Jeffords and Ford. According to Martin, a legislative strategy did emerge from this meeting:

> In order to maximize the financial return to our states, and for equity purposes, we decided to use the SIE as our data base and to redefine the definition of poverty according to the national median income level.
> We counted votes on a pure self-interest level, without regard to potential Presidential arm-twisting or other factors which might hurt or help us.
> We looked at the history of committee and floor votes and decided we could do it. We also developed several alternative plans for the full committee markup.
> Our first proposal would be to count all the Title 1 money and all new money over the fiscal 1978 levels under SIE. That would have amounted to about $600 million in benefits for the coalition states. Our first back-up proposal, the one many of us felt we would get, was to have SIE used for only new money which amounted to about a $200 million benefit.[26]

The problem of "soft" or questionable data that arose at the task force meeting was also resolved at this time, as Quie authorized his personal staff to request from the Library of Congress Congressional Research Service reliable data concerning the distribution of funds under the various alternative formulas under consideration (see Table 4.1).

The Research Service findings were of particular interest to Ford, as their study indicated, as did John Martin's study and the study conducted by the National Institute of Education, that thirteen states would gain funds through the adoption of the full count of AFDC children while thirty-seven states would lose funds. In terms of percentage gain, five states stood to receive substantially more funds under the revision: Hawaii, Michigan, New York, Connecticut, and Wisconsin. According to the study, all of the southern states and most of the western states stood to lose funds as a result of the revision, Texas being the biggest loser with a reduction of

Table 4.1 Title I Funds: Gainers and Losers Under HR 15

This table shows the estimated changes in state allocations of Title I compensatory education funds as a result of two formula changes made by HR 15. The first change would count in the funding formula all children from families receiving AFDC payments above the poverty level, instead of two-thirds as under existing law. The first set of figures shows how funds would be redistributed in fiscal 1980 if the same amount of money were available as in fiscal 1979 ($2.35 billion). The second change bases the count of low-income children on the 1976 Survey of Income and Education (SIE) instead of the 1970 census. This change would apply only to funds added in fiscal 1980 (estimated at $229,328,000). That allocation is shown in the second set of figures.

	AFDC Change				SIE Change			
State	Present Formula (AFDC at 2/3)	New Formula (AFDC at 100%)	Difference	% Change	Present Formula (based on 1970 census)	New Formula (based on 1976 poverty survey)	Difference	% Change
	(in millions of dollars; figures rounded)				(in millions of dollars; figures rounded)			
Alabama	$ 63.8	$ 62.2	−$ 1,561,000	− 2%	$ 6	$ 3.9	−$2,137,000	− 35.4%
Alaska	4.7	4.6	− 50,000	− 1	.4	.3	− 183,000	− 40.9
Arizona	23.5	22.9	− 575,000	− 2	2.2	2.6	+ 426,000	+ 19.2
Arkansas	36.3	35.4	− 888,000	− 2	3.4	3.1	− 343,000	− 10
California	196.3	200.4	+ 4,090,000	+ 2	19.4	23.3	+ 3,883,000	+ 20
Colorado	21.6	21.2	− 420,000	− 2	2.1	2.1	+ 31,000	+ 1.5
Connecticut	20.7	21.4	+ 767,000	+ 4	2.1	2.4	+ 296,000	+ 14.3
Delaware	6.1	6	− 107,000	− 2	.6	.6	+ 3,000	+ 0.6
District of Columbia	14.1	14.2	+ 111,000	+ 1	1.4	.9	− 434,000	− 31.4

State									
Florida	80.7	78.7	–	1,974,000	–2	7.6	11.2	+ 3,531,000	+ 46.3
Georgia	68.9	67.2	–	1,686,000	–2	6.5	6.4	– 84,000	– 1.3
Hawaii	8.4	9.2	+	793,000	+9	.9	.7	– 170,000	– 19.2
Idaho	5.7	5.6	+	111,000	–2	.5	.6	+ 95,000	+ 17.5
Illinois	102.1	102.4	–	321,000	0	9.9	12.1	+ 2,190,000	+ 22
Indiana	31.7	31	–	700,000	–2	3	3.6	+ 638,000	+ 21.2
Iowa	22.5	22.2	–	298,000	–1	2.2	2.1	– 92,000	– 4.3
Kansas	18.4	18	–	402,000	–2	1.7	1.6	– 100,000	– 5.8
Kentucky	49.2	48	–	1,200,000	–2	4.7	4.5	– 189,000	– 4.1
Louisiana	72.6	70.8	–	1,774,000	–2	6.9	5.3	– 1,586,000	– 23.1
Maine	9.1	9	–	104,000	–1	.9	1.1	+ 227,000	+ 26
Maryland	40.8	39.8	–	990,000	–2	3.9	4.4	+ 587,000	+ 15.2
Massachusetts	46.8	47.7	+	857,000	+2	4.6	5.9	+ 1,322,000	+ 28.6
Michigan	95.1	102.5	+	7,381,000	+8	9.9	9.3	– 651,000	– 6.6
Minnesota	34.5	34.2	–	242,000	–1	3.3	3.4	+ 99,000	+ 3
Mississippi	60.9	59.4	–	1,490,000	–2	5.8	4.4	– 1,364,000	– 23.7
Missouri	42.9	41.9	–	1,048,000	–2	4.1	4.1	+ 80,000	+ 2
Montana	8	7.8	–	195,000	–2	.8	.8	+ 57,000	+ 7.5
Nebraska	13.3	13	–	288,000	–2	1.3	1.3	+ 45,000	+ 3.6
Nevada	3	2.9	–	72,000	–2	.3	.6	+ 299,000	+105
New Hampshire	3.8	3.7	+	77,000	–2	.4	.6	+ 226,000	+ 63.1
New Jersey	61.9	62.9	+	975,000	+2	6.1	8	+ 1,923,000	+ 31.5
New Mexico	19.8	19.3	–	484,000	–2	1.9	1.8	– 77,000	– 4.1
New York	233.1	245.3	+	12,141,000	+5	23.8	23.1	– 648,000	– 2.7
North Carolina	73.7	71.9	–	1,802,000	–2	7	6	– 909,000	– 13
North Dakota	6.6	6.5	–	133,000	–2	.6	.5	– 156,000	– 24.8
Ohio	72.3	70.8	–	1,597,000	–2	6.9	8.4	+ 1,572,000	+ 22.9

Table 4.1 (Continued)

State	AFDC Change				SIE Change			
	Present Formula (AFDC at 2/3)	New Formula (AFDC at 100%)	Difference	% Change	Present Formula (based on 1970 census)	New Formula (based on 1976 poverty survey)	Difference	% Change
	(in millions of dollars; figures rounded)				(in millions of dollars; figures rounded)			
Oklahoma	29	28.3	− 671,000	−2	2.7	2.5	− 256,000	− 9.3
Oregon	21.9	22.2	+ 316,000	+1	2.2	2.2	+ 2,000	+ 0.1
Pennsylvania	110.9	111.7	+ 789,000	+1	10.8	12.5	+ 1,624,000	+ 15
Puerto Rico	80	80	0	0	8.8	(SIE not conducted)		
Rhode Island	8.3	8.2	− 30,000	0	.8	.8	+ 32,000	+ 4
South Carolina	48.5	47.3	− 1,186,000	−2	4.6	3.7	− 861,000	− 18.8
South Dakota	8.7	8.5	− 195,000	−2	.8	.6	− 196,000	− 23.7
Tennessee	57.7	56.3	− 1,412,000	−2	5.5	5.7	+ 277,000	+ 5.1
Texas	154.2	150.4	− 3,771,000	−2	14.6	15	+ 397,000	+ 2.7
Utah	7.8	7.8	+ 2,000	0	.8	.7	− 74,000	− 9.8
Vermont	3.9	3.9	− 26,000	−1	.4	.6	+ 256,000	+ 68.2
Virginia	56.1	54.7	− 1,360,000	−2	5.3	4.7	− 624,000	− 11.8
Washington	27.3	27.4	+ 105,000	0	2.7	2.7	+ 52,000	+ 1.9
West Virginia	25.4	24.8	− 622,000	−2	2.4	1.9	− 508,000	− 21.1
Wisconsin	38.5	39.5	+ 974,000	+3	3.8	4.1	+ 292,000	+ 7.6
Wyoming	3.4	3.3	− 80,000	−2	.3	.3	− 2,000	− 0.7

SOURCE: Congressional Quarterly, Weekly Reports (June 10, 1978), p. 1481. Reprinted with the permission of Congressional Quarterly, Inc.

$3.8 million.[27] Since the five states that stood to obtain substantial percentage increases under the change were represented by nine members on the Education and Labor Committee and the Sunbelt was represented by ten members, Ford knew that a fight for the adoption of the full count of AFDC children would be close. As a senior member of the committee, however, Ford felt that he had established a long-standing personal relationship with many committee members and that he could count on several votes that on a purely self-interest basis might have been expected to be cast against the full count of AFDC children. Since the adoption of either of the coalition's two proposed SIE formula revisions would mean only a slight increase in funds for Michigan while the adoption of the AFDC revision would provide Michigan with an added $7.38 million,[28] Ford contacted coalition leaders Harrington and Jeffords and insisted that the coalition support the AFDC change as well as the SIE revisions. Since adoption of the AFDC amendment represented a regional benefit to the coalition's states of $60 million, and Ford was so strongly committed to the AFDC revision, Harrington and Jeffords agreed to support the AFDC revision as well as the SIE revisions.[29] It was still Jeffords's understanding, however, that the adoption of the SIE data base as the determinant of where the poor live was the prime objective of the coalition, because both of the coalition's SIE formula revisions represented a much larger ($600 million and $200 million, respectively) benefit for the coalition states than did the AFDC revision ($60 million).[30]

Armed with the results of the Congressional Research Service findings that backed up the coalition's study, Jeffords and Ford thought they had a good chance to revise the formula in committee. They even hoped to adopt changes in both the SIE poverty count and the AFDC eligibility formula, especially since twenty-six of the thirty-six members of the House Education and Labor Committee were members of the coalition. The two congressmen recognized, however, that Carl Perkins, chairman of both the Committee and the Subcommittee on Elementary, Secondary and Vocational Education, would oppose their efforts to change the bill. They also knew that many of the fourteen committee members who had been on the committee in 1974 did not want to reopen the formula fight over Title 1 funds.

Despite the fact that Jeffords and Ford knew that they had the votes on a self-interest basis to implement even the $600 million SIE proposal (which benefited the districts of twenty-nine of the thirty-six members of the committee), they were not overly confident about the upcoming markup session. They knew that most Education and Labor Committee members liked and respected Chairman Perkins, and this personal relationship made life on the committee relatively pleasant rather than combative, as in the past.[31] Thus, Jeffords and Ford knew that many committee members would question whether the benefits to be gained purely in terms of dollars by backing the coalition's proposals would be worth straining their personal relationships with those members who would lose funds under the proposals, particularly since the person most hurt by the changes would be Carl Perkins. Despite the recent weakening of the powers of congressional committee chairmen, it was of course still in a committee member's interest to maintain a good working relationship with him.[32] If Perkins remained adamant in his opposition to the revisions, Jeffords and Ford knew that many of their northeastern colleagues would go along with him in the hope of gaining his favor for their pet projects in the future. As Roberta Stanley, aide to William Ford, commented:

> The members of the committee like to think of themselves as a big family. In 1974 there was a lot of name calling and no one wanted to repeat that again. Most people simply did not want to upset the apple cart.[33]

THE HOUSE CONFRONTATION: THE TRIUMPH OF COMMITTEE POLITICS OVER CAUCUS POLITICS

When the subcommittee markup session got under way in late March 1978, Chairman Perkins made his position on the formula revisions perfectly clear by refusing to hear any amendments to the existing language concerning Title 1's formula. As a result, when the full committee met in early May to consider the extension of the Elementary and Secondary Act of 1974, the coalition leaders were surprised when their first SIE proposal (representing a $600 million benefit to the Snowbelt) passed easily as introduced by Jeffords.

The sequence of events that immediately followed the vote, however, was to surprise the coalition leaders even more—and is a classic example of the chairman's power of persuasion and of the advantage of having a thorough understanding of parliamentary procedures. John Martin, who was present at the markup session and felt that victory had been achieved, recalled what occurred:

We were shocked by the [initial] vote. At that point, the chairman broke off the markup session for lunch. He never does this, we found out later, unless something goes wrong, but Mr. Jeffords and the rest of us went off to eat and returned to the markup session about three minutes after it had been scheduled to begin.

While we were at lunch, Perkins had gone to various committee members [including several northeastern representatives] and expressed his displeasure on the results of the vote and, in the meantime, had convinced Congressman LeFante [D-N.J.] who was unclear on one point of our amendment, that the only way to get clarification was to bring the whole thing up for reconsideration.

Another vote was taken and we lost on a tie. Believe me, it came as a great shock to us. At that time I had only been on the Hill for about three months and Mr. Jeffords about three and a half years. We just didn't know. [34]

Ann Elmore, federal liaison representative for North Carolina, who was also present during the markup session, commented on Chairman Perkins's action during the lunch recess:

All I can say is that there was a lot of politicking in that Democratic caucus room.
. . . We made some phone calls, contacted some members and got their proxies in to Mr. Perkins. [35]

Roberta Stanley, who like Martin felt that they had achieved a major victory, commented:

It was a terrible shock to us all. Mr. Perkins carried with him a lot of proxies, including some [northern] votes which probably would have gone with us if they had been there to vote. [36]

After the vote was taken and the coalition-sponsored $600 million SIE revision seemed dead, the committee recessed for the day. Jeffords and Martin spent that entire evening reviewing their strategy in hopes of attempting to salvage the $600 million revision. They realized that the chairman had made a number of promises they could not match, but they felt that two of the northeastern members who had voted against the revision might change their minds if approached in the right way. They did not know, however, that the Carter administration had also taken stock of the committee's action and, in an effort to have its proposal (which called for no changes in the Title 1 formula) adopted, contacted several Democratic committee members that evening to urge them to oppose any efforts to amend its proposal. At the same time, Ford, who had been busy lining up support for his AFDC formula revision, prepared to introduce an amendment to that effect. Also, the Northeast–Midwest Congressional Coalition, sensitive to the New York delegation's opposition to the adoption of the SIE standard, sent a letter to its members urging them not to support the Jeffords amendment.

Reflecting upon these developments, Martin stated: "I guess that you could say at this time we had a crack in the alliance."[37]

The next day Jeffords reintroduced the coalition's $600 million SIE formula revision only to see it roundly defeated. This was a clear example of logrolling politics defeating caucus-style politics. Jeffords could not offer the committee members any future favors. He could only point out to them how this particular amendment would affect their districts. When the members compared the value of Perkins's offer with that of the Jeffords' amendment, however, the amendment lost. Ford then introduced the coalition's backup SIE formula, which affected only new money allocated to the program and represented a $200 million benefit for the coalition states. It passed 21–14 as a means to end the fight. While a disappointment to the coalition, no one outside the coalition expected that even this revision would be adopted. When viewed in terms of expectations, the adoption of the $200 million compromise was a victory for the coalition.

In the meantime, Ford had distributed charts to the other members of the committee indicating how their respective districts would fare under the adoption of the full count of AFDC children. Since the committee had just experienced a trying battle over SIE, he knew the vote would be close, as it was. On the first vote his proposal was defeated on a tie (17–17), but upon reconsideration it, too, was accepted 18–17.[38] As a result, the coalition had accomplished what few had believed it could: it had revised Title 1's formula.

On May 11, 1978, the House Education and Labor Committee reported the bill for floor action. Despite the South's defeat on the SIE and AFDC changes, leaders of the southern representatives on the committee announced that they would not reopen the fight over the Title 1 formula on the House floor. In an interview with *Congressional Quarterly*, John Buchanan (R-Ala.) commented on his decision not to reopen the fight: "[To do so] would endanger the balanced bill the committee has reported and would unnecessarily excite regional chauvinism in education."[39]

Also interviewed by *Congressional Quarterly* at that time was Ann Elmore, who said: "Who knows what would happen if they opened it up on the floor. It could have been a whole lot worse."[40]

When asked what she meant by this remark, Elmore said that if the Jeffords amendment had been introduced on the floor, it probably would have passed. In fact, if it were not for the efforts of Chairman Perkins, she insisted, it would have been adopted in committee. When questioned about the possibility of the Jeffords amendment being adopted on the floor of the House, Martin said that since the amendment would have provided 274 districts with extra funds, it probably would have been adopted. He pointed out that to introduce it on the floor after having defeated it in committee, however, would have been considered bad form, so that most members of the Education and Labor Committee opposed the idea. Chairman Perkins was reported to have contacted several members of the committee and reminded them that one does not legislate on the floor of the House, one legislates in committee. In effect, he was trying to prevent outside forces, especially the Northeast–Midwest Congressional Coalition, from further undermining the hegemony of his committee in education policy.

While the SIE revision went unchallenged on the House floor, Ford's AFDC formula revision was challenged. On July 12, 1978, Mickey Edwards (R-Okla.), a junior member of the Education and Labor Committee, introduced an amendment that would have stricken the full count of AFDC children from the formula and restored the original two-thirds count. In support of his amendment,

Edwards stated on the House floor:

> . . . that change [to 100 percent] will benefit a very few states at the great detriment of the rest of the country. Only 14 states will gain under the committee change.
>
> . . . according to the HEW report of the President, in New York City in 1974 more than one-fourth of all AFDC cases had total incomes of more than $7,000 a year and about ten percent had incomes exceeding $10,000 a year.
>
> It does not make sense to weight so heavily the AFDC recipients because an area like New York that goes overboard in giving away AFDC.[41]

In response to Edwards's argument, Michigan Representative William Ford stated:

> It is true there is an adjustment of funds towards California, Illinois, Michigan, Pennsylvania and New York. . . . But why does that happen? Our figures show us since 1970 the number of poor people in these states had enormously increased.[42]

The House rejected the Edwards amendment, 175–212.[43] On first examination, the vote seemingly reflects a stark regional alignment as the fourteen Sunbelt states supported the Edwards amendment, 92–45, while the eighteen Snowbelt states opposed it, 45–151. On closer examination, however, it is clear that it was not regional self-interest that guided this vote but district self-interest. California, for example, despite its Sunbelt status, would have lost $4 million if the Edwards amendment had been adopted. Not surprisingly, not a single California representative supported the Edwards amendment and thirty-four Californians opposed it. The Snowbelt states were also divided on this state-by-state breakdown of benefits. Ten of the eighteen Snowbelt states would have had their Title 1 funds increased if the Edwards amendment had passed [44] These Snowbelt representatives voted against the region's interests by supporting the Edwards amendment, 37–23. It was the representatives of the remaining eight Snowbelt states who were benefited by the committee's needs formula who opposed the Edwards amendment, 8–128. Because these eight states have larger delegations than the other ten Snowbelt states, the overall vote seemed to reflect a regional rather than a more parochial, state interest.

The fact that district rather than regional self-interest determined the outcome of this vote raises the question of whether regional coalitions exist at all. The vote suggests that regional coalitions are loosely associated aggregates of local interests rather than cohesive regional voting blocs. This question will be addressed later in this chapter.

On July 13, 1978, the House adopted the five-year, $51.6 billion Elementary and Secondary Education bill, 350–20. The program's high authorization reflected the fact that the Appropriations Committee funded the program at less than half the authorization level sought for the years 1974 through 1978.[45]

THE SENATE HUMAN RESOURCES COMMITTEE'S SNOWBELT BIAS

While the coalition was battling for the AFDC and SIE revisions in the House, the Senate Human Resources Committee began to discuss the elementary and secondary education bill. Unlike the House committee, the Senate Human Resources Committee was chaired by a northeasterner, Harrison Williams (D-N.J.). Also, the chairman of the committee's Subcommittee on Education was from the Northeast, Claiborne Pell (D-R.I.). Even the ranking minority member of the committee was from the Northeast, Jacob Javits (R-N.Y.). The Senate, however, did not have a coalition (though one would be formed later in the year) to push these senators into taking aggressive action concerning Title 1's formula. Also, these senators, unlike the coalition's activists, did not view this program as being redistributive. They sought compromise, not victory. Williams, for his part, was still sensitive about his committee's reversal on the floor of the Senate in 1974, he did not want that to happen again. He was willing to forgo any major revisions in the formula, as Pell was. Pell, having developed a cohesive relationship with all the members of his subcommittee, was appalled by the fight over the formula within the House Education and Labor Committee. He did not want Title 1's formula to disrupt the collegial atmosphere of his subcommittee, and Javits was of a like mind. He suggested that they push only for the AFDC change instead of for both the SIE and AFDC formula changes. This was agreed to because New Jersey, Rhode Island, and New York were benefited by the full counting of AFDC recipients. The SIE proposal, on the other hand, did not significantly alter aid to New York or Rhode Island, and Williams reportedly did not believe that the coalition's figures indicating that New Jersey would be a big winner under the SIE revision were accurate.[46] (Williams and all other northeastern senators had received a copy of Martin's study.) In order to appease those on the committee who might have wanted to see more aid flow to the Northeast, the committee's leaders decided to make their AFDC revision effective as of fiscal 1979, a year earlier than allowed for by the House.

The Williams-Pell-Javits compromise measure proved to be politically astute, as it was adopted without dissent within the Human Resources Committee and passed by the full Senate on August 24, 1978, 86–7. Not a single amendment was offered to change Title 1's formula.[47]

THE HOUSE-SENATE CONFERENCE: PERKINS PULLS ANOTHER SURPRISE

As the House-Senate conference committee prepared to meet, the Southern Growth Policies Board held its annual fall meeting of the thirteen southern governors. At this meeting the elementary and secondary education bill was discussed, and a letter signed by the thirteen governors was sent to each of the conferees urging them to accept the Senate version of the bill. Also, Governor James Hunt of North Carolina, who was elected to succeed George Busbee as chairman of the Southern Growth Policies Board, sent a personal letter to all the conferees urging them to accept the Senate version of the bill.

When the House-Senate conference opened in mid-September, the coalition leaders thought that the House conferees had a very good chance of preserving the House version of the bill. Their optimism was soon destroyed by Carl Perkins. As chairman of the House Education and Labor Committee, Perkins opened the conference with a surprise compromise offer to the Senate that if implemented, would have wiped out nearly all the gains for the Snowbelt made by Jeffords and Ford. The Perkins compromise would have postponed implementation of the full count of AFDC children until fiscal 1980, as mandated by the House version of the bill. In return for this concession to the Senate, which had mandated that the full AFDC count commence in fiscal 1979, the House would delete the use of SIE data as an indicator of where poor children reside from its version of the bill. Instead, as mandated by the Senate, the 1970 Census Bureau's survey of poverty would be used.

This compromise offer set off some vicious infighting among the House conferees. Many felt that Perkins had overstepped his authority in presenting such a compromise. The result of the offer, however—despite the fact that it would never be approved by the House conferees—was to place the House Snowbelt representatives in a defensive posture throughout the conference and severly hampered their bargaining position relative to the Senate conferees who opposed the SIE revision.

After two weeks of attempting to defend the House version of the bill, the House conferees reluctantly agreed to accept a compromise offered by Senator Javits. In return for postponing implementation of the full count of all AFDC children until 1980, as mandated in the House version of the bill, Javits's compromise allowed the use of SIE data to determine where eligible poor children reside but limited its application to one half of new money appropriated in excess of the fiscal 1979 level rather than, as mandated by the House, all new money appropriated in excess of the 1979 level. In an effort to reduce the negative effect of the use of SIE data on the South, Senate conferees accepted a provision of the House bill that directed the commissioner of education to use the most recent poverty data available or to conduct a new poverty survey in any state where SIE data indicated a decline of greater than 25 percent in the number of poor children eligible for funding purposes. The compromise continued the payment policy of awarding grants according to the number of children eligible multiplied by 40 percent of the average per pupil expenditure in the state, provided that the average could be no less than 80 percent nor more than 120 percent of the national average per pupil cost.[48]

The conference committee filed its report on October 10, 1978. The Senate approved the report by voice vote on October 12, 1978, and the House approved it, 349–18, on October 15, 1978. On November 1, 1978, President Carter signed the five-year, $52 billion extension of the Elementary and Secondary Act.[49]

CONCLUSION: SOME SUCCESS AT THE SUBGOVERNMENT LEVEL

Unlike the revisions made in the formula granting procedures of the housing and community development bill in 1977, the revisions made in the elementary and secondary education bill in 1978 were initiated by the Northeast–Midwest Congressional Coalition and were not initially supported by the Carter administration. The coalition's position also lacked the strong support of the Education Committee's primary interest group, the National Education Association. In addition, the coalition was opposed by the chairman of the Education and Labor Committee and lacked the advantage of surprise, to which many in the Sunbelt had attributed the coalition's housing and community development victory.

Despite all these barriers, and especially the active opposition of Chairman Perkins, the coalition was able to secure provisions that would increase the Snowbelt's share of Title 1 funds by $394 million during the program's five-year existence if appropriations for the program followed the pattern established during the 1974–78 period. The coalition had exercised clout in setting the rules for distribution of federal assistance funds. It had stood alone, against the drift of conventional wisdom, against the Carter administration, against the allied efforts of the South, against the prevailing urge of many northeastern congressmen on the Education and Labor Committee not to rock the boat, yet had successfully revised the legislation's formula so that it sent more money to the Snowbelt.

Despite this accomplishment, which erased many doubts concerning the coalition's political strength at the subgovernment level, there was a prevailing feeling among the coalition's participants that they had failed to fully mobilize their forces. In short, they felt that they could and should have done better. They were haunted by the number of ifs that had developed during the course of the bill's passage. If Jeffords and Ford had been able to reconcile their differences during the coalition's Education Task Force meeting, perhaps the Title 1 formula could have been restructured along lines even more favorable to the Snowbelt. And if at this meeting the New York representatives could have reconciled their differences with Jeffords and Ford, forming a package deal that included the New Yorkers' concentration program, perhaps the final legislation would have included revisions that would have been more beneficial to the Snowbelt than the package deal that eventually passed. If Jeffords had returned to the markup session in time to discover the efforts of Chairman Perkins to reverse the favorable vote on the coalition's first SIE proposal, perhaps he could have saved it. Finally, if the New York delegation had not pressed its cause so strongly, perhaps the coalition would not have sent out its letter asking its members not to support the Jeffords $600 million SIE proposal and he would have been able to find a congressman willing to switch his vote and save the proposal despite his late return to the markup session.

These ifs serve to place the coalition's activities in proper perspective. The impression with which one is left after reading the various articles that concern its successful revision of the needs formula in the housing and community development bill of 1977 is one of a highly disciplined army of newly aroused northeastern congressmen eager to battle the "greedy forces" of the South. The fact that the Elementary and Secondary Education Act had experienced a regional confrontation over the allocation of Title 1 monies in 1974, and that the northeastern members of the committee then used many of the same arguments the coalition presented in 1978 (including the need to consider cost-of-living differentials in the education formula) indicates that it was not the coalition alone that aroused northeastern congressmen to oppose southern congressmen. Regionalism has long been a facet of congressional life. What the coalition had done, rather adroitly, was to provide an outlet for some of this regional debate to be heard by legislative actors outside any given committee as well as by the public at large.

It is this broadening of the audience, this raising of regional consciousness that is the coalition's real power. By making more political actors aware of the long-term consequences of decisions made at the subgovernment level, the coalition had made more actors sense a personal stake in the deliberations of subgovernments that may be quite remote from the subgovernments with which that particular actor may normally concern himself. Policies that are normally viewed in distributive terms (no losers) are now being viewed in redistributive terms (the Snowbelt is "losing" to the Sunbelt). Consequently, actors outside as well as within a given subgovernment are now more prone to challenge its decisions both before and after that decision reaches the floor of the House or the Senate. It is worth noting again what Mickey Edwards (R-Okla.) said on the House floor when he introduced his amendment to strike his own committee's decision to fully count AFDC-eligible children in the Title 1 formula: "that change [to 100 percent] will benefit a very few states to the great detriment of the rest of the country."[50] Edwards clearly viewed this issue in redistributive terms, as an issue that allocated resources from one section of the country to another. This comment indicates that the coalition raised the regional consciousness not only of Snowbelt representatives but of Sunbelt representatives as well, thereby making the decisions reached at the subgovernment level prone to challenges from Sunbelt as well as Snowbelt representatives.

This new regional awareness, however, had not reached the point where everyone was voting on the floor of the House only according to how well their region fared under whatever proposal was under consideration. Many representatives, as the analysis of the Edwards vote indicated, were still willing to vote against their short-run self-interest, that is, to logroll, in order to protect their own subgovernment's decisions. While in this particular circumstance the tendency to logroll helped the Snowbelt's position (the same was true of the vote on the Hannaford amendment), the fact remained that although the coalition had proved that it could be very effective at the subgovernment level, many questions remained concerning its effectiveness on the floor of the House. What the coalition had proved was that it had the ability to (1) determine how specific options influenced the regional flow of funds, (2) get that information to its members, and (3) have those members respect that information as being accurate and use it as a voting cue. Most of the coalition's members, however, still did not view these programs as being redistributive. Instead, each member still looked at each program as it arose and asked how the program affected his district rather than his region. Also, although the members did use the coalition's information as a voting cue, they were not yet prepared to abandon the practice of logrolling as a viable option. They still felt that logrolling enhanced their districts' self-interest. On the Edwards vote, and the Hannaford vote earlier, this tendency to logroll had not hurt the coalition because it had been able to get the respective subgovernments to enact policy options favorable to the Northeast. Logrolling was not a problem so long as the Coalition continued to "win" at the subgovernment level, but the biggest share of federal aid and the aid most "biased" in the direction of the Sunbelt was defense expenditures. Most defense expenditures during the Ninety-fifth congress were under the jurisdiction of committees and subcommittees that were not only led by, but were primarily composed of, Sunbelt representatives. If the Title 1 formula fight was any indication of what the coalition would face in these committees, it was clear that it would not be as successful in these areas as it had been with the housing and community development and education subgovernments. If the coalition hoped to get a larger share of defense funds for its region, it would have to establish its effectiveness on the floor of the House, and Defense Manpower Policy Number Four provided it with an opportunity to do so.

The Sunbelt forces, for their part, were not going to let the coalition alter the flow of defense funds without a fight. Unlike Title 1 funds, both the West and the South had a great deal at stake in this issue. As the outgoing president of the Southern Growth Policies Board, Governor George Busbee, put it: "The South had been caught with its eyes closed and its britches down. . . . [But now] the South was ready to end this nonsense."[51]

What was missing from all this rhetoric, of course, was any consideration of a national educational or defense policy for the nation as a whole. Each actor was working to enhance his own position. This is not evil; it is power politics in operation. The Congress envisioned by the founding fathers where enlightened representatives debated the great issues of the day and discovered the common good has never fitted reality. The difference between then and now, however, is that the decisions made by the Congress today can radically alter the economic prosperity of entire regions in any single Congress. While the call can be made for the emergence of enlightened statesmen to solve the Sunbelt/Snowbelt controversy, the call itself may be unrealistic.

Staff Initiative and Procurement Policy: The Case of Defense Manpower Policy Number Four

On March 28, 1977, the Northeast–Midwest Research Institute released its first position paper, entitled "Federal Procurement and Regional Needs: The Case of Defense Manpower Policy Number Four." The author of this paper, Laurence Zabar, was a young staff member at the institute who had formerly served as Michael Harrington's director of constituent services. His paper dealt with a relatively forgotten and disused executive order (DMP-4) that provided for the issuing of certain preferences in the awarding of federal procurement contracts to businesses located in areas of high unemployment.

The Northeast–Midwest Congressional Coalition's efforts to have DMP-4 implemented serve to illustrate that the coalition is much more than a paper organization. It has not only encouraged a growing awareness of the regional implications of policy decisions but has provided a vehicle for a large number of congressmen to have their voices better heard within both their own and other committees' jurisdictions.

This chapter's specific lesson, however, does not lie in an examination of the coalition's activities per se but of the activities undertaken by staff member Laurence Zabar. There were dozens of people to be influenced, and Zabar, as much as any elected official played a crucial role in the attempt to enforce the provisions of DMP-4; substantiating the recent recognition of the important role played by congressional staff in the policy process.

ZABAR'S FIRST STUDY: THE CATALYST

Unlike the Housing and Community Development Act of 1977 and the Elementary and Secondary Education Act of 1978, DMP-

4 was not an ongoing legislative program already on the decision-making agenda. It was a dead political issue. Interest groups did not rush to lobby to protect their share of DMP-4's benefits. There were no such benefits—yet. For that matter, few congressmen or government officials even knew that DMP-4 existed. Zabar, however, had learned of DMP-4 shortly after the coalition's formation from aides of Representative John LaFalce (D-N.Y.). LaFalce had introduced a bill in 1975 (H.R. 10940) that would have given priority to bids on defense procurement contracts to businesses located in areas of high unemployment and another in 1976 (H.R. 13517) that would have done the same for bids on nondefense procurement contracts. But hearings on these bills never took place because the House Government Operations Committee (where the bills were referred) gave the bills low priority and never got around to them. Also, only a few of LaFalce's colleagues expressed an interest in using federal procurement policy to enhance the economic stability of declining areas. This reluctance was evidenced by the fact that no one was willing to cosponsor H.R. 10940, and only eight others were willing to cosponsor H.R. 13517.[1] According to LaFalce's aides, even he considered the issue dead. Zabar, however, knew that the federal government would spend nearly $60 billion in 1977 on the procurement of goods and services by contract and another $40 billion through discretionary grants. Since DMP-4 would target procurement monies to areas of high unemployment and the northeastern states were experiencing the highest rates of unemployment in the nation, it was clear that enforcement of the objectives and provisions of DMP-4 would help accomplish the coalition's basic objective. It would redirect billions of federal dollars from growing areas (most of which were located in the Sunbelt) into the declining areas of the Northeast. Not only would more funds be directed into the coalition states, but the enforcement of DMP-4 would provide the Northeast with millions of additional procurement-related jobs, which unlike short-term federally funded jobs, possessed a reasonable expectation of permanency. In Zabar's mind, DMP-4 represented one of the single most important issues the Coalition could address. As a result, he asked for and received permission from Thomas Cochran and John Moriarty to undertake an analysis of

DMP-4 to determine what, if any, action the coalition should take regarding it.

Zabar discovered that Defense Manpower Policy Number Four was issued by the Office of Defense Mobilization on February 7, 1952, pursuant to the order of President Truman. Issued during the Korean War, the order was to "provide for procurement by negotiated contracts and purchases with responsible concerns which are in an area of current or imminent labor surplus."[2] The reasons given for the issuance of DMP-4, which holds the force of law, was to prevent any possible shortages should an industry concentrated in one area be destroyed by an enemy attack as well as to maintain an industrial mobilization base in case certain products had to be produced in vast quantities in a short period of time.[3] DMP-4 was to stabilize the economic situation of labor surplus areas by providing preferences in the awarding of federal procurement contracts to firms located in areas of persistent or substantial unemployment, as determined by the Department of Labor. As the national unemployment rate was approximately 3 percent at the time, the Labor Department defined substantial unemployment as being 6 percent or greater.

The DMP-4 preference program was to be enforced and governed by an interagency Surplus Manpower Committee that was to include representatives of the Departments of Defense and Labor, the Atomic Energy Commission, the Defense Production Agency, the General Services Administration, the Small Defense Plants Administration, and the National Production Authority.[4] The committee was to determine the maximum price differential considered appropriate to insure a wide geographic distribution of federal contracts, while at the same time insuring that the government was not paying exorbitant prices. Once this differential was determined, the committee would inform the director of defense mobilization of its finding, and he would then notify the appropriate executive agency that such a price differential or preference was in the national interest. The executive agency was to "take all practical steps, consistent with other procurement and military objectives, other than price, to locate procurement in the areas covered by the Committee's findings."[5]

Shortly after the issuance of DMP-4, Senator Burnet Maybank (D-S.C.) successfully offered an amendement during Senate consideration of the defense appropriations bill of 1953 that prevented the Defense Department from awarding a price differential, if the purpose of the differential was to relieve economic dislocation. This amendment was introduced by Maybank in order to protect the southern textile industry, which had been the recipient of a substantial portion of the department's procurement contracts of cotton and woolen products. It was Maybank's belief that the Defense Department, which had already been deliberately purchasing a portion of its textile needs from New England despite the fact that southern textiles were less expensive, would be forced, under DMP-4, to purchase a much greater portion of its textile needs from New England, thereby preventing the growth of the southern textile industry, including the South Carolina textile industry.[6] The amendment reads, in part:

. . . no funds herein appropriated shall be used for the payment of a price differential on contracts hereafter made for the purpose of relieving economic dislocation, except where the Secretary of Defense has specifically determined that sufficient price competition exists to insure a reasonable price to the government.[7]

The Maybank amendment's "reasonable-price" language was interpreted to mean the lowest price available as determined by competitive bidding. As a result, Zabar discovered that the Department of Defense, despite the fact that by 1977 its procurement budget approached $50 billion, had since 1953 spent, on the average, only $23 million per year under the provisions of DMP-4.[8] In 1975, for example, the department spent $40 billion in defense procurement but only $74.4 million under the provisions of DMP-4, or 0.2 of 1 percent of its procurement budget.[9]

The coalition states' share of Defense Department prime contract awards is exemplified in Table 5.1. However, because of Defense Department policies, these figures do not reflect subcontracting and locations are listed according to the site of companies' headquarters rather than according to the site of production. Sunbelt supporters claim that much of the subcontracting occurs in the Northeast, thus causing the data to understate the Snowbelt's share

Table 5.1

Region	1955	1960	1965	1970	1975	1979
DOD Procurement (billions)	$13.9	$20.5	$24.3	$30.7	$39.4	$57.6
Snowbelt (% share)	53.9	44.8	41.6	41.4	38.4	41.2

SOURCE: Paul Travis and Laurence Zabar, "A Case of Inequity: Regional Patterns in Defense Expenditures, 1950–1977" (Washington, D.C.: Northeast-Midwest Research Institute, August 1977), p. 22.
NOTE: 1979 figures appeared in *Budget Analysis Series* (Washington, D.C.: Northeast–Midwest Research Institute, February 1981), p. 3.

of funds. Snowbelt supporters counter by stating that the Northeast has many corporate headquarters in its region, thus causing the data to overstate its share of the funds. In either case, the available data convinced Zabar in 1977 that DMP-4 was a potential and needed windfall for the Northeast.

Zabar also discovered that while the procurement policies of the various civilian agencies, such as the Labor Department and the General Services Administration, were not legally affected by the restrictions of the Maybank amendment, the Office of Emergency Preparedness determined in 1952 that in order to insure uniformity in procurement practices, civilian as well as defense agencies would be bound by the language of the Maybank amendment. As a result of this ruling, the status of DMP-4 remained uncertain and disused.

In 1972 an effort was undertaken to increase the use of DMP-4. The interagency Surplus Manpower Committee in cooperation with the General Accounting Office determined that DMP-4 would never be utilized unless a way around the Maybank amendment were found. This goal, they reasoned, could be accomplished only by remaining in compliance with the Maybank amendment's lowest-price requirement. Accepting the idea that the lowest price for a contract can be determined only by inviting bids from all firms, regardless of location, the Surplus Manpower Committee decided that all contracts had to be bid upon by all interested firms; as a result, a total contract could not be set aside for bidding and awarded to firms located only in labor surplus areas. However, the Surplus Manpower Committee did determine that it was acceptable for only half of a contract to be awarded to the firm with the lowest price and the other half of the contract "reserved" for a firm located in labor surplus areas, provided that this reserved half of the contract was fulfilled at the same price as the unreserved half of the contract. In this way, firms located in labor surplus areas had an opportunity to receive federal procurement contracts and still remain in compliance with the lowest-price requirement of the Maybank amendment.[10]

While this interpretation of the usage of DMP-4 confined its application to those contracts that were splittable into two production runs such as food, clothing, and medical supplies and exempted more expensive and complex items such as tanks, planes, and rockets, which cannot be produced in two production runs, the Surplus Manpower Committee's new interpretation offered the possibility that DMP-4 would be utilized to provide an economic stimulus to areas of substantial unemployment. As Zabar neared completion of his study, however, he found that not only had no one undertaken a study of the effect of the 1972 interpretation on the federal procurement practices of the government but that, to his astonishment, very few procurement officials were even aware of the existence of DMP-4. Even the Federal Preparedness Agency, which had jurisdiction over the implementation of DMP-4, was uncertain, at first, whether or not it held jurisdiction over DMP-4, or even what DMP-4 was. As the aides of Representative LaFalce had warned, the issue seemed dead.

In concluding his study of DMP-4, Zabar made a number of recommendations. First, he recommended that the Department of Labor revise its definition of a substantial unemployment rate, since 91 percent of all labor areas in 1976 had unemployment rates of 6 percent or more. A revision to a higher figure, he reasoned, would provide a more realistic advantage to firms located in areas especially hard hit by the recession. Second, he recommended that the two-production-run requirement be eliminated so that entire procurement contracts could be set aside for labor surplus areas. To accomplish this, the Maybank amendment would have to be repealed. Finally, he recommended that the executive branch should undertake a more rigorous attempt to enforce the objectives and provisions of DMP-4.[11]

THE PRESS PROVIDES A HELPING HAND

After publication and distribution of Zabar's study to the members of the coalition and the press, nothing happened for a week or two, and Zabar began to believe that LaFalce's pessimisim had been justified. However, as Zabar put it:

> After releasing the study nothing happened for awhile, but then the *New York Times* ran a full column article on the study. Suddenly, everyone was calling for a copy of it.[12]

While DMP-4 was still a far cry from being a household word, suddenly thousands of influential people across the nation were aware of DMP-4 and its potential impact on the flow of federal funds. Aides of representatives from the Northeast-Midwest region now looked for Zabar's study from among the countless reports piled on their desks, read it, and reported to their superiors what DMP-4 would offer their congressional district. At the same time, several northeastern newspapers, sensing the local benefit of DMP-4, endorsed the concept of targeting federal procurement contracts to areas of economic distress and urged their state congressional delegations to join the coalition in its efforts to implement DMP-4. Zabar had gotten DMP-4 back onto the political agenda.

On May 25, 1977, Harrington sent a "Dear Colleague" letter to coalition members urging them to endorse the objectives of DMP-4 and to join him in the fight that would repeal the Maybank amendment by cosponsoring his bill (H.R. 5944). During this period, Zabar was busy talking to officials in the Federal Preparedness Agency, principally James Delaney, in order to urge a revision in its established policy of enforcing the restrictions of the Maybank amendment on civilian as well as defense procurement policies.

As the agency considered the coalition's pleas, Zabar, Harrington, and several other coalition members met with Charles Duncan, Jr., deputy secretary of defense, to discuss the Department of Defense's apparent opposition to the increased utilization of DMP-4. At the meeting, Duncan reportedly outlined the department's opposition to DMP-4 on the ground that it would force the department to spend a great deal more money on its equipment without increasing its quality or quantity.

Despite the Defense Department's opposition and the realization that the Congress, which normally acts in a slow, incremental fashion, would most likely not rejuvenate this sleeping giant of an executive order, Harrington persisted because he believed that these would be the first steps taken on a long road toward achieving full implementation of DMP-4. This political strategy of breaking ground for future action, however, was soon supplanted by the real possibility of altering the language of the Maybank amendment, as Senator William Hathaway (D-Maine) became aware of Harrington's efforts to repeal the amendment. Hathaway had attempted in each of the last three sessions of Congress to modify the amendment's restrictive language so that an entire procurement contract, rather than half, could be set aside for firms located in labor surplus areas. Each attempt, however, while accepted by the Senate Finance Committee, had been rejected by House Appropriation conferees in the conference committee.[13]

Hathaway told Harrington that the House conferees had explained to him that they had rejected his modification of the Maybank amendment because of the apparent conflict between the surplus labor set-aside program and the current national policy of setting aside portions of federal contracts for small businesses regardless of the economic condition of the area in which they were located. In order to make this argument moot, Hathaway intended to introduce an amendment that would not only modify the Maybank amendment to allow total set-asides to firms located in labor surplus areas but would also provide a first priority for small businesses as well. To further insure that House conferees could not deny the modification on the ground that it conflicted with the small business set-aside program, Hathaway (who was chairman of the Government Procurement Subcommittee of the Senate's Select Committee on Small Business) also included his priority structure in Title 4 of the Senate's amendments to H.R. 692, the Small Business Administration's authorization bill.

Hathaway, however, had a problem he hoped Harrington might be able to help him with. On February 9, 1977, the House had passed its version of the Small Business Administration's authorization bill, 381–0, and had not included any modification of the preferences awarded to small businesses. As Procurement Subcommittee chairman, Hathaway was certain to be chosen as a Senate conferee, but since the House bill had passed without his priority structure and because his priority structure was such a great departure from the traditional manner of awarding contracts to small businesses, he was not very confident of his ability to convince House conferees to accept his new plan.

THE FIRST LEGISLATIVE HURDLE IS CLEARED: THE SMALL BUSINESS COMMITTEE

Until contacted by Hathaway, Harrington believed that the implementation of DMP-4 was years away, but after speaking with the senator he realized that a modification of the Maybank amendment could be realized during the Ninety-fifth Congress. Therefore, Harrington decided to back the political strategy as outlined by Hathaway and to abandon his efforts to completely repeal the Maybank amendment.

At this point, Hathaway's political strategy was already well under way. He had introduced his bill (S. 1380) to modify the Maybank amendment (which provided a priority structure in the awarding of procurement contracts that were to be totally set aside for firms located in areas of labor surplus), and the Senate had accepted his priority structure in Title 4 of the Senate's amendments to the Small Business Administration's authorization bill on May 19, 1977. But time was of the essence. The conference committee that would decide if Senator Hathaway's priority structure would be retained in the authorization bill was scheduled to convene in June, which meant that Harrington had only three weeks to find support for the Hathaway priority structure. One of the coalition's members who was certain to be selected to serve on the conference committee, however, Joseph Addabbo (D-N.Y.), a senior member of the House Small Business and Appropriations Committee, had read Zabar's study on DMP-4 and let Zabar know that he was willing to help the coalition in its efforts to implement DMP-4. When Zabar told Addabbo of Hathaway's efforts to modify the Maybank amendment by amending both the Small Business Administration's authorization bill and the defense appropriations bill, Addabbo let Zabar know that he would support the small business amendment in the upcoming conference session. In the meantime, John LaFalce, another member of the House Small Business Committee, and also the originator of the DMP-4 issue, indicated that he would also support Hathaway's priority structure if he was selected to serve on the conference committee.

As it turned out, both Addabbo and LaFalce served on the Small Business Conference Committee. With their help, and the informational assistance of Zabar, Hathaway successfully protected his priority structure, and it was adopted as part of the conference committee report that was reported on July 26, 1977. Both the House and the Senate routinely adopted the committee's report, and on August 4, 1977, President Carter signed the Small Business Administration Amendments of 1977 (P.L. 95–89). The legislation included in Title 4 Senator Hathaway's priority structure that, Hathaway believed, would now take precedence over the Maybank amendment for both civilian and defense procurement policies.

ZABAR'S SECOND STUDY: THE PROBLEM OF
IMPLEMENTATION

While the Small Business Administration's authorization bill was being acted on in the conference committee, Zabar began a study of the use of DMP-4 by civilian agencies. As already noted, the Office of Emergency Preparedness had determined in 1952 that civilian as well as defense agencies would be bound to the restrictions of the Maybank amendment. Since this was the case, Zabar expected that compliance with DMP-4 would be slight, as it was.

Zabar's study examined the use of DMP-4 by the Energy Research and Development Administration; the National Aeronautics and Space Administration; the Department of Health, Education, and Welfare; the General Services Administration; the Veterans Administration; and the Department of the Interior. Collectively, these six agencies spent $13 billion of the $18 billion spent by all civilian agencies of the federal government on the procurement of goods and services by contract. Of this $13 billion, only $75 million, or

0.5 of 1 percent of the total amount spent on procurement contracts, were awarded under the provisions of DMP-4 in fiscal year 1976.[14]

After interviewing a number of federal procurement officials, Zabar reported that they attributed the minimum use of DMP-4 to two interrelated factors.

. . . the Maybank amendment requiring that purchases be made at the lowest possible price, and the General Accounting Office—intra-agency Surplus Manpower interpretation that the items purchased be "splittable" into two production runs to insure payment of the "base price".[15]

It was Zabar's opinion, however, that the real cause of the lack of compliance with the provisions of DMP-4 was only partly attributable to the administrative order itself. Part of the blame also had to be shared by the procurement officials of the various civilian agencies, many of whom, when initially contacted by Zabar, were, as in the defense agencies, unaware of the existence of DMP-4. He specifically cited the General Services Administration and the Veterans Administration as two agencies whose procurement needs were easily divisible into two production runs and thereby suitable for DMP-4, even under the intraagency Surplus Manpower Committee's "splittable" requirements.

In an attempt to get DMP-4 implemented, Zabar made a number of recommendations in the conclusion of his second study. He recommended that the Federal Preparedness Agency allow total set-asides of government contracts to firms located in areas of economic need (as allowed by the passage of the Small Business Administration Amendments of 1977); revise the "triggering" mechanism for DMP-4 by raising the level of unemployment designation of labor surplus areas; permit self-certification by firms eligible for preference under DMP-4, thus reducing bureaucratic red tape; and require government prime contractors to be bound to the same requirements when awarding subcontracts so that the work in fulfilling the contracts was actually undertaken in labor surplus areas, rather than simply on paper. Many firms, as indicated earlier, have corporate headquarters in the Northeast and Midwest, and when awarded contracts the money involved is statistically tabulated as being spent in these labor surplus areas when in fact these firms are relocating or subcontracting large percentages of the work to firms located in areas not experiencing labor surplus and sometimes even to firms not located in the Northeast and Midwest.[16]

In concluding his study, Zabar indicated that these changes would not be enough to enable DMP-4 to be fully utilized. Without the support of the administration in enforcing the provisions of DMP-4, it would remain ineffective. In this regard, he recommended that the administration increase the training of federal government procurement officials in the use of DMP-4 guidelines, increase the staff of DMP-4 administrators, increase public encouragement and technical assistance to interested firms, and require government agencies to set and meet dollar quotas in the implementation of DMP-4.[17]

Armed with the conclusions of Zabar's study, Senator Hathaway opened hearings before his Senate Subcommittee on Government Procurement on October 6, 1977, in order to question federal procurement officials concerning their efforts to implement DMP-4 in light of the passage of his priority structure in the Small Business Administration Amendments of 1977. While these hearings were taking place, Zabar again contacted Jim Delaney of the Federal Preparedness Agency to make various suggestions concerning revisions in the Federal Code that would have to be made in light of the enactment of the Small Business Administration Amendments of 1977 and the resulting modification of the Maybank amendment. Zabar also met with Addabbo who, as a member of the House Appropriations Committee, was willing to oppose the addition of the Maybank amendment in the upcoming defense appropriations bill of 1978. Addabbo, however, soon discovered that George Mahon (D-Tex.), chairman of the House Appropriations Committee and its Subcommittee on Defense, would oppose any effort to strike the Maybank amendment from the upcoming bill. As a result, Addabbo, in deference to Mahon's influence on the committee, especially in relation to defense matters, did not bring the issue to a vote and, as had been the case since 1953, the defense appropriations bill once again included the Maybank amendment.

While Addabbo had run into difficulties in the Appropriations Committee, on November 3, 1977, new federal regulations concerning the awarding of procurement funds (DMP-4A) appeared in the *Federal Register*. These new regulations not only allowed the total set-aside of a contract for a labor surplus area as required by the Small Business Administration Amendments of 1977 but also subjected all federal procurement discretionary grants and executive agreements to the provisions of DMP-4A. This meant that an additional $40 billion of procurement expenditures were now susceptible to total surplus labor area set-asides.[18]

The only obstacles remaining that would prevent the full utilization of DMP-4A was the Labor Department's designation of labor surplus areas as being any labor area that had an unemployment rate of 6 percent or greater and the realization by procurement officials of the changes resulting from the enactment of the Small Business Administration Amendments of 1977. Since these obstacles were administrative in nature, Harrington appealed to President Carter to endorse the concept of DMP-4A. Harrington reminded the president that the Democratic platform of 1976, which had been approved by the president, endorsed the concept of targeting federal resources to areas of greatest need.

While Harrington appealed directly to the president, Thomas Cochran, director of the Northeast–Midwest Research Institute, contacted both Robert Embry, Assistant Secretary for community and urban development, and Robert Duckworth, staff director for the Urban and Regional Policy Group (both in the Department of Housing and Urban Development), urging them, in light of their private indications of support for the concept embodied in DMP-4, to contact the president on behalf of the full implementation of DMP-4A.

While the coalition tried to overcome the administrative obstacles to the utilization of DMP-4A, an even larger obstacle arose when the Defense Appropriations Act of 1978 became law. Upon the request of the Office of Federal Procurement Policy, the Department of Defense and the Small Business Administration, the comptroller general of the United States was asked to determine which law held preference, the Small Business Administration Amendments of 1977 (which modified the Maybank amendment) or the Defense Appropriations Act of 1978 (which reaffirmed the Maybank amendment).

The comptroller general's opinion was rendered on October 31,

1977, and soon became known within the coalition as the "Halloween massacre." It was the comptroller's opinion that since the Defense Appropriations Act involved only the Department of Defense, the Maybank amendment held precedence over the Small Business Administration Amendments of 1977 in regard to defense procurement policies for all monies appropriated for 1978 but not for any monies appropriated prior to 1978 that might not have been already spent. The modification of the Maybank amendment in the Small Business Administration Amendments, did, however, hold precedence over the Defense Appropriations Act in all civilian agencies' procurement policies. What the ruling meant was that the provisions of DMP-4A now affected 31 percent of the total federal procurement expenditures by contract (approximately $18 billion) but could not be used in determining where the other 69 percent of all federal procurement expenditures by contract were awarded (approximately $40 billion).

While DMP-4A now theoretically affected the distribution of all nondefense procurement contract awards and all of the $40 billion spent on discretionary grants and executive agreements involving procurement, little, if any, real effect on the distribution of federal procurement monies was possible until the Labor Department revised its definition of a labor surplus area. The Defense Department, for example, which operated under the restrictions of the Maybank amendment in 1977, was still able to award $18.5 billion, or 47 percent of its defense procurement contracts, to firms located in labor surplus areas.[19] The reason this occurred was because 91 percent of the country's labor market areas, as determined by the Labor Department, had unemployment rates exceeding 6 percent in 1977. In brief, the Defense Department awarded 53 percent of its procurement budget to only 9 percent of the country's labor market areas, and even if the department was subject to the modifications made by the Small Business Administration Amendments of 1977, this practice was entirely within the limits of the law.

Realizing that DMP-4A was still not being implemented, LaFalce, as chairman of the Subcommittee on Capital, Investment and Business Opportunities of the House Small Business Committee, held hearings with Department of Labor officials in order to prod them ppropriations bill, Dr. Diane DeVaul, another analyst at the institute, assumed Zabar's role and met with Harrington, John Morarty, and Thomas Cochran, in order to decide whether to try to repeal the Maybank amendment altogether or just revise it. Since President Carter had called for an experimental program in the use of DMP-4A in the procurement policies of the Defense Department and the coalition's leaders were well aware of the influence Mahon would have on the floor vote, it was decided that it would be politically wise to try to revise the amendment rather than attempt to delete it. Consequently, the coalition's leaders decided to introduce an amendment to the defense appropriations bill mandating that 10 percent of the Defense Department's procurement budget be subject to the provisions of DMP-4A.

This figure was selected for three reasons. First, it would enable the amendment to correspond with the stated policy of the president, which called for an experimental use of DMP-4A. Coalition members hoped that the administration (which remained neutral on this question) would be willing to express its support for the measure. Second, they realized that many conservative members of the House were inclined to oppose any "inflationary" expenditures. Since the coalition's amendment allowed price differentials in the awarding of procurement contracts, its leaders knew that the amendment would be labeled inflationary. It was hoped that the 10 percent figure would suppress that effectiveness of the inflationary argument. The coalition was prepared, in this regard, to point out that the Federal Preparedness Agency had run a procurement simulation study indicating that, when contracts were targeted to labor surplus areas, the average price differential paid to the lowest bidder from labor surplus areas was only 0.7 percent. The third reason the coalition's leaders chose this 10 percent figure was that they realized that not all of the procurement contracts awarded by the Defense Department could be targeted to labor surplus areas because of the nature of the department's needs. Large aircraft and rocketry, for example, are made only in certain areas of the country, the contracts awarded for their construction cannot be targeted to labor surplus areas if there are not a sufficient number of firms capable of completing the contract in such areas to insure the government a reasonable price.

into revising their designation of labor surplus areas. Despite these hearings, and numerous letters sent to the department by various members of the coalition, the department did not release new regulations concerning the unemployment rate needed to designate a labor surplus area until March 3, 1978. These regulations redefined labor surplus areas to labor market areas with an unemployment rate at least 1.2 times the national unemployment rate. As a result of this revision, the number of surplus labor areas was reduced from 91 to 36 percent of all labor market areas.[20] At last, the utilization of DMP-4A could be achieved, since the entire mechanism for wide implementation of DMP-4A was finally in place for civilian agencies.

According to coalition staffers, the Labor Department was slow in revising its designation of labor surplus areas because the Carter administration was not certain that it wanted to endorse the concept of DMP-4A. Like the Congress, the executive branch is not immune to regional considerations. Some agencies, such as HUD, have strong ties to the Northeast; others, such as the Defense Department, have strong ties to the Sunbelt (because of the composition of their respective subgovernments). Also, most of Carter's staff, as well as the president himself, were from the South. In this case, DMP-4A reduced the South's share of procurement funds. Many of the president's southern presidential advisors reportedly cautioned him against backing DMP-4A on the ground that by doing so he would be threatening his southern political base. Still other political advisors, on the other hand (many of whom were from the Northeast), were reportedly advising the president to endorse the coalition's program because his political posture in the Northeast and Midwest was not as strong as it should be in light of the Snowbelt's electoral strength.

In an effort to break this deadlock, Harrington met with Stuart Eizenstat, assistant to the president for domestic affairs and policy, in February 1978. Harrington hoped to secure Eizenstat's support for inclusion of federal procurement targeting in the president's urban program, which was scheduled to be announced at the end of March. At this meeting, Eizenstat expressed cautious support for the implementation of DMP-4A. He subsequently recommended to the president to encourage the use of DMP-4A in civilian procurement policies and to create a one-year experimental program for the use of DMP-4A in defense procurements.

While Harrington was meeting with Eizenstat, several members of the coalition's staff again contacted Embry (assistant secretary of housing and urban development) to urge him to exert whatever influence he had with the president and the secretary of housing and urban development, Patricia Roberts Harris, to persuade them to adopt the objectives of DMP-4A in the upcoming urban policy plan.

Partly as a result of Eizenstat's and Embry's support of DMP-4A, the president instructed the Labor Department to revise the definition of labor surplus areas and, on March 27, 1978, issued a major urban policy statement endorsing the objectives of DMP-4A. The president announced that he advocated the full utilization of DMP-4A in the awarding of civilian procurement contracts and an experimental use of DMP-4A, for a one-year period, in the awarding of defense procurement contracts as well.

In light of this development, LaFalce again conducted hearings in his Small Business Subcommittee in order to monitor the implementation of DMP-4A on civilian agencies. At this time (April 5, 1978), LaFalce found that none of the executive agencies had yet made any substantial numbers of set-asides to labor surplus areas. In light of President Carter's urban policy plan, however, executive procurement officials assured him that they intended to make maximum use of DMP-4A in the near future.

THE SECOND LEGISLATIVE HURDLE:
GEORGE MAHON

As already noted, while the implementation of DMP-4A was now well under way for civilian agencies, the defense procurement program was still operating under the restrictions of the Maybank amendment. Secretary of Defense Harold Brown informed the president that, because of the Maybank amendment, the Department of Defense could not undertake even an experimental use of DMP-4A as announced in his urban policy plan. It was now evident to the coalition's leadership that the Defense Department's $40 billion

procurement budget could be made subject DMP-4A only if the Maybank amendment v revised in the upcoming defense appropriation.

Since the Senate Finance Committee had ac efforts to revise the Maybank amendment in th gresses, Harrington, Moriarty, Cochran, and Zab that the Senate would once again accept Hathawa to modify the amendment. The question now was amendment deleted or revised on the House side. leaders realized that, owing to congressional operating they now had three options. The coalition could attemp Addabbo, to delete the Maybank amendment in the Appr Committee markup session; it could wait until the defens priations bill reached the House floor and attempt to delete the amendment there; or it could wait until the House vers the defense appropriations bill reached the conference comm and attempt to delete or revise the amendment there. It was qu decided, however, that two of these options—the markup sess and the conference committee—were certain to fail because of t composition of the Appropriations Committee and Chairma Mahon's opposition to the deletion or revision of the Maybank amendment. Thus, the only remaining alternative was to fight for the deletion or revision of the amendment on the floor of the House. As Zabar explained:

We left the Senate alone because we knew Senator Hathaway would be successful in offering his amendment and we were right.

. . . We decided not to try to delete the Maybank language in committee, but on the House floor, instead. We felt Mahon would be more vulnerable on the floor of the House than he is on his own committee. The power of the Chairman of Appropriations is impressive. He has been around for a long time and members of his committee generally do not buck the Chairman.[21]

In anticipation of a difficult floor fight, Harrington sent a series of "Dear Colleague" letters to coalition members informing them of the potential benefits the deletion of the Maybank amendment would have for their districts. At this time, Zabar left the Northeast-Midwest Research Institute on an extended leave of absence. As the date approached for floor consideration of the 1979 defense

The Defense Department's appropriations bill of 1979 (H.R. 13635) reached the floor of the House on August 4, 1978, where debate centered on the inclusion of a $2.1 billion nuclear aircraft carrier that the president opposed.[22] As debate on the carrier dragged on, the vote on the coalition's amendment was delayed until August 8, 1978, the same day of the Georgia, Idaho, Indiana, and Michigan primaries. Since Georgia, Indiana, and Michigan at that time had unemployment rates well above the national average—meaning that they would have benefited from the approval of the coalition's amendment—the timing of the vote meant that thirty to thirty-five representatives the coalition had expected to vote for adoption of its amendment would not be present to vote. Also, this was the day on which President Carter signed the New York City Loan Guarantee Act of 1978 in New York City, so that many New York representatives were in New York to be present for the signing. This situation, coupled with the opposition of Chairman Mahon, virtually assured the defeat of the coalition's amendment.

The coalition's amendment, introduced by James Howard (D-N.J.), represented the coalition's first attempt to amend a subgovernment decision on the floor of the House. It failed, 165–213. Fifty-four representatives were absent at the time of the vote; 28 represented districts located in coalition states.[23] As expected, most (134) of the 185 coalition members who did vote, voted in favor of the Howard amendment, and most (113) of the 140 Sunbelt representatives who voted opposed it. So many coalition members broke ranks, however, that even if all of the absent coalition members had been present and had voted for the amendment, it still would have failed.

The fact that so many Snowbelt congressmen defected while so many Sunbelt congressmen did not is explainable in terms of several interrelated factors. First, voting for the Howard amendment was contrary to the norm of committee reciprocity. Mahon (as chairman of one of the most powerful committees in the Congress) had established a long-standing and mutually beneficial relationship with many in the Congress, particularly Sunbelt representatives. These representatives were inclined to logroll with Mahon on this one in the expectation that he and his committee's members would reciprocate (or "punish" them by decreasing their pet projects' funding levels) in the future.

While the norm of committee reciprocity was clearly a factor in the Sunbelt's cohesiveness (where the amendment hurt more districts than it helped), it was also a factor in the Snowbelt's non-cohesiveness, as nearly half (94 of 213) of the districts there did not have a qualifying labor surplus area in them.[24] These Snowbelt representatives, therefore, had little personal stake in supporting the Howard amendment, other than the fact that the amendment would help their region as a whole. Thus, the coalition failed to establish its effectiveness on the floor of the House. If the 94 Snowbelt representatives had voted with the coalition's position (and ignored the urge to logroll), this would have indicated that the coalition could create a cohesive voting bloc based upon regional interests. Instead, it demonstrated that it could use its informational expertise only to aggregate local districts into an appearance of regional solidarity. A caution is in order, however: this was the coalition's first attempt to overthrow a subgovernment decision, and 56 of the 94 Snowbelt representatives that were not helped by the Howard amendment voted for it nevertheless. The coalition's efforts were clearly evident in these representatives' decision to buck the norm of committee reciprocity.

The major reason the coalition failed on this vote was Chairman Mahon. His strategy was to present the Howard amendment as poor public policy. He claimed that the amendment was not only inflationary (attracting conservative opposition to the amendment) but contrary to the national security interests of the United States as well. What the amendment presented, he argued, was parochial interest versus the national interest. He was able to do this by indicating that (1) the price differential would result in the Department of Defense receiving less defense for the nation for its dollar and (2) that the objectives of the amendment were not appropriate for inclusion in a defense bill, since the government already had numerous programs dealing with unemployment. A defense bill, he effectively argued, was meant to deal with the national defense of the United States: if you want to talk about unemployment, talk about it elsewhere. Speaking in opposition to the Howard amendment on the floor, Chairman Mahon stated:

. . . it seems to me to be very, very important that we do not make a relief program out of the defense appropriation.

. . . the Department of Defense has consistently held the view that removal of the Maybank amendment is not in the national interest.

. . . What our defense people need is the best possible equipment from the very best suppliers in the nation. We do not want inferior equipment made by firms that are incapable of getting a job done.[25]

The success of Mahon's strategy was reflected in the fact that Republicans (generally considered more conservative than Democrats on domestic fiscal policy and more sensitive to any weakening of American defense posture) were strongly opposed to the amendment. Of the 51 Snowbelt representatives who opposed the amendment, 36 were Republicans. An examination of those who voted in support of the coalition's amendment, however, does indicate that the parochial view did have an impact. More than half (16 of 27) of the Sunbelt representatives who voted for the amendment were from high unemployment areas in California, a state that, as a whole, stood to lose from the adoption of the amendment because of its high concentration of defense industries located in non-labor-surplus areas. Other Sunbelt delegations, however, were strongly opposed to the Howard amendment because it was contrary to their local interests, contrary to the norm of committee reciprocity, and seen as being inflationary and contrary to the national security interests of the United States. With all of these factors working against the amendment, it is not surprising to discover that the Sunbelt, although lacking a coalition, was able to secure such solid opposition to the Howard amendment. These same factors, of course, also worked to frustrate the coalition's efforts to secure a regional voting bloc in favor of the Howard amendment.

At the same time the coalition was defeated on the floor of the House, the coalition met with a huge success in its dealings with the executive branch. On August 16, 1978, President Carter finally ordered (Executive Order 12073) procurement officials to implement DMP-4A in relation to civilian procurement policy.

. . . in order to strengthen the economic base of our nation, it is hereby ordered as follows:

Executive agencies shall emphasize procurement set-asides in labor surplus areas in order to strengthen our nation's economy.

Labor surplus area procurements shall be consistent with this Order and, to the extent funds are available, the priorities of Section 15 of the Small Business Act, as amended by Public Law 95-89.[26]

Since civilian procurement officials had not received direct orders from the president to implement DMP-4A until August 16, 1978, the effect of the order on 1978–79 procurement dollars has not yet been accurately determined, but the added revenue to the Snowbelt in the 1980s will be measured in the billions of dollars and represents the coalition's most impressive victory during the Ninety-fifth Congress.

CONCLUSION: NATIONAL SECURITY CLOUDS THE ISSUE

Compared with the coalition's victories in the housing and community development and elementary and secondary education cases, this victory was attained in an unorthodox manner. Instead of working in conjunction with the coalition's task force (in this case, the Task Force on Military Installations), Zabar worked independently, despite the fact that DMP-4A's implementation was obstructed by the Department of Defense and that the department's procurement budget represented the largest single source of revenue challenged by the coalition during the Ninety-fifth Congress.

The reason this task force never became involved in the effort to get DMP-4A implemented was that it never existed in any meaningful, concrete sense. All the coalition's task forces are meant to be fluid organizations—active when their respective legislative interests are being acted upon, inactive when they are not—but the Task Force on Military Installations never really got organized. Representative Donald Mitchell (D-N.Y.), cochairman of the Military Installations Task Force, conceded in an interview that many task force members rarely attended meetings, preferring to take positions on issues rather than work on them. He insisted, however, that the task force did not become involved in the implementation of DMP-4A because it was recognized that DMP-4A was Harrington's "pet project" and that Harrington was, in many ways, a "task force" unto himself and could handle the needed work without any task force' assistance. This may have been a contributing factor in the defeat of the Howard amendment. Since there were fewer representatives actively engaged in working for the Howard amendment, there were fewer resources available to support the coalition's position. In the two previous cases, for example, members of the Housing and Community Development Task Force and the Education Task Force were instrumental in the coalition's efforts; they were the ones who put the coalition's information into the right hands. They not only carried the coalition's information but, in presenting it to certain preselected members, lent that information a certain measure of personal prestige. Information coming from a trusted friend or partisan or ideological compatriot is usually more highly regarded than information provided by strangers or from those of an opposing party or ideological camp. Because DMP-4A was handled by a relatively small number of individuals within the coalition, however, there were relatively few representatives available to spread the word about the Howard amendment with any significant degree of enthusiasm and even fewer who were willing to go the next step—to logroll votes with their colleagues in order to get the Howard amendment adopted.

While the coalition's task force system failed to provide DMP-4 any significant political support, Zabar's study, coupled with his efforts and Harrington's, attracted the support needed to get DMP-4 back onto the political agenda and to achieve a significant victory concerning civilian agencies' procurement practices. Zabar's study not only broke the issue's inertia that had prevented Representative LaFalce from pushing the issue; it also attracted Representative Addabbo to the issue; and, finally, it provided Senator Hathaway with the backing he needed in the House. It goes without saying that without the formation of the Northeast–Midwest Congressional Coalition and the efforts of those involved, DMP-4 would still be in the dormant state in which it was found in 1977.

The large number of Snowbelt votes (51) against the Howard amendment and the failure of the Military Installation Task Force to organize indicate that the coalition's efforts during the Ninety-fifth Congress, as also indicated by the elementary and secondary education case study, fell far short of resembling the media-inspired image of a highly disciplined army ready to do battle with the Sunbelt forces. The coalition has few resources, unlike committee chairmen or even the party leadership, to influence the votes of its congressional members. Its real source of power—information— simply was not enough on this specific vote. The national security argument was devastating.

Surprisingly, in view of the potential effect DMP-4 would have on regional distribution of federal procurement funds, the Southern Growth Policies Board did not commission a study on the effects DMP-4 would have on southern monies. When questioned about this, officials at the board's Washington office admitted that it had simply failed to recognize the significance of DMP-4 (recall that even defense procurement officials did know what DMP-4 was all about at first), but promised to look into the subject during the Ninety-sixth Congress.

Despite the lack of counterorganization evident by the lack of activity on the Southern Growth Policies Board's part, the Sunbelt position was once again well represented by a senior member of the House of Representatives, George Mahon. He was the right man in the right place at the right time.[27] His retirement at the end of the Ninety-fifth Congress, however, radically altered the Sunbelt's position vis-à-vis the Maybank amendment. While Mahon's successor as chairman of the Appropriations Committee, Jamie Whitten (D-Miss.), is also from the Sunbelt, the new chairman of the Appropriations Subcommittee on Defense is Joseph Addabbo!

On September 16, 1980, Addabbo introduced an amendment to the defense appropriation bill for fiscal 1981 that would totally repeal the Maybank amendment. The Addabbo amendment was adopted, 220–179. After two years of lobbying from the coalition, the coalition's members voted 172–23 in favor of the amendment. The fourteen Sunbelt states opposed it 29–118.[28] The final version of the bill, signed by President Carter on December 15, 1980, modified the Maybank amendment by establishing a one-year, $3.4 billion procurement targeting program to begin on February 26, 1981.

The regional solidarity evidenced on the Addabbo amendment can be accounted for, at least in part, by the realization of many Snowbelt representatives that the coalition had something important to say about regional expenditures. The earlier battles of the Ninety-fifth Congress had opened their eyes to the regional flow-of-funds issue. The coalition, in this regard, kept the Snowbelt

Table 5.2   Federal Balance of Payments Fiscal 1975–79 (millions of dollars)

Region	1975	1976	1977	1978	1979	Cumula-tive
Snowbelt	− 30,623	− 33,508	− 30,983	− 34,289	− 35,636	− 165,039
Sunbelt	+ 21,934	+ 24,072	+ 21,072	+ 22,466	+ 22,001	+ 111,949

SOURCE: Northeast–Midwest Institute, *The Federal Balance of Payments: Regional Implications of Government Spending* (Washington, D.C., August 1980), p. 4.
NOTE: These figures include all noncoalition states as Sunbelt states. Interest payments on the national debt are excluded.

representatives abreast of the latest developments in the regional balance of payments (the latest figures are represented in Table 5.2) and convinced many who were unwilling to engage in regional politics in 1978 to do so in 1980.

While the housing and community development, elementary and secondary education, and Defense Manpower Policy Number Four cases all indicate that the coalition met with success in its efforts to redistribute federal funds, not all of its efforts were successful (as evidenced by the figures in Table 5.2). Two of President Carter's major policy initiatives of the Ninety-fifth Congress, for example, promised to provide the Snowbelt with substantial financial benefits, but neither program survived the Ninety-fifth Congress in the form desired by the coalition. We now turn to these two initiatives—energy and urban policy.

CHAPTER SIX *The Formation of the*

Carter Urban Program, 1977–78: The

Efficacy of Administrative Lobbying

Since the Northeast-Midwest region has, for the most part, developed its industrial and manufacturing base within the boundaries of its major cities, the economic vitality of the entire region obviously depends on the economic conditions existing within its urban communities. According to a 1977 study by the Treasury Department, however, eight of the nation's ten most financially pressed cities were located in the Northeast-Midwest region.[1] Another study, conducted in 1978 by Chase Econometric Associates, Inc., a company specializing in economic forecasting, indicated that the ten cities with the worst future employment opportunities were all located in the Northeast-Midwest region.[2] A report presented to the House Committee on Banking, Finance and Urban Affairs in 1977 by two Brookings Institution researchers, Richard Nathan and Paul Dommel, indicated that the most accurate way of predicting the economic condition of a city was determining its location.

> The most troubled cities—those with what can be called "urban crisis conditions"—are concentrated in the Northeast quadrant, the Northeastern and Midwestern states combined. Typically, these troubled cities are old cities with boundaries encompassing a relatively small proportion of their total metropolitan area and characterized by problems of aging structures and a concentration of high cost, low income population. Conversely, the less troubled cities and those with brighter prospects for the future tend to be the newer cities [of the Sunbelt] with a growing middle-income population.[3]

It was for these reasons that the substance of the federal government's approach to solving the economic and social problems of the nation's urban centers was regarded at the Northeast–Midwest Congressional Coalition as one of its most important policy concerns during the Ninety-fifth Congress. Michael Moriarty, executive director of the coalition, recalled that President Carter's urban program was "one of the Coalition's highest priorities in the 1977–78 period."[4] Michael Harrington, commenting before the Northeastern Regional Conference of the National League of Cities, declared:

America's cities, particularly those in the Northeast and Midwest, today face a hidden crisis which in some areas threatens disaster at nearly any moment—the decay of our urban infrastructure. Dotting the urban landscape across our region are signs—some readily apparent, some not—of steadily deteriorating sewers, water lines, utilities, streets and bridges. Our collective disinclination to squarely address these hidden problems has created a series of urban "time bombs" where inevitable detonation will impose replacement costs two to three times as great as current repair costs.[5]

This chapter examines the efforts undertaken by the coalition to influence the formation of President Carter's urban proposals; the next chapter examines the fate of these proposals once they were sent to Congress. As will be indicated in this chapter, the coalition's efforts to influence the president's proposals were overshadowed by the struggle over the control of the substance of urban policy between the White House and executive officials, principally those from the Department of Housing and Urban Development. As was indicated in the previous chapter, HUD had strong ties to its subgovernment partners—representatives of the House and Senate Banking Committees and their clientele interest groups. Both of these subgovernment partners were disproportionately located in the Northeast, and many HUD officials also came from that area. The White House, on the other hand, consisted of persons who were disproportionately from the South. The White House, therefore, tended to have an empathy for the needs of the southern, growing cities, whereas the bureaucrats at HUD tended to have an empathy for the needs of the northeastern, declining cities. As a result, the formation of the administration's urban policy became an internal debate over what constituted "real" need. The White House insisted that need included the problems associated with growth; HUD insisted that need was primarily associated with decline. Since the president had determined that no new funding would be made available for urban programs, the White House position actually would have lowered the absolute level of urban funds allocated to the Northeast. HUD's position, on the other hand, would have further shifted the current allocation patterns that were already generally favorable to the Northeast.

The coalition, of course, supported HUD's position on the definition of need. The White House ignored the coalition's pleas, however, as evidenced by the decision to force HUD to abandon its efforts to define need as being primarily associated with decline, because the White House had determined that its position was not only the correct one but also the one that would prevail on Capitol Hill. In other words, as far as the White House was concerned, the coalition was not as powerful a group as some might have thought. Before the White House was going to adjust its policy positions, the coalition would have to prove that it was an organization powerful enough for the White House to have to alter its policy positions.

THE FEDERAL ROLE IN RESCUING THE CITIES

For years, experts had argued that the cities of the Northeast-Midwest region were in dire need of fiscal assistance. It was not until the 1960s, however, that the federal government began to provide significant amounts of federal funds to the nation's cities. In 1952, for example, only 9 percent of the federal government's grant-in-aid budget of slightly over $2 billion was in the form of direct payments to local governments. By 1975, however, $14.44 billion, or 29 percent of the federal government's grant-in-aid budget of nearly $50 billion, took the form of direct payments to local governments.[6] A major reason the federal government deliberately bypassed the various state governments was that state governments had ignored their urban centers when doling out state revenues and because the urban crisis of the mid-1960s convinced the nation's lawmakers that the nation's urban centers were in dire need of financial help.[7] Whatever the reason, the point is that because the federal government had assumed a significant role in the determination of the economic well-being of the nation's cities, the coalition was in a position to funnel billions of added federal dollars to the cities of the Snowbelt.

THE COALITION: ONE VOICE AMONG MANY

President Carter had indicated on several occasions during his presidential campaign that he did not see his administration giving any special attention to the needs of the northeastern cities. Urban problems, according to Carter, were widely spread throughout the country. In an interview in the *New York Times*, for example, Carter indicated that while energy and the growing obsolescence of the region's factories were special problems of the Northeast, he felt that targeting urban aid only toward the Northeast was unconstitutional.[8] On June 29, 1976, however, Carter did promise before the National Convention of the U.S. Conference of Mayors that he would continue the Democratic tradition of aiding the nation's major urban centers. He also repeated his campaign pledge to create a national urban policy that would clearly map out the responsibilities of the federal, state, and local sectors as well as provide some directions to the potpourri of programs in existence.[9]

While urban advocates of all regions agreed with Carter on the need for organizational reform, neither the Northeast nor the Sunbelt interests were quite certain who would benefit financially from Carter's reorganization pledge, especially since he had thrown in a caveat during his speech that "we cannot just throw money at programs."[10]

Following Carter's election, John Moriarty assigned Shelly Amdur and Laurence Zabar to gather relevant data that would substantiate the Northeast's claim of special need. As Amdur and Zabar examined the numerous urban programs coming up during the Ninety-fifth Congress, Michael Harrington began to contact various coalition members in order to build a political base of support from which its staff findings could be presented to the president. But as the coalition prepared to present its case, so did numerous other groups. Whereas the coalition had played a singular role in the transformation of Defense Manpower Policy Number Four from an executive order near oblivion into an executive order influencing the direction of billions of federal dollars, it was just one voice among many as the newly elected president set out to create his urban policy plan. This was largely due to the fact that urban programs provide separate government subsidies to a large number of groups. This meant that a number of other interested parties (those receiving subsidies) were as concerned about the determination of who got what share of the funds as the coalition was. Among these interested parties were the National Urban League, the U.S. Conference of Mayors, the National League of Cities, the National Association of Counties, and the Associated Builders and Contractors. Each of these organizations was eager to establish friendly relations with the new Carter administration, especially because of the president's often repeated campaign pledge to continue federal assistance to the nation's urban centers.

PRESIDENT CARTER'S URBAN POLICY GETS A SLOW START

The process of forming the Carter urban policy plan began in March 1977. At that time, President Carter sent a memorandum to his Cabinet officers informing them that HUD Secretary Patricia Harris was to head a Cabinet-level, interdepartmental task force, the Urban and Regional Policy Group. The task force was charged with the responsibility of drafting an urban policy plan for the president.[11]

The group was to consist of representatives of the six Cabinet departments that dealt with urban programs—Housing and Urban Development; Commerce; Health, Education, and Welfare (HEW); Labor; Transporation; and the Treasury. The president's memorandum did not set a strict timetable for the completion of the urban policy draft but did call for an interim report by early summer. However, as the task force began its deliberations, the White House failed to follow up this initial memorandum with further directives, and the president failed to indicate to the task force whether he intended to present to the Congress any formal statement on the status of the numerous urban programs in existence. As a result, the Urban and Regional Policy Group was not very active. For its first six months it made little progress toward developing a comprehensive urban program and, instead, spent considerable time fighting over which agency would gain administrative and budget control over any emerging proposals.[12]

As the summer of 1977 drew to a close without the formation of an urban policy statement from the president, Vernon E. Jordan, Jr., executive director of the National Urban League, publicly denounced the administration for "dragging its feet" and abandoning the cause of the nation's urban centers and their residents, many of whom were black and had supported Carter during the 1976 presidential election.[13]

In response to Jordan's denunciation of the administration, Carter ordered Stuart Eizenstat to take responsibility for speeding up the deliberations of the Urban and Regional Policy Group. Eizenstat then instructed the Urban and Regional Policy Group to complete its urban policy proposal in time for a major presidential announcement in March 1978 and to have an outline of its final proposals ready for President Carter's State of the Union message in January 1978.[14] Eizenstat, however, did not become personally involved in the task force' deliberations at that time. The fact that no one at the White House got involved in the formation of the proposals until much later in the deliberations was seen as an indication by many urban advocates that President Carter did not view his urban policy as having a very high priority. As the mayor of Boston, Massachusetts, Kevin White, stated:

. . . I think his [President Carter's] heart is not in [his urban program]. There are some things my heart is not in and it isn't that the thing doesn't need attending. I try and take care of a lot. But you get extra enthusiastic about those things either of which you have knowledge or you're drawn to it and then respond to it and that has not been the case with him.
. . . The bottom line, I think is, one, there's a lack of understanding or empathy and the second thing, I think, is that he has obviously been preoccupied with foreign concerns.[15]

Since the president was still not pressuring his task force to complete action on its urban policy recommendations and was not taking a leading role in settling the jurisdictional "turf battles" that were still holding up progress on the policy, the task force did not complete and send its first draft of the national urban program ("Cities and People in Distress") to Eizenstat for his approval until October 1977.[16] The draft reflected the unresolved internal jurisdictional battles between the executive departments in that it consisted of a laundry list of existing programs. It advocated only one new proposal, the establishment of an urban development bank that would provide low-interest loans to firms located in distressed areas. Since President Carter had indicated during the presidential campaign that he wanted a new urban strategy and not a rehash of existing programs, Eizenstat rejected the task force' recommendations and ordered another, more comprehensive draft prepared.

As the Urban and Regional Policy Group began to work on the second draft, a noticeable absence of activity existed on the part of the Northeast–Midwest Congressional Coalition and other urban public interest groups. Unlike the congressional process, where the coalition, comprised of congressional members, has within its power the ability to initiate and to influence the outcome of any particular piece of legislation of interest, the executive formation process can be, if the administration so desires, largely immune from the direct interference or influence of any nonexecutive entity. In this case, the administration chose not to allow any outside, direct "interference" with the initial deliberations of the Urban and Regional Policy Group. The reason was that, as Donna Shalala, assistant secretary for policy development and research of HUD recalls, the Carter administration was attempting to do something that had never been done before: to construct a national urban program, encompassing both project and formula grants.[17] Not only had this never been done before, but the individuals assigned to do it were, for the most part, newly appointed by the Carter administration. They were still in the process of trying to understand the current operating procedures of their respective agencies and had little idea of how to go about creating new ones. In this sense, the isolation of the urban formation process during the 1977–78 period was less of a power play by the administration and more of a forced isolation, one that had to occur as the administration's agency heads "got their act together."[18] As a result, clientele interest groups, the coalition, and Congress, faced with a new administration attempting to determine its own policies, were forced to wait and see what emerged from the internal convulsions that accompany the turnover of one president to the next. Frank Godfried, legislative aide specializing in urban affairs for House Speaker O'Neill, for example, indicated that while the Speaker's office was kept abreast of developments concerning the president's urban program, the Speaker made little effort to influence the formation process, choosing instead to use his influence to get whatever emerged enacted once it reached the Congress.[19]

The coalition and other urban interest groups were forced to wait until the Urban and Regional Policy Group submitted its drafts; this of course did not mean that the president's task force was unaware of the influence the coalition and other urban interest groups have on the legislative process. Each member of the group possessed a unique set of subgovernment partners. Nearly all of these subgovernment partners, however, were from the Northeast. It was not surprising, therefore, that in its first draft the group stressed the concept of targeting existing aid to the nation's most distressed cities. While the draft did not specify what criteria would determine eligibility requirements for being designated a distressed city, it was clear that any such designation would benefit cities of the Northeast and Midwest.

THE OFFICE OF MANAGEMENT AND BUDGET: CARTER CHANGES THE PARAMETERS

In November 1977 the Urban and Regional Policy Group submitted its second urban policy draft to Eizenstat; but again he did not believe that the task force' draft had created an overall urban strategy. Consequently, Eizenstat instructed his own staff to draft an urban policy statement for the president. In the meantime, the Office of Management and Budget (OMB) was preparing President Carter's fiscal 1979 budget, and the financing of the urban program became a major issue at the White House.

President Carter knew that in order to please his urban constituents, who had been instrumental in his election in 1976, he would have to increase the amount of federal aid that had been offered to cities under the two previous Republican administrations. The U.S. Conference of Mayors, for example, had already called for an $11.3 billion increase of Federal spending in fiscal 1979 for urban programs.[20] President Carter also knew, however, that while increasing the amount of federal aid to urban areas would solidify his support among urban and black constituencies, this action would not be viewed favorably by the majority of the public who wanted to see the federal government spending less, rather than more on cities. Carter knew that he had been nominated and elected largely on the strength of his promises to control government programs and to balance the federal budget. He also knew that Congress was not in a spending mood; particularly, Congress was not disposed to support any new spending proposals if most of the benefits of these proposals were directed at a particular section of the country. As a result, the president let it be known to the Urban and Regional Policy Group, through Eizenstat, that in order to work toward a balanced federal budget no new significant funds would be made available for urban programs.

This development flew in the face of the pattern of exponential growth that had marked the development of urban policies. In the past decade there had always been more money available for these programs. Because of this, urban subgovernments, dominated by representatives from the Northeast, were able to adopt policies that were favorable to the Northeast, yet still provided increased levels of spending for the Sunbelt as well. Because everyone received more funding year after year, everyone at the subgovernment level was relatively pleased and there were few challenges to urban subgovernment decisions. As a result of the Carter announcement, however, if federal aid were to be channeled directly to those cities most in need (defined as being in decline), as earlier drafts of the urban policy plan indicated, funds that had been directed to other urban areas would have to be reduced. In effect, Carter's position made HUD's proposals redistributive rather than distributive in nature; that is, aid that had previously been given almost without limit would now have become subject to choice among particular classes of beneficiaries. This development, of course, produced an immediate outcry from the urban public interest groups of the Sunbelt that did not want to see their federal aid reduced. On December 7, 1977, HUD Secretary Patricia Harris addressed the National Convention of the National League of Cities one of the affected urban interest groups. In an obvious appeal for support, Secretary Harris declared that she would endeavor to make certain that the Sunbelt cities would not be shortchanged when the final version of the Urban and Regional Policy Group's recommendations was presented to the President. To the enthusiastic applause of the crowd she declared that the Carter administration "will not rob St. Petersburg to pay Minneapolis–St. Paul" and that "we will have an urban policy that addresses need, not greed."[21]

CARTER TAKES A STAND: AN URBAN POLICY FOR EVERYONE

The Harris speech reflected a shift in emphasis that had quickly developed as a result of President Carter's "no new spending" directive and Eizenstat's strong disapproval of the early drafts of the Urban and Regional Policy Group's urban program. The shift was away from targeting aid so narrowly that the most distressed cities (most of which were located in the Northeast) would receive the bulk of urban aid funds. Instead, the various urban programs' formulas were to be constructed in such a way as to provide aid for growing Sunbelt cities as well. The reasoning behind this White House decision to shift HUD's initial direction of resources was that urban problems were caused by growth as well as by decline. Critics of the White House shift, however, were quick to argue that the shift in emphasis was a political move to attract additional support for the president's urban program and that the shift actually diluted the effectiveness of the program instead of strengthening it.[22]

The urban development bank provides an excellent example of the effect this White House-induced shift in emphasis had upon the formulas being constructed at HUD. As presented in the Urban and Regional Policy Group's first two drafts, the urban development bank would have provided low-interest loans and marketing assistance to private businesses that were located in distressed cities. The designation of distressed city was so narrowly focused in the second draft that cities in only seventeen states would qualify for these services.[23] While this proposal would have directed federal urban aid to areas of particular need, it was not politically expedient, as the proposal did not offer enough congressional districts a share of the urban aid pie to insure congressional approval. This was especially the case since other portions of the urban grant-in-aid program would not, in light of President Carter's "no new spending" directive, provide compensatory aid to the other thirty-three states. The formula that was finally introduced to the Congress, on the other hand, awarded aid to 30 percent of the nation's local governments, and every state had at least one recipient.

On December 23, 1977, Secretary Harris sent a lengthy memorandum to Stuart Eizenstat that reflected an acceptance on HUD's part of the White House preference for broad targeting of aid. The memorandum was meant to supersede the group's second urban draft, the one that had been so poorly received at the White House that one White House aide had reportedly called it a "piece of sh––."[24] The memorandum clearly stated that the president should not concentrate on the older, distressed cities of the Northeast and Midwest, but should also provide aid to the newer cities of the South and West.[25]

The presidential shift away from providing aid only to declining cities and toward all cities in "distress" was a result of (1) the conviction on the president's and his personal staff's part that urban distress was too narrowly defined, and (2) their political assessment that the coalition (which was then still in its infancy as an organization) and the urban subgovernments could be maneuvered into a position where they could not prevent this shift once the legislation reached the Congress.

The White House strategy was to open up the urban policy process near its conclusion (after the administration had decided what it wanted to do) so that virtually every interest group and governmental agency involved with the management of urban programs would be consulted before the formal announcement of the administration's urban policy. The administration hoped to gain the support of these executive agencies and of their chief interest groups by making them feel they were a part of the formation process. In this way, many of these groups might be willing to accept policy positions that were not as beneficial as they might have hoped, because they would feel as if the administration had met them halfway, as confidants, not antagonists. If successful, the administration's strategy would gain the support of two of the three partners within most urban subgovernments without having to significantly alter its policy preference. The congressional members of these urban subgovernments (who supported HUD's initial position) would then be pressured to adopt the administration's position on need without major revision. Also, the administration would gain the support of groups responsible for implementing the programs once they were enacted. Bert Carp, aide to Eizenstat, commented that President Carter's urban process was intended to avoid the "consistent difficulties presidents have had getting programs enacted or administered."[26]

THE COALITION'S APPEAL TO THE WHITE HOUSE FALLS ON DEAF EARS

This White House-initiated shift in emphasis, of course, was not well received at the Northeast–Midwest Congressional Coalition. Early drafts of the national urban program had not only stressed targeting aid to northeastern cities but had also included the implementation of DMP-4 (see Chapter 5) and a proposal to locate a greater portion of federal facilities, both civilian and military, in areas of economic distress. Now, on one of the most important issues facing the Northeast, the coalition was not certain of anything. The time had come to act.

On January 10, 1978, the day before Eizenstat would send the final urban program draft to the president, Michael Harrington sent Eizenstat a memorandum reminding him of the coalition's successful efforts in the past year in restructuring the community development block grant program, Defense Manpower Policy Number Four, and the food stamp program. The memorandum clearly was intended to indicate to Eizenstat that the coalition would have to be reckoned with as the urban program worked its way through the Congress.[27]

The next day, however, January 11, 1978, the final draft of the urban program was sent to President Carter in the form of a ten-page memorandum, developed from the December 23 Harris memorandum and the work of Eizenstat's staff. The draft advocated five general principles around which a more detailed urban proposal would be constructed. While the draft clearly indicated that growth as well as decline should be used as a criterion of urban need, it also surprisingly cited as one of the underlying causes of urban decay the wide dispersal of federal aid that resulted in less aid being sent to distressed cities than would otherwise be the case.[28]

Responding to the urban draft, President Carter, on January 25, 1978, sent a memorandum to Harris and Eizenstat that read, in part:[29]

. . . proceed on urban policy . . . but

(a)   include all cities
(b)   analyze existing programs first
(c)   encompass federal, state, local Governments [sic] and private and neighborhood groups and volunteers.

I would like to place a major emphasis on (c) and try to do it in an inspirational and exciting way if possible.

The president also added his own views to the ten-page Harris-Eizenstat memorandum and arrived at a final figure of fourteen general principles around which the urban program was to be constructed. These principles, however, were still of a very general nature. For example, one of the principles was to "help urban areas respond to housing and neighborhood revitalization needs", another was to "strengthen the private sector economic base of urban areas, and improve their physical facilities."[30] This kind of vagueness indicated to the coalition leaders that specific program details had not yet been worked out.[31] The coalition still had time to exert whatever influence it had to offset this new emphasis on targeting to both declining and growing areas of need, rather than only to declining cities. The fact that the president chose to indicate in his memorandum that he wanted all cities included and not just needy cities, however, signaled that convincing the administration would be difficult if not impossible.

In a final effort to urge the administration to rethink its drift away from targeting aid to only the most distressed cities, Michael Harrington led a contingent of the coalition's leading members in a face-to-face meeting with Eizenstat on February 21, 1978. [32] During the meeting, Eizenstat was reportedly polite but unmoved by their arguments for a narrower dispersion of funds. His position reflected the fact that the president had made up his mind not to target aid to the older cities of the Snowbelt.[33]

On March 21, 1978, the Urban and Regional Policy Group submitted its final draft of urban recommendations to the president. Despite the nearly year-long formative process, the final draft still presented the president with seventy options concerning specific programs. The draft provided the president the freedom to choose his own definition of need and at what level of spending the entire program would be funded. At this time, Israeli Prime Minister Menachem Begin made an emergency visit to the White House to discuss the Middle East situation, forcing the president to set aside his urban proposals for another few days.

On March 24 the president finally sat down to complete his urban proposals. While he later denied it, it was reported that he initially rejected nearly all of the task force program recommendations and cut the amount of aid offered to urban areas by billions of dollars. The president reportedly changed his mind only after Eizenstat and his chief political advisor, Hamilton Jordan, convinced him that such actions would be political suicide.[34]

On March 27, 1978, President Carter officially announced his urban program to the Congress. While the president's announcement dispelled the rumors that had spread across Capitol Hill that he would decimate the national urban program, he called for only nominal increases in federal spending for urban needs; $742 million more in fiscal 1979, $2.9 billion more in fiscal 1980, and $2.8 billion more in fiscal 1981. In addition, the president announced that when he introduced to the Congress the specific legislative proposals of his national urban program (detailed in Chapter 7) he would target the funds to distressed cities. He did not, however, indicate what his definition of distress was—one that would target aid to the older cities of the Snowbelt or one that would include the needs of the growing cities of the Sunbelt.[35]

While the size of the increase in federal spending was disturbing to all urban interests groups, including the coalition, the reported action of the president on March 24 convinced them all that the president would not actively support his urban program, even at this modest level of spending. Thus, at this time, activist members of the coalition, who accepted the fact that the president was certain to introduce formulas that would spread the limited amount of urban aid throughout the nation were faced with a question: Could the coalition rewrite his proposal's formulas within the legislative process—or failing that, as was most likely given the antispending mood of the Congress—should the coalition concentrate on protecting what little there was to offer the Snowbelt in the president's program? This question and the Coalition's answer will be examined in Chapter 7.

CONCLUSION: CARTER CONCLUDES THAT THE COALITION CAN BE BEATEN

President Carter's urban program recommended more than 160 changes in thirty-eight existing urban programs that were designed to make them more urban-oriented. Most of these changes did not require legislative action. They were administrative changes that, unlike the president's legislative proposals, were initiated and acted upon by the executive bureaucracy in relative independence of the White House. These changes did not attract the attention that was focused upon the president's legislative proposals, but they did have a profound effect on the regional distribution of urban funds, more than the legislative proposals, most of which were not passed. For example, the Environmental Protection Agency was instructed to change its guidelines for granting water and sewerage funds (one of the largest of all grant programs) so that more funds would be allocated to sewerage facilities in need of rehabilitation rather than to the development of new sewerage systems. This would redirect sewerage funds from developing areas to older urban areas.[36]

While these administrative changes were applauded by the coalition, the coalition had little to do with the decision to make these changes. It was the Department of Housing and Urban Development bureaucrats, coined the "Administration's left wing" by Donna Shalala, who were pushing for more aid to the older, declining cities of the Northeast.[37] It was their belief that need was the most prevalent in the Northeast. According to analysts for the Southern Growth Policies Board, many of these bureaucrats had been educated in, and were natives of, the northeastern states and tended to define need in terms that benefited the Northeast.

Along with these administrative changes, President Carter also allowed the Urban and Regional Policy Group to continue working on four major administrative changes the president felt would provide the foundation allowing him to gain some measure of control over the cornucopia of urban programs. Among these changes was the establishment of urban and community impact analyses by all federal agencies. As Donna Shalala, assistant secretary at HUD who was responsible for initiating this change, commented:

> Every time Treasury changes the Tax Code, every time Congress alters a welfare program, every time the Defense Department awards a military contract, urban policy is being made.[38]

These urban and community impact analyses, used for the first time on an experimental basis during the formation of this urban program, were designed to inform the White House how these normally considered nonurban federal actions affected urban areas.

Other administrative changes encouraged by the president were the implementation of DMP-4 (see Chapter 5), providing priorities to locating civilian and defense facilities in "distressed" areas, and the establishment of an interagency Coordinating Council that would use the information gained from the urban and community impact analyses and other studies to coordinate the actions taken by all federal agencies whose programs affected urban areas. The coalition supported all of these changes and anxiously awaited the issuance of the executive orders that would implement these proposals, but it was not in a position to play a decisive role in the resolution of these issues.

The Northeast fared so well in the determination of these administrative policies because the executive branch can, if the president cooperates with the bureaucracy, circumvent the disparate political considerations that are so often crucial to the legislative branch. In this particular circumstance, HUD officials desired to coordinate administrative practices so that they would be in a better position to eliminate the antiurban bias of federal actions. They were given the means to do so because the president viewed these executive orders as a means of securing some measure of control over a distributive policy area that had proved to be resistant to presidential interference. As a by-product of this executive deal between the bureaucracy and the president, the Northeast happened to be the major beneficiary.

Although the coalition was not a major factor in the determination of the outcome of these administrative changes, it was a factor in the determination of the president's legislative proposals. The White House respected the coalition's potential impact on urban policies through its membership in many urban subgovernments. The fact that the White House decided to force the bureaucracy to redesign its programs' formulas anyway, however, indicates that the White House did not share the *National Journal's* opinion that the coalition was a "well-oiled, bipartisan lobbying machine."[39] The White House believed that the coalition would be unable (1) to rewrite the formulas at the subgovernment level despite the fact that the committees handling these formulas were dominated by representatives of the Northeast-Midwest region, or (2) to rewrite the formulas once they reached the floor of the House.

The White House confidence derived from several interrelated factors. First, and perhaps most important, was that given the administration's "no new spending" directive, the coalition's efforts to target funds more narrowly clearly altered a distributive policy and made it redistributive over geographic lines. While most of the representatives on the subcommittees dealing with urban programs were from the Northeast, all of the Sunbelt representatives on these subcommittees were aware of this potential alteration (because of the just-concluded fight between the White House and the bureaucracy). These Sunbelt legislators were already threatening to challenge any of their subcommittees' decisions that were redistributive once they reached the floor of the House. As Patricia Dusenbury, program analyst for the Southern Growth Policies Board specializing in urban affairs, recalled, most Sunbelt legislators remained silent during the formation of the urban program in the executive branch because it was expected that the Northeast would do slightly better than the Sunbelt in the determination of who got what share of the funds.[40] But now that the process had been completed, and as expected no new funding was forthcoming, these Sunbelt representatives were willing to fight for their share of the program's subsidies. Many of them were still angry over their loss in the housing and community development fight. In that case (see

Chapter 2), the Sunbelt had lost only in a relative sense, since the program's funding level for all regions had been increased. This time, however, any rewriting of the administration's formulas would mean an absolute loss of funds for the Sunbelt. In their eyes, the stakes were now higher than they had been in the housing and community development formula fight. The Sunbelt representatives on each subcommittee (acting independently of one another) were willing to abandon the traditional committee practice of supporting the subcommittee's decision if that subcommittee backed the coalition's efforts. The Snowbelt leaders of these urban subgovernments knew this, as did the administration and the coalition leaders.

The administration believed that the leaders of the various urban subcommittees would reject the coalition's efforts to turn their programs into redistributive policies and that they would adhere to the norm of logrolling that is associated with distributive policies. The administration took this position because it believed that these urban subcommittee leaders knew that even if they accepted the coalition's position, as opposed to the administration's, the mood of the Congress was to reject such policies on the floor of the House. The easy route to follow, the one that had been followed before, was to go along with the administration's proposals, particularly since they continued to direct a sizable portion of urban aid to the Northeast.

While the coalition's leaders knew that the administration's broad definition of need was politically more palatable than their own narrower definition, their belief that these urban policies were part of a larger, redistributive system of federal aid demanded that they at least try to get these subcommittees to reject the administration's policies. They recognized, however, that not all of the urban subcommittees were led by a coalition activist and that even some of the activists were reluctant to disrupt their relatively friendly subcommittee environments and turn them into regional battlegrounds.

CHAPTER SEVEN *President Carter's Urban Program, 1977–78: The Legislative Confrontation*

President Carter's urban message to the Congress on March 27, 1978, provided only the outline of his urban program. The president did not send specific pieces of legislation to Congress until much later in the session because the White House and the federal agencies continued to be divided over the definition of need. The bureaucrats were still advocating a definition of need that favored the older, declining cities of the Northeast, and the White House was still pushing for aid to all cities. The Northeast–Midwest Congressional Coalition, in the meantime, as well as other northeastern urban interest groups (especially big-city mayors), braced themselves for what they perceived as a rough fight over urban funds. They felt that Patricia Harris's speech—especially her vow that "we will not rob St. Petersburg to pay Minneapolis–St. Paul"—was an indication that the White House was not going to let the bureaucrats get their way.[1] As it turned out, they were right. All four of the president's major urban bills—supplemental fiscal assistance, national development bank, investment tax credit, and public works— contained formulas that more broadly defined need than the formulas that had been proposed by the executive agencies.

As coalition leaders assessed their chances of rewriting these formulas at the subgovernment level, they realized that several obstacles lay in their path. Not only were the White House and Sunbelt representatives strongly opposed to a more narrow definition of need, but only one of the four bills, the national development bank bill, was referred to a committee that was chaired by a representative from the Northeast-Midwest region. Also, of the three bills referred to committees chaired by a representative of the Sunbelt, only one, the public works bill, was referred to a subcommittee that was chaired by a representative from the Northeast-Midwest.

On the positive side, however, urban funds were easily translated into subsidy terms alone. Contrary to the case with defense procurement funds, the first question representatives from the Snowbelt asked was how each of their districts fared in the determination of who got what, not whether or not the national security interests of the United States were being threatened. Also, since urban funds were easily translated into subsidy terms alone, partisan and ideological divisions within the coalition were mute. The coalition's leaders thus knew that their major weapon on floor votes—information—would be of vital importance on these issues. If they could devise formulas that aided the Snowbelt, they could inform their members of this fact and, most likely, overrule any "hostile" subgovernment decisions on the House floor. The problem, however, was that the president's "no new spending" directive made it impossible for them to devise a formula that allocated aid to all, or nearly all of the Northeast's districts while still targeting the aid to those cities most in need. The coalition could redefine need on the House floor without increasing these programs' funding levels only by convincing Snowbelt representatives who were not benefited by the narrower definition of need to vote for the new formulas anyway. The coalition, however, had no weapons to force these representatives to vote against their local and for their regional interests.

THE SUPPLEMENTAL FISCAL ASSISTANCE BILL: A GALLANT EFFORT FALLS SHORT

The supplemental fiscal assistance bill would have provided $2 billion over a two-year period to cities and communities that were in an economic state of "distress." It was introduced by the Carter administration to replace the anti-recession fiscal assistance program that was to expire on September 30, 1978. This program, commonly referred to as the countercyclical revenue-sharing program, had been enacted in 1976 and extended in 1977 as a means of providing direct federal aid to states, cities, and communities experiencing high unemployment as a result of the recession.[2]

The countercyclical revenue-sharing program's funds were distributed quarterly to eligible state and local governments whenever the national unemployment rate exceeded 6 percent; state governments received one third of the available funds and local governments two thirds.[3] Because eligibility depended upon having at least 4.5 percent unemployment for both state and local governments and funds were allocated by "excess" unemployment over the national average, the Snowbelt, as a region experiencing high unemployment rates in fiscal 1977 and 1978, received the bulk of the available funds.[4] New York State, for example, received $487 million during the program's two-year existence, more than the fourteen states of the South, which received a combined total of only $473 million during the same period.[5]

Recipient governments of the countercyclical revenue-sharing program's funds used them to subsidize their employees' salaries and to hold down property taxes while continuing essential services. Many recipient governments, despite the fact that the antirecessionary program was scheduled to expire, had already written into their budgets monies that were expected to be allocated by the program. Failure to enact the president's or some alternative program would have caused local governments to cut governmental services, to lay off public employees, and/or to increase their property taxes.

The Carter administration's proposal was introduced in the House of Representatives on April 24, 1978, by L. H. Fountain (D-N.C.), chairman of the Government Operations Subcommittee on Intergovernmental Affairs (the subcommittee of jurisdiction). The president's proposal made several major changes in the program, confirming the coalition's fear that he intended to spread urban aid more widely. Among the revisions the president proposed was the elimination of the 6 percent national unemployment rate "triggering" mechanism so that the program's funds could continue to be allocated even if the national unemployment rate declined below 6 percent, as was expected, in fiscal 1979.[6] The president also proposed to retain the 4.5 percent unemployment criterion for determining aid eligibility for local governments. He did add an alternative eligibility formula, however, that would allow a local government whose unemployment rate was below 4.5 percent to be eligible if that government's growth rates were below the national average during the previous five years in two of three categories:

Committee wanted to save the bill because many local governments, especially of larger cities, had already included the proposal's funds in their operating budgets. When Fountain's subcommittee vote was made public, representatives of these local governments and from the National League of Cities, the U.S. Conference of Mayors, and the National Association of Counties began to call their senators' offices to find out if the president's bill, or some facsimile of it, could be saved. Each of these groups preferred a slightly different formula for the program, but they joined together in pressuring their senators in the fear that nothing would be adopted.

With this political pressure flooding into Washington, the Senate Finance Committee members decided that a scaled-down version of the expiring countercyclical aid program was in order. As a result, the Finance Committee substituted a modified version of the expiring countercyclical aid program for the text of H.R. 2852, a minor tax bill.[16] House Speaker O'Neill, who supported the concept of countercyclical aid, could now circumvent the Government Operations Committee by asking for a vote of concurrence to the Senate amendments to the minor tax bill on the floor of the House.[17] Before the Speaker could do this, however, the House Rules Committee would have to issue a rule on the bill. Surprisingly, James Delaney (D-N.Y.), chairman of that committee, refused to schedule a committee meeting so that it could grant the bill a rule. Delaney's action reportedly stemmed from the fact that the Speaker had neglected to attend a farewell party that was given in honor of Delaney, as he was to retire at the end of the Ninety-fifth Congress.[18]

It should be noted that the coalition, while responsible for setting these events in motion by forcing Fountain's subcommittee to vote on the president's proposal, had little to do with the Senate's decision to circumvent the Government Operations Committee or with the negotiations which ensued between O'Neill and Delaney to grant the bill a rule. This is not meant to belittle the importance of the coalition's role in this series of events, but it does indicate that its efforts often work in concert with, rather than in isolation of, other political forces that work in the interests of the northeastern states.

As O'Neill attempted to pacify Delaney, Fountain and Brooks realized that the Senate Finance Committee's action would most

per capita income, population, or unemployment.[7] The president also proposed to limit the amount of aid provided to any government to the amount of aid received under the provisions of the countercyclical aid program in fiscal 1978.

While the second, alternative formula put forward by President Carter promised to target more funds to the Snowbelt (because the Sunbelt had experienced rapid growth during the 1970s), it also allowed approximately 10,000 additional local governments to become eligible for funds.[8] Since the president placed a ceiling on the aid received by previously eligible governments and his proposal called for the expenditure of nearly $250,000 less in fiscal 1979 than was spent under the countercyclical aid program in fiscal 1978, the most economically distressed cities of the Snowbelt were slated to receive less aid in fiscal 1979 than in fiscal 1978.[9] This situation, of course, was not well received at the Northeast–Midwest Congressional Coalition or by the public interest groups that represented the affected cities. The Carter administration, however, argued that since the unemployment rate was expected to fall below 6 percent in 1979, the proposal at least offered some aid to those cities that would otherwise receive no funds.

Hearings on the president's proposal commenced in the Senate Finance Committee's Subcommittee on Revenue Sharing, chaired by William Hathaway (D-Maine), on May 3, 1978, and in the House Government Operations Subcommittee on Intergovernmental Affairs, chaired by L. H. Fountain (D-N.C.), on May 4, 1978. At both of these hearings, the administration's chief witness, Robert Carswell, deputy secretary of the Treasury Department, was asked by the respective subcommittee chairmen to explain why the administration chose to target aid under the program so broadly that 26,211 local governments (nearly 70 percent of all local governments) were eligible for aid under the supplemental fiscal assistance program. In contrast, under the expiring countercyclical aid program, only 17,003 local governments were eligible.[10] Carswell defended the program, stating:

> . . . This program is an essential element of the President's recently announced policy for distressed areas and is aimed at alleviating fiscal stress of local governments throughout the nation.[11]

Later in the hearings, Carswell once again defended the program's distribution of funds, stating that under the proposals, "the top ten [distressed cities] still get one-quarter [of the funds] and the top fifty get 33 percent."[12] Carswell had made the administration's position clear. The bulk of the program's funds was still to be directed at the most distressed cities, but a significant portion of the funds would be dispersed throughout the nation.

Most members of the House and Senate subcommittees considering the president's proposal realized that its revised formula was designed to attract additional political support, yet the formula actually caused two normally antagonistic groups—fiscal conservatives and urban representatives—to join together to oppose the bill. Fiscal conservatives in the committees, many of whom represented nonurban areas and received little of the program's funds, felt that since inflation was now the dominant national concern, it was unwise to dole out urban funds to communities whose distress was questionable. If such funds had to be allocated, they believed, the administration should spend such funds only on the very neediest cities and at substantially lower levels of spending than proposed. On the other hand, urban representatives on the committees, from both the Snowbelt and the Sunbelt states believed that the increased number of eligible local governments, coupled with the lower level of spending, so diluted the program's effectiveness that they could not support it. Several members of the House Government Operations Committee who represented urban districts decided to introduce an alternative bill whose formula targeted aid more narrowly so that more of the available funds would be awarded to the larger, more "needy" cities. This alternative bill (H.R. 11298) was introduced by William Moorhead (D-Pa.), a leading coalition member. The program would have retained the expiring countercyclical aid program's formula, except that the national unemployment trigger would be lowered from 6 to 5.5 percent.[13]

At this point, the coalition's staff members and leaders recognized that its point of view corresponded to Moorhead's and offered him whatever support he felt the coalition could provide. As the hearings on the program progressed, however, it became clear that there was little that the coalition or Moorhead could expect to accomplish on the issue at this level because L. H. Fountain, the subcommittee chairman, announced his opposition to both Moorhead's and the president's bill on the ground that both were inflationary.

Fountain refused to bring either of the bills to subcommittee. Although the other members of th could have forced Fountain to consider the bills, agreed with his views of the bills and supported his bring them to a vote. The fact that the chairman Government Operations Committee, Jack Brooks (I opposed the two bills as being inflationary meant that h try to induce Fountain to consider the bills. Therefore, ings on the president's supplemental fiscal assistance prog on May 5, 1978, no further action on the program was within the House Government Operations Committee meantime, the Senate Finance Committee also postponed islative action on the program as it waited for the House to

As the session rapidly headed to a close, it appeared as Sunbelt's positioning in the committee structure had again trated the efforts of the coalition's activists. The longer the F Government Operation Committee ignored the president's Moorhead's bills, the less time was available for both the House Senate to complete all the necessary steps required for a bill become law. With time running out, Harrington decided that t coalition had to act. Recognizing that any bill, even the president' was better than none, he circulated a petition among the coalition membership that asked Fountain to schedule a markup session on the president's bill. The petition was signed by forty-eight coalition members, including House Speaker O'Neill, and was delivered to Fountain on August 1, 1978.[14]

In response to this petition, Fountain brought the matter to his subcommittee for consideration. According to one legislative aide who was present at this session, Fountain agreed to have the bill considered only after he had made certain, by asking the members, that the proposal would be defeated. Once he was sure that it would be killed, Fountain recognized the motion of his friend, Elliot Levitas (D-Ga.), who offered the bill (also knowing that it was going to be defeated). Then, stating that he was in the mood to "dispose of it," Fountain happily recorded a 7–6 vote to table the president's proposal.[15]

The Senate Finance Committee now recognized that the president's bill was finished unless it acted and so decided to take a somewhat unorthodox move to save the bill. The Senate Finance

likely result in enactment of a countercyclical aid program because the program's clientele interest groups were so aggressively lobbying on the Hill. In an effort to kill the Senate's bill, on October 10, 1978, they mailed to each member of the House a "Dear Colleague" letter arguing that the bill was inflationary and "an irregular vehicle [used] to circumvent the integrity of House procedures."[19]

In the effort to get Delaney to allow the Rules Committee to grant the bill a rule before the House adjourned for the upcoming congressional elections, House Speaker O'Neill had President Carter pay Delaney a personal visit. As a result of this visit, Delaney finally allowed the Rules Committee to consider the bill. The elapsed time, however, was great, as the bill was not given a rule until the early hours of October 15, 1978, the last day Congress would be in session, and a time when congressmen were frantically trying to complete action on a half dozen other major pieces of legislation.

As the final day of the Ninety-fifth Congress began, conservative Republican Robert Bauman (R-Md.), realizing that the Senate's bill was certain to be adopted on the House floor, informed the Speaker that he and his fellow conservative Republicans, who opposed the bill as being inflationary, would begin various legislative maneuvers to hold up legislative business. Since the energy and tax bills, as well as a number of other important pieces of legislation, had yet to be voted on, the Speaker agreed not to call up the countercyclical aid bill for consideration until after the energy and tax bills had been voted on. The Speaker refused, however, to take H.R. 2852 off the schedule. But that afternoon, once the energy, tax, and several other bills were voted upon, most members of the House hurriedly left the Capitol to begin their final campaign drives. It was impossible to gather a quorum for a vote on the countercyclical aid bill, and it died.

THE NATIONAL DEVELOPMENT BANK: COMPLICATIONS DELAY ACTION

On June 21, 1978, William Moorhead (D-Pa.) and Henry Reuss (D-Wis.), chairman of the House Banking, Finance and Urban

Affairs Committee, both prominent members of the Northeast–Midwest Congressional Coalition, introduced what many considered the centerpiece of the president's urban program, the national development bank proposal. The bill, H.R. 13230, would have established a federal interagency "bank" that would, over a three-year period, provide the private sector with incentives to locate and expand within distressed areas by reducing the cost of capital investment through grants ($1.6 billion), loan guarantees ($8 billion), and interest rate subsidies on bonds ($13.8 billion).[20]

The concept of an urban development bank as a means of stimulating economic activity within the nation's economically distressed cities was not new. The idea had been kicked around on Capitol Hill for a number of years. Each of the bank's advocates, however, had a different idea about how the "urbank" should be administered, what types of aid the bank should provide, and who should have responsibility for running the program. Since the northeastern states had the highest incidence of distressed cities, most of the urbank advocates were members of the Northeast–Midwest Congressional Coalition. William Moorhead, for example, was a longtime advocate of the urbank concept and had introduced legislation in past Congresses that would have provided public funding not only for private development, as provided in the president's proposal, but also for the subsidization of various governmental functions. Michael Harrington also had long favored the urbank concept and had introduced a bill during the Ninety-fourth Congress that would have established a system of regional urban development banks.[21]

While Moorhead's and Harrington's proposals differed, both men had a keen interest in the president's urban development bank proposal, as both viewed the bank as a means of slowing the relocation of businesses from the cities to the suburbs as well as from the Snowbelt to the Sunbelt. As indicated in the previous chapter, however, the president's national development bank proposal had undergone a massive metamorphosis by the time it was introduced in the House. The Urban and Regional Policy Group's early emphasis on providing aid only to the most economically distressed cities was no longer in force. The final Carter proposal provided federal aid to induce private sector investment in distressed cities (termed "leveraging") in both large and small urban areas, in both declining and growing urban areas, and even in some rural areas. As Vice President Walter Mondale stated before the U.S. Conference of Mayors, the bill now provided a little aid for just about everyone:

The bank can serve the economic need of all areas of our country. The bank can serve a big city like Atlanta or a rural county like Hancock. It could serve New York City and it could serve a pocket of poverty in a city like Houston.[22]

The specific requisite for eligibility for aid in the president's proposal was the possession by any local government, regardless of population size, of a per captia income level not exceeding 125 percent of the national average and meeting three criteria of economic distress during the most recent five-year period: unemployment greater than the national average, population growth rate below the national average, and any increase in absolute dollars in per capita income less than the national average.[23] Also, 10 percent of the available funds were to be set aside for providing aid to the private sector to invest in "pockets of poverty," defined as being any areas of at least 10,000 persons located within an ineligible local government of at least 50,000 persons.[24]

Of the approximately 40,000 local governments (or "jurisdictions," as defined by the bill) in the United States, 12,000 were eligible for funding.[25] While this bill's formula spread the available funds to a number of recipients, most of the program's funds were still directed into the Northeast–Midwest region. As Patricia Dusenbury, program analyst for the Southern Growth Policies Board, indicated in an issue paper that was sent to the governors of the South concerning the bill:

. . . Because growth lag determines basic eligibility, the interregional variations among eligible cities will reflect recent growth trend variations between regions; most major cities in the Northern Tier will be eligible to participate, while in the Southern States, eligible areas will be mostly small [under 10,000] towns.

. . . [Of cities with greater than 100,000 persons] only nine of 57 . . . in the South are eligible . . . while 46 of the 54 major cities in the ten Northern Tier states qualify.[26]

Despite the fact that the national development bank proposal would provide billions of added federal dollars to the Snowbelt and it had been referred in the House to a "friendly" committee and subcommittee, neither the Carter administration nor John Moriarty, executive director of the coalition, felt that the president's bank bill would pass during the Ninety-fifth Congress.[27] One unnamed administration official was quoted by *Congressional Quarterly* as saying: "We'd be naive to think we could get it through this year."[28] John Moriarty concurred:

> The problem with the National Development Bank was that it was not proposed until well into the fall and . . . it was the least organized and thought out program submitted in the entire urban program.
>
> We hired a consultant [Michael Barker] to prepare a working model for a National Urban Bank [because the Carter proposal was so poorly structured]. We wanted hearings on the Development Bank to take place so that we could have the evaluation process begin and so we [the coalition] could be a part of that process.[29]

The problem faced by the coalition and other urban interest groups from the Northeast that wanted an urbank adopted was clearly not positioning in the committee structure of Sunbelt or nonurban representatives; the problem was with the bill itself. From the moment the concept of a federal urban bank was raised by the Urban and Regional Policy Group as a possible ingredient in the president's urban program, the administration of the program became a major source of controversy. Both the Departments of Commerce and Housing and Urban Development claimed that they should administer the program. The president sidestepped this "turf battle" by having the bank run by a tripartite board of directors composed of representatives of both of these departments as well as of the Treasury Department. However, most members of the House Banking, Finance and Urban Affairs Committee believed that this unusual administrative apparatus would cause considerable delays in the delivery of the program's aid and was unacceptable.[30] Since the president's bill was introduced late in the session, most members of the committee felt that this administrative question would not be resolved in time for the bill to be enacted. It was also recognized that many of the committee members, including the chairman, Henry Reuss, would challenge the president's allocation formula as being unresponsive to the needs of America's larger cities. Since the resolution of this issue also required time (the one commodity the bill lacked), few, if any, believed that the president's proposal would be adopted during the Ninety-fifth Congress. In fact, preliminary hearings on the proposal were held by the House Banking, Finance and Urban Affairs Committee on August 1 and 2, 1978, but the bill was never reported for committee or House floor action. The coalition lost round two.

THE 5 PERCENT INVESTMENT TAX CREDIT: THE SENATE COALITION LENDS A HELPING HAND

Congress was in recess when the president announced his urban program on March 27, 1978. When the Congress reconvened on April 3, 1978, the president's entire urban message was scrutinized by the House Budget Committee whose task was to construct the first fiscal 1979 budget resolution by May 15. The Budget Committee's Task Force on State and Local Government, chaired by Elizabeth Holtzman (D-N.Y.), was especially interested in the president's proposal to extend the current 10 percent investment tax credit program that was awarded to any firm to offset the cost of purchasing new machinery and equipment so that the credit would also cover the construction of new plants and the renovation of existing ones. The task force was also interested in the proposal because it called for an additional 5 percent tax credit to offset expenses incurred by companies that built or renovated plants already located in areas of economic distress.[31]

Elizabeth Holtzman was not the only member of Congress interested in the president's tax program. Michael Harrington immediately recognized the potential benefit the enactment of this tax credit would mean to companies in the Northeast that were contemplating a move to the Sunbelt. This was exactly the type of governmental program the Northeast–Midwest Congressional Coalition felt would keep many of these firms from relocating. Harrington thus met with Holtzman to see if they could work together to enhance the proposal's chance for adoption.

The investment tax credit program, first adopted in 1962 at 7 percent and temporarily extended to 10 percent in 1977, was designed to reduce the cost of capital investment and thus stimulate more capital spending. While the consensus at the coalition was that the current investment tax credit program was effective and approved of the president's intention to make the credit permanent, the across-the-board nature of the credit was viewed negatively. Since the credit was not targeted to areas of distress, it was reasoned that the credit contributed to the long-run decline of the northeastern and midwestern economy.[32]

While the across-the-board nature of the 10 percent tax credit was suspect, the coalition's leaders viewed the president's proposal to extend the 10 percent tax credit to new plant construction as being potentially disastrous to the economic well-being of the region's major cities[33] In their view, this portion of the president's proposal would encourage firms to abandon existing facilities currently located in northern cities and move to the surrounding suburbs or even to the Sunbelt where property taxes and other conditions offer businesses lower operating expenses. This development, of course, would exacerbate the already acute problem of declining tax bases within the region's major metropolitan areas as well as the downward economic trend in the region.

Pointing to a study undertaken by the Congressional Budget Office indicating that extending the tax credit to new structures would hasten the exodus of firms located in central cities, Representatives Michael Harrington, Elizabeth Holtzman, Henry Reuss, and Paul Simon, all coalition members, wrote to the president on February 21, 1978, urging him to withdraw this portion of his tax credit proposal. The president's subsequent decision to retain the extension of the tax credit to new construction in his urban message and his decision to allocate $1.4 billion to the credit while allocating only $200 million for the 5 percent "targeted" portion of the tax credit insured that his proposal would receive a thorough examination before Holtzman's Task Force on State and Local Government.

During the hearings on the investment tax credit proposal before her task force on April 3, 1978, Holtzman questioned HUD Secretary Patricia Harris about the administration's decision to allocate so much money for the across-the-board tax credit while limiting the targeted 5 percent "bonus" credit to only $200 million.[34] Harris replied that the 5 percent differential would still have "some significant" effect in stimulating investment in distressed areas but admitted that she did not have any data to substantiate her claim.[35]

Believing that the administration's 5 percent targeted tax credit was introduced as an afterthought, Holtzman heatedly stated later in the hearing that the administration's proposal was a "dagger pointed at the heart of cities."[36] Robert Edgar (D-Pa.), testifying before the task force on behalf of the coalition, stated that the president's "proposal to extend the investment tax credit to new structures is decidedly negative from an urban perspective and is hardly offset by the inclusion of an additional credit for building renovation."[37]

While the House Budget Committee, chaired by Robert Giaimo (D-Conn.), another coalition member, provided an excellent opportunity for it to publicly attack the tax credit proposal, the real political decision-making body on this issue was not the House Budget Committee but the Ways and Means Committee, which would consider the proposal as part of the fiscal 1979 revenue bill.

Only seventeen of the thirty-seven members of the Ways and Means Committee represented districts located in the Snowbelt. It was clear that the coalition could not expect this committee to be as receptive as the Budget Committee had been to its opposition to the president's proposal to extend the 10 percent tax credit to new construction or share its support of the additional 5 percent tax credit for new construction and rehabilition of existing plants in distressed areas.[38] In fact, as the Ways and Means Committee prepared to begin the markup session on the president's tax bill in July, the president's proposal had not been referred to any of the Ways and Means Committee's subcommittees, and it appeared that the proposal would not even be brought up for consideration.

One member of the House Ways and Means Committee, however, William Cotter (D-Conn.), chairman of the coalition's Tax Expenditures Task Force, refused to concede defeat for the targeted aspect of the proposal. He met with several other northeastern representatives on the committee in hopes of determining a means of salvaging what he perceived as being the beneficial aspects of the president's investment tax credit.

As the markup session on the 1979 revenue bill opened before the entire membership of the Ways and Means Committee on July

27, 1978, it had become clear that the chairman, Al Ullman (D-Oreg.), was not going to allow the President's investment tax credit revisions to be considered. Instead—and only as a conciliatory gesture to Cotter and several other northeastern representatives on the committee—he allowed consideration of an amendment to the revenue bill that would make permanent the across-the-board 10 percent investment tax credit on new machinery and equipment while including as eligible for the credit the rehabilitation of existing commercial and residential structures, provided that the buildings to be renovated were in use for at least 5 years. This amendment, called the Cotter amendment, was adopted, 23–13.[39] This amendment, of course, would benefit the Northeast and the Midwest to some extent, despite the continuation of the across-the-board nature of the investment tax credit, because the North's housing and commercial structures are older than the South's and West's and are therefore more likely to qualify for rehabilitation funds.

The full House routinely adopted the Cotter amendment as part of the revenue bill that was passed, 362–49, on August 10, 1978.[40] Because the House revenue bill (H.R. 13511) came under consideration in the Senate Finance Committee, however, chaired by Russell Long (D-La.), there was little hope that a measure that would extend the 10 percent investment tax credit to the rehabilitation of older structures would be adopted. Like the House Ways and Means Committee, the Senate Finance Committee was composed mainly of members from the Sunbelt states that had little to gain by adoption of the Cotter amendment. At this time, only four of the Senate Finance Committee's eighteen members were from the Snowbelt. It was also unlikely that any of the Finance Committee's members would create a fuss over the matter as Cotter had done in the House.

Even before the twelve-day markup session on the 1979 revenue bill ended on September 27, 1978, Long confirmed the suspicions of the coalition as he declared that he would oppose any effort to include the Cotter amendment in his committee's bill and would do everything in his power to keep it out of the revenue bill when it reached the Senate floor for consideration.[41]

Since it was clear that the Senate Finance Committee was going to complete action on the bill without including the Cotter amendment, Michael Harrington and John Moriarty decided to ask Senator Howard Metzenbaum (D-Ohio), the newly elected chairman of the new Northeast–Midwest Senate Coalition, to attempt to amend the Senate version of the revenue bill when the bill reached the Senate floor.[42] If successful, this would force Long to accept the Cotter amendment in the upcoming conference session.

In response to Harrington's plea, Metzenbaum called a meeting of the Northeast–Midwest Senate Coalition on September 15, 1978, to discuss the revenue bill, and at the meeting it was decided that Metzenbaum would offer a modified version of the Cotter amendment on the Senate floor.[43] Eight other senators present agreed to speak on behalf of the amendment when it was brought up for consideration.[44]

On October, 5, 1978, the Senate began debate on the Finance Committee's version of the revenue bill that, as predicted, did not include the Cotter amendment. On October 7, 1978, Metzenbaum introduced his amendment to the bill (number 2020), claiming that the revision would cost the Treasury only $60 million, "a pittance as compared to what it costs the people of America in trying to bring back our downtown communities."[45]

Although Long rose in opposition to the Metzenbaum amendment, stating that it "discriminates in favor of the old parts of the country against the new parts of the country,"[46] the Metzenbaum amendment was adopted 38–31.[47] Of the twenty-three members of the Northeast–Midwest Senate Coalition who voted, only two, Edmund Muskie (D-Maine) and William Roth (R-Del.), voted against the amendment.[48] Of the twenty members of the Sunbelt who voted, ten voted for the amendment and ten opposed it.

On October 10, 1978, the Senate adopted the Metzenbaum amendment as part of the fiscal 1979 revenue bill, which was passed 86–4. As a result of the earlier vote on the Metzenbaum amendment, Long did not oppose its adoption during the conference committee's meeting when House conferees offered to substitute it for the Cotter amendment. The conference committee's subsequent report on the revenue bill was sent to the Senate and the House on October 15, 1978, where it was accepted, 72–3 in the Senate[49] and 337–38 in the House.[50] On November 6, 1978, President Carter signed the revenue bill into law (P. L. 95–600).

The adoption of the Metzenbaum amendment was the first (and

only) victory for the coalition in the legislative consideration of the president's urban proposals. Surprisingly, this victory was achieved despite the fact that the 5 percent investment tax credit proposal was under the jurisdiction of two of the most hostile committees in the Congress, as far as the coalition was concerned. While this was the first (and only) major cooperative effort between the House and Senate coalitions during the Ninety-fifth Congress, their success on this measure suggests that more cooperative ventures by the two organizations will occur in future Congresses. This suggests not only a general heightening of the coalition's power but also that the coalition's efforts to alter subgovernment decisions within hostile as well as friendly subgovernments may prove increasingly successful.

THE LABOR-INTENSIVE PUBLIC WORKS PROPOSAL

On March 27, 1978, President Carter asked the Congress to provide $1 billion a year for three years for labor-intensive public works projects that were targeted to communities with high unemployment. The program's intent was to provide employment opportunities for minorities and youths who were unemployed for long periods of time by requiring that all approved projects have a high labor cost ratio (thereby making the president's proposal labor-intensive). This contrasted with the then existing local public works program that funded projects requiring large expenditures on equipment, materials, and planning and relatively little on the actual cost of labor (making the program capital-intensive).[51]

The president's proposal would have used the $3 billion for the renovation of existing public facilities such as sewers, schools, public buildings, and roads. Collectively, these renovation projects were aimed at bolstering urban infrastructure. Since, as Michael Harrington indicated, the decay of the Northeast-Midwest region's urban infrastructure was a major priority at the coalition, it might be assumed that the coalition would have heartily endorsed and supported the president's proposal.[52] The president's March 27, 1978, proposal, however, was not fully worked out in respect to such matters as what unemployment criteria would be used to establish eligibility, what the labor cost ratio would have to be in order to qualify for funds, and what the administration's definition of long-term unemployment would be. The unemployment targeting mechanism was of particular concern at the coalition, since this feature of the program would determine what region would receive the bulk of the program's funds. Given the president's actions prior to the submission of his urban message, the coalition's staff and executive officers were, at best, cautiously optimistic as they awaited the introduction of the president's legislative proposal.

The resolution of the program's specifics within the administration took another two months, and the president's labor-intensive public works program was not introduced in the House until June 5, 1978 (H.R. 12993), and in the Senate on June 8, 1978 (S. 3233). In the House, the bill was referred to the Public Works and Transportation Committee, chaired by Harold J. Johnson (D-Calif.), and its Subcommittee on Economic Development, chaired by Robert Roe (D-N.J.). In the Senate, the bill was referred to the Environment and Public Works Committee, chaired by Jennings Randolph (D-W.Va.), and its Subcommittee on Regional and Community Development, chaired by Quentin Burdick (D-N.Dak.).

Since the introduction of the proposal had been delayed, hearings on the bill were quickly convened by both the House and the Senate subcommittees considering the bill. The first hearings were conducted by the Senate's Subcommittee on Regional and Community Development on June 15, 1978, where Robert Hall, assistant secretary of commerce for economic development, explained that the president's labor-intensive public works program was aimed at "conserving and improving existing public facilities"[53] and had as its objective the targeting of "half of the construction jobs generated to the long-term unemployed from low income families."[54] Hall also indicated that the program's funds would be distributed according to a two-step formula. First, the program's funds were allocated to the states according to the following criteria: 65 percent awarded on the absolute number of unemployed persons and 35 percent awarded on the extent which the state exceeded the national unemployment rate. Each state was guaranteed $2.5 million a year, and no state was to receive more than $125 million a year. After this step, the money would then be distributed within each state according to a second formula. First, 6 percent of the funds were given to the state's government, with the remaining 94 percent of the funds distributed to cities and counties whose population exceeded 50,000 persons, using the same criteria that determined state eligibility.[55]

While the president's proposal to guarantee each state $2.5 million a year spread the program's funds toward the Sunbelt, the coalition was pleased to discover that 47.8 percent of the program's funds were still going to be awarded to the eighteen coalition states.[56] The fact that the money was to be distributed within the states according to the same criteria for awarding money among the states was also viewed favorably by coalition leaders. They realized that the bulk of the funds was to be directed to the respective states' cities and not their suburbs. As a result, the coalition's leaders decided that they would not attempt to rewrite the president's public works formula even though they would have preferred a formula that targeted the funds more narrowly.

The three major reasons why the coalition did not attempt to rewrite the public works formula were: (1) the bill's formula was not that unfavorable to the coalition states; (2) both the House Public Works Committee and the Senate Environment and Public Works Committee were led by, and primarily composed of, Sunbelt representatives (meaning that the coalition should concentrate its small cadre of activists on other portions of the urban program); and (3) the one member of the House Public Works Committee from the coalition who was in a position to affect the outcome of the president's proposal, Subcommittee Chairman Robert Roe, was not an active member of the coalition. Given the fact that the coalition had activists on the committees considering the president's three other urban proposals, the public works proposal was a logical choice to leave unchallenged at the subgovernment and committee level. The coalition's staff, however, was given responsibility for monitoring the progress of the president's proposal and for suggesting any appropriate action once the bill reached the House floor.

As it turned out, the president's labor-intensive public works proposal, like his national development bank and supplemental fiscal assistance proposals, never reached the floor of the House. The

members of the House and Senate Public Works Committees preferred the expiring capital-intensive public works program to the
president's labor-intensive program and refused to vote on the president's measure. As the markup sessions on the president's proposal
were delayed, the House and the Senate Budget Committees, which
were required to submit the second budget resolution for fiscal 1979
by September 15, were left without any indication as to which public
works program would be enacted or what level of spending the two
Public Works Committees would seek for the program. As the September deadline approached and the two committees had still not
acted on the bill, the Budget committees were forced to act. The
House Budget Committee chose to allot $700 million for the pres-
ident's proposal, but the Senate Budget Committee, chaired by
Edmund Muskie, took the matter to the floor of the Senate for
instructions.[57]

On September 14, 1978, Muskie introduced a resolution (S. Res.
562) on the floor of the Senate that asked the Senate to reject any
funding for any public works programs.

> . . . The "soft" public works program was originally proposed by the
> President as a way to provide public sector jobs for disadvantaged work-
> ers. . . . That is why I was for it. . . . However, in the past few months,
> the heart of the proposal has been compromised away. . . . Senate amend-
> ments would cost $175,000 a year for every disadvantaged worker, and the
> House amendments cost even more.
> . . . Back in 1976, when the Nation was in a severe recession, heavy
> public works spending did seem justified. . . . But if fiscal policy is to be
> responsible, these programs must not only be turned on when they are
> needed, they must turn off when the need passes.[58]

Senator Daniel Patrick Moynihan (D-N.Y.) rose in opposition to
Muskie's resolution, stating that the vote on the resolution would
have to be considered a vote of confidence on the president's entire
urban program, since it would be the first vote taken on any aspect
of the president's urban package on the Senate floor.[59] He was
joined in opposition to the resolution by his New York colleague,
Jacob Javits, who stated that New York was "broke" and needed the
economic stimulus the public works proposal would provide.

Senator Jennings Randolph (D-W.Va.), chairman of the Environment and Public Works Committee, and Senator Quentin Bur-

dick (D-N.Dak.), chairman of the Subcommittee on Regional and Community Development, also rose in opposition to the resolution, but on the ground that any decision made on the legislation should be made by the authorization committee and not by the Budget Committee.[60] Burdick also indicated that his subcommittee had not held a markup session on the bill and that since this session was scheduled for September 19, 1978, it was premature for Muskie to say that his subcommittee had abandoned the president's proposal.

Despite these arguments against the resolution, it passed, 63–21.[61] The magnitude of the vote indicated that the Senate, in this period of rising inflation, was not inclined to vote for any significant new urban spending programs, especially since, as Muskie had indicated, the federal government was already spending close to $40 billion in 1978 to create jobs and to provide urban aid to the nation's urban communities.[62]

Senator Burdick, viewing the Senate's vote on the Muskie resolution as being instructive to him as well as to the Budget Committee, canceled the scheduled September 19 markup session on the president's labor-intensive public works proposal, and as a result the program died.

CONCLUSION: 1978, NOT A GOOD YEAR FOR URBAN PROGRAMS

The president's urban program did not fare very well on Capitol Hill. Except in its one success on the investment tax credit proposal, the coalition fared poorly. It is clear that the coalition made every feasible effort to salvage what it could out of the president's urban program but that it could not overcome several obstacles. First, it is not clear that the Carter administration put its best effort into presenting and promoting its own legislative program. The administration's four major proposals were sent to the Congress very late in the session, despite the fact that the formation process had begun in the executive branch nearly a year prior to their submission. Once submitted, the president's proposals were often poorly drafted, as was the case of the national development bank proposal. Also, they were not aggressively lobbied for, as evidenced by the lack of

White House contact with congressional leaders and the presentation and defense of several of the urban proposals by junior members of the executive departments rather than by those departments' secretaries at congressional hearings.

While the Carter administration deserves some of the blame for the urban program's failure to be enacted, an equally important cause of the failure was the political realities of that time. The year 1978 was not a good one for promoting spending on urban concerns. Depending on whose figures are used and what is determined as representing urban aid, the federal government was already spending between $40 billion and $60 billion a year on employment and other forms of aid in urban areas. Many of the aid programs were recently expanded during the recession, but in 1978 the recession had ended for many parts of the country and inflation had become the primary concern. Any additional spending strictly for urban areas, especially with the fall elections only a few months away, was seen by many nonurban members of the Congress as being politically unwise.

During legislative consideration of the supplemental fiscal assistance proposal, for example, L. H. Fountain and Jack Brooks opposed it on the ground that it was inflationary. This opposition delayed action on the proposal, which ultimately led to its death. In 1976, when the countercyclical revenue-sharing program was first introduced, both Fountain and Brooks opposed the bill on the ground that it was inflationary, but the bill was adopted anyway because other nonurban representatives viewed the bill as an old-fashioned distributive porkbarrel proposal. They logrolled with their urban colleagues because inflation was not a primary concern in 1976; unemployment was. In 1978, however, most nonurban representatives from both the Sunbelt and the Snowbelt were no longer willing to logroll on these urban issues. They wanted to tell their constitutents that they were taking steps to cut the federal budget, which, it was reasoned, would cut inflation. Since these nonurban congressional members received only a small share of the countercyclical aid program's funds, this program was one they could oppose at little cost to themselves and at the same time enhance their electoral position with their constituencies.

This reluctance on the part of nonurban Sunbelt and the Snowbelt representatives to vote for any urban spending indicates that the coalition's efforts to convince its nonurban representatives that the president's programs were redistributive had failed. The coalition's nonurban members were unwilling to vote for any funds, targeted or not. They apparently felt that the opportunity to enhance their electoral strength more than outweighed the benefits their region would receive from enactment of these programs. In previous cases, such as that of the housing and community development bill, these nonurban Coalition members were willing to join their urban colleagues in the coalition in support of measures that enhanced the region's interests. They supported the housing and community development formulas, however, because their local as well as their regional interests were enhanced by the formula revisions (because funding was increased). Now that their local interests were at odds with their regional interests (because of Carter's "no new spending" directive), they chose to protect their local interests and therefore opposed the president's and the coalition's efforts.

This abandonment of the coalition's efforts by its nonurban representatives clearly indicates that the coalition is far from being a well-oiled machine. It has no means of disciplining its members. Information can be an effective political weapon, but in the determination of the outcome of these urban programs, during the Ninety-fifth Congress, the coalition's information alone was not enough. The coalition failed to convince enough of its members that these distributive policies were actually redistributive to enact policies that did not benefit all (or nearly all) in the region. Local interests still superseded regional interests in the determination of one's voting behavior. In this sense, the fact that it took the unorthodox intervention of the Northeast–Midwest Senate Coalition and the efforts of William Cotter within the Ways and Means Committee to press for a measure that provided only $60 million in added revenue to the Snowbelt was not so surprising, nor was the fact that the Metzenbaum amendment was the extent of the coalition's gains during legislative consideration of the president's urban proposals.

While the coalition's success record on the urban proposals was a checkered one, the president's legislative and administrative policies did reflect a new approach that the coalition has supported since its inception: that public policy should attack unemployment and urban decay by bringing jobs to where people currently live rather than encouraging the migration of the jobless and businesses to other areas. The investment tax credit program, the executive orders mandating that priority be given to siting federal facilities in distressed urban areas, and the implementation of DMP-4—all were examples of the administration's commitment to providing federal assistance to areas in economic distress. Until this time, federal policy generally encouraged migration as the cure for economic distress by subsidizing canals, turnpikes, railroads, and homesteading.[63] Now the federal government was beginning to look for solutions to economic problems where they exist by generating new investment there, rather than by encouraging workers and businesses to migrate to the suburbs or to the Sunbelt. While it is difficult to give total credit to the coalition for this development, it can be said that the coalition has been—and still is—the single strongest proponent of this trend.

CHAPTER EIGHT   *The Crude Oil*

Equalization Tax: The Effect of

Redistributive Policies on the Coalition

When President Carter took office in 1976, one of his first priorities was to put together a comprehensive energy program for the nation. While the nation's energy shortage (and its long gas lines) had lessened since the Arab oil embargo (October 13, 1973–March 18, 1974), a fundamental change in energy had occurred as a result of the embargo: oil was no longer a bargain. The Organization of Petroleum Exporting Countries (OPEC), recognizing the advantages of monopolistic collusion, would never again allow a 72-gallon barrel of oil to be sold for just $3.00, as had been common prior to the embargo. Instead, OPEC abruptly raised the price of its oil to $11.65 on January 1, 1974, and continued to raise the price systematically, so that at the outset of the president's term the price was more than $20.00 a barrel.[1]

Because oil is used in the production of other sources of energy, particularly electricity, Americans had to face the prospect of paying higher utility bills and more for other petroleum-based products as well. Gasoline, for example, which is processed from crude oil, had been selling in the United States at an average price of 35 cents a gallon in January 1973. By August 1974 the price of gasoline had risen to an average of 56 cents a gallon and has generally been rising since.[2]

Despite the escalating cost of imported oil, domestic consumption continued to rise. At the same time, domestic production of oil began to decline, despite the fact that the price of domestic oil (which was under federal control) was allowed to increase from $3.89 a barrel in 1973 to $7.99 a barrel in 1976. At the outset of the Carter administration, for example, domestic oil production stood at 8.2 million barrels a day, down by more than 1 million barrels compared with production in 1973.[3] During this same three-year period, United States dependence on the more expensive OPEC oil actually doubled as a percentage of oil imports, as Canada, which had supplied one third of American oil imports in 1973, severely cut back its exportation of oil to the United States to use the oil for its own domestic needs. As a result, in 1976 the United States was forced to import approximately 45 percent of its oil needs, 7 million barrels of oil each day, at an average price of $13.40, quadruple the average price in 1973, which was $3.27.[4]

These escalating energy prices resulted in escalating trade deficits and in a weakening of the American dollar and of the American economy. While the entire economy was adversly affected, the already economically troubled cold weather states of the Northeast were hardest hit. The economy of these states, lacking any significant oil or natural gas resources of their own, was very precarious. Since the region's economy depended on oil for nearly 80 percent of its energy needs, each increase in the price of domestic and foreign oil also increased the region's capital outflow problem. This outflow, coupled with the growing obsolescence of the region's industrial base, made the creation of a national energy policy to keep domestic energy prices from skyrocketing crucial for the continued economic stability of the Snowbelt. Sunbelt representatives, on the other hand, viewed such measures as the deregulation of natural gas and oil prices as conducive to increasing domestic resources and an enhanced local economy. As such, the resolution of national energy legislation possessed all the ingredients of a regional battle— with the energy-rich Sunbelt opposed to the energy-poor Snowbelt. The importance of the energy issue to the Northeast was reflected in the fact that one of the original five task forces formed by the Northeast–Midwest Congressional Coalition at its inception was its Task Force on Energy.

Because the adverse impact of higher domestic energy prices was unevenly distributed within the United States, it might have been expected that the battle lines over domestic energy policy, particularly those affecting its price, would have been distinctly regional in nature and that the coalition's information resources should have been sufficient to persuade the representatives from the Northeast-Midwest region that it was in their common regional interest to oppose any policies that resulted in higher energy prices. The battle lines that actually emerged over domestic energy prices, however, were not distinctly regional in nature, and the coalition's informational resources were insufficient to persuade the Snowbelt representatives to vote as a group against policies that raised energy prices.

The reason for these surprising developments was that energy policy could not be translated into subsidy terms alone. Energy policy, unlike any of the other policies examined in this book, was redistributive on other than a geographical basis. Because redistributive policies allocate resources along class and/or group lines, party and ideological considerations (which were of secondary importance in the other issues examined) were very important. Also, because energy policy was redistributive, every representative sensed that he had a stake in the outcome of this policy and endeavored to have his views prevail. The coalition's activists, who opposed higher domestic energy prices as being contrary to the region's interests, thus discovered that its spectator members were unwilling to listen to their arguments. Instead, the coalition's membership was divided along partisan and ideological lines.

Because of this internal division, the coalition's leaders decided not to press for any regional actions on any of the "controversial" parts (the redistributive portions) of the president's energy program. Instead, they, in concert with the coalition's Task Force on Energy, determined that it was in the best interests of the coalition (then just a few months old) to address itself only to those portions of the president's energy package that were not controversial (the distributive portions). The president's crude oil equalization tax was in the first category. The crude oil equalization tax's home heating oil rebate plan, however, was in the second category. The coalition, therefore, did little to affect the outcome of the oil equalization tax but worked very hard to affect the outcome of the rebate plan.

CARTER ANNOUNCES THE "MORAL EQUIVALENT OF WAR"

On April 18, 1977, President Carter announced to a skeptical American public on national television that the national energy crisis was real.[5] He opened his speech with the sober statement that:

Tonight I want to have an unpleasant talk with you about a problem unprecedented in our history. With the exception of preventing war, this is the greatest challenge our country will face during our lifetimes. The energy crisis has not yet overwhelmed us but it will if we do not act quickly.[6]

Later in the speech, the president warned that:

Our decision about energy will test the character of the American people and the ability of the President and the Congress to govern this nation. This difficult effort will be the "moral equivalent of war"—except that we will be uniting our efforts to build and not to destroy.[7]

Two days later, on April 20, 1977, the president appeared on national television again as he announced his energy program before a joint session of the Congress. In order to reach seven specific energy goals that were, collectively, aimed at achieving relative energy independence for the United States by 1985, President Carter announced a multifaceted energy program that was designed to (1) promote conservation, (2) increase domestic production, (3) promote conversion from oil and natural gas to coal, (4) develop new energy resources, particularly solar energy, while (5) maintaining what the president referred to as "fairness," so that "None of our people must make an unfair sacrifice" and that "None should reap an unfair benefit."[8]

Among the president's proposals was a standby tax on gasoline; a graduated excise tax on new "gas-guzzling" cars; a sliding-scale tax on large industrial users of oil and natural gas; a reduction in the licensing period for the construction of nuclear power plants; a tax credit for those purchasing solar-powered water and space heaters, and the crude oil equalization tax, which many referred to as the centerpiece of his energy program.[9] This tax, often referred to as the wellhead tax, would have caused the price of newly discovered domestic oil to rise over a three-year period to the 1977 world market price. The president announced that the revenues collected by the tax would be rebated to the public, but he did not specify exactly how this would be done. He was very specific, however, about his position regarding the ending of federal controls on the price of domestic oil.

proposals for immediate and total decontrol of domestic oil and natural gas prices would be disastrous for our economy and for working Americans, and would not solve long-range problems of dwindling supplies.[10]

The president did not anticipate a warm response to his program on Capitol Hill. During his address before the joint session of Congress, he stated that the development of a national energy policy was a "thankless job."[11] In his opening remarks, the president also said he did not expect much applause. He was right; he did not receive much.[12]

THE INSTITUTIONAL SETTING: ENERGY, A REDISTRIBUTIVE ISSUE

The reason the president did not expect and did not receive much applause is simple. The energy proposals, unlike any of the distributive programs examined in this book, did not do things for people— they did things to people. They were redistributive policies that in an immediate, material sense increased fuel prices to the detriment of all, but particularly to those of the lower income levels.[13] The proposals also adversely affected numerous interest groups, particularly the "powerful" oil and automobile lobby groups, as well as nearly every constituent of every senator and representative in Congress.

Thomas O'Neill, Jr., the newly elected Speaker of the House, put the president's energy proposals in a proper political perspective when he commented shortly after the president's speech before the joint session of the Congress that the president's energy plan would lead to "the toughest fight this Congress has ever had."[14] The reason for this lies in the fact that unlike distributive policies, which have clientele interest groups fighting for enactment of the program under consideration, this program had almost every major lobby group in the country trying to defeat one aspect of the program or another, if not the entire package.

The political struggle to enact the president's national energy package was destined to occupy the efforts of the Ninety-fifth Congress and to continue into the Ninety-sixth Congress, despite the fact that House Speaker O'Neill made the passage of the president's energy program his number one priority. The extended political struggle that took place over these energy proposals is a subject that can be approached from many angles and perspectives and is deserving of commentary that cannot be supplied within the constraints of one chapter. As a result, this chapter does not attempt to provide an overall evaluation of the political, social, and economic effects of the energy proposals; it does attempt to offer an insight into the proposals' effects upon the Northeast and Midwest, the manner in which northeastern and midwestern representatives reacted to the proposals as directed by the coalition, and the success or failure of the coalition in achieving its goals with respect to the president's energy proposals.

Since, like the president's urban program, this energy program contained numerous proposals and a detailed examination of each would be inappropriate in this study, this chapter will present a detailed examination of the coalition's efforts concerning the president's centerpiece proposal—his crude oil equalization tax and its consumer rebate plan.

THE EXECUTIVE BRANCH FORMS ITS ENERGY POLICY IN SPLENDID ISOLATION

Given the potential adverse economic impact the president's energy proposals presented to the energy-consuming Snowbelt, one might expect that the coalition would have been in constant contact with James Schlesinger and his staff as they pieced together the administration's energy program. The coalition, however, as well as numerous other interested parties, was denied an input into the executive formation process because Schlesinger and his staff, given a presidential mandate to complete the program in ninety days, were too busy writing the energy proposals to consult with virtually any outside group. The energy staff was working on the proposals with such speed that even key congressional leaders such as Al Ullman, chairman of the House Ways and Means Committee, and House Speaker O'Neill were not given the opportunity to make any substantive contribution to the executive's energy formation process.

Despite this exclusion of the coalition's influence on the formation of the president's energy proposals, the proposals anticipated many of its preferences. The president, for example, chose to cushion the economic impact of higher energy prices on the Northeast-Midwest region by using various tax mechanisms to rebate the increased energy costs back to consumers as well as by providing tax credits to these who insulated their homes and businesses. Since the northeastern states are high energy-consuming states, most of the benefits of these provisions would go to persons and firms located in the Northeast and Midwest. Thus, the president's energy package promised to keep a large portion of the revenues collected from the higher domestic energy prices in the Snowbelt and would prevent, as had been feared, an acceleration of the region's capital outflow problem.

THE COALITION'S RESPONSE TO THE PRESIDENT'S PROGRAM

In order to closely study the implications of the president's energy program on the economy of the Northeast and Midwest, the coalition set up an Energy Task Force, cochaired by Representatives William Brodhead (D-Mich.) and Stewart McKinney (R-Conn.). Eleven other coalition members volunteered to serve on the task force, and a series of organizational meetings was held in early May 1977.[15] At these meetings (which were not attended by the congressional members of the task force but by members of their respective legislative staffs) it was discovered that little consensus, other than the agreement that the president's energy proposals could have been worse relative to the Northeast's needs, could be reached. According to Dr. William Boxall, legislative aide specializing in energy-related matters for Brodhead, the energy issue (as a redistributive issue) split the coalition along partisan lines.

The whole energy bill was explosive. The Republicans and the Democrats just could not agree.
. . . There was a reluctance to push too hard on energy as it was not known if the Coalition could survive the stress.
. . . There was a conscious effort not to push too hard or the advancements being made on Community Development and Food Stamps [two distributive issues where partisanship is muted] might be shattered.[16]

Larry Halloran, legislative aide to Stewart McKinney, concurred with Boxall's assessment of the task force' situation.

The Northeast–Midwest Congressional Coalition was still in the formative stage in early 1977—forming the bonds between the Northeast and Midwest regions. The energy bill, however, threatened to split the Coalition in half, destroying those bonds before they had had a chance to come together.
. . . [As a result] we [the coalition's Energy Task Force] concentrated our efforts on the "give me" [distributive] aspects of the energy bill, like the home heating oil rebate . . . and limited ourselves to providing information on the other aspects of the bill as it was proposed by the President.[17]

Because the energy bill elicited such a partisan division within the coalition, the Energy Task Force decided not to challenge any of the president's energy proposals. Instead, the task force planned to monitor the progress of energy legislation and serve as an information resource for coalition's members by informing them when votes of interest were to take place and by issuing periodic update memoranda that would outline the effect of specific energy proposals on the Northeast-Midwest region. The task force also decided not take any formal positions on most of the energy issues except on those that were clearly beneficial to all representatives from the northeastern states. The home heating oil rebate plan that was part of the president's crude oil equalization tax was such a proposal. On this issue, party labels and ideology made little difference. Each of these representatives represented a cold weather district, with high home heating oil consumption. They could stand together on this issue because all of them recognized that the adoption of this measure would provide them with a governmental subsidy without any political loss. On the other energy issues, however, such as the deregulation of natural gas and oil prices, the positions taken on these measures not only involved the question of governmental interference in the private sector (an ideological consideration) but also promised to elicit political pressure from within the home district both pro and con. As a controversial issue as well as an ideological issue, these redistributive portions of the energy package were not conducive to consensus. Consequently, McKinney and Brodhead decided not to force the Energy Task Force to address the redistributive portions of the president's package.

While the coalition was preparing to address the energy issue, numerous other regionally based groups were doing the same thing. The governors of sixteen western states (a region that produces most of the nation's low-sulfur-content coal) decided to form a regional energy policy group to monitor the progress of federal energy legislation with an eye toward protecting the region's environmental standards.[18] The Southern Growth Policies Board, representing a region that produced 70 percent of the nation's domestic energy supplies in 1975, also monitored the progress of federal energy legislation so that its member states would be kept abreast of the latest developments in Washington.[19] These two regional groups, however, were not in a position, as was the coalition, to actively lobby on energy. The western group, headquartered in Denver, Colorado, was still unstaffed and disorganized when the energy bill entered the legislative policymaking process, and the Southern Growth Policies Board did not open its Washington office until August 1977. There was one other regionally based group that was in a position to lobby on the energy bill, however—the New England Congressional Caucus.

Eclipsed in many respects by the coalition as a lobbying force within the Congress, the New England Congressional Caucus focused most of its research and lobbying efforts on the president's energy proposals. The New England Caucus even formed its own energy task force, independent of the coalition's, which was chaired by Paul Tsongas (D-Mass.) and the coalition's Energy Task Force cochairman, Stewart McKinney (R-Conn.). Unlike the coalition, which chose to let its task force' cochairmen's staff direct its energy research (thereby freeing the coalition's staff to work on the urban program), the New England Caucus had its research arm, the New England Economic Research Office, prepare its economic impact analyses of the president's energy proposals.

O'NEILL AND THE AD HOC COMMITTEE ON ENERGY

Even as the president's staff was putting together the president's energy program, House Speaker O'Neill decided that unless something was done the Congress was not going to enact energy legislation that was not biased toward the domestic oil and natural gas interests. As a representative from the Northeast, well aware of the future consequences a failure to enact a comprehensive energy program would have on the economy of the Northeast as well as on the nation as a whole, Speaker O'Neill decided to place his reputation and his place in history on the line by adopting a major innovation. He decided to seek the creation of a special ad hoc committee that would consider the legislative actions taken by the various committees considering each of the energy proposals and be given the responsibility of molding the pieces into a comprehensive whole before they were sent to the floor of the House for consideration.[20] While the leaders of the coalition had nothing to do with the Speaker's decision to take this dramatic action, they fully endorsed the idea. They recognized that the formation of this committee provided the opportunity for circumventing the Sunbelt's positioning on many of the committees considering energy.

On April 21, 1977, just two weeks before the energy bill was introduced in the House, the Speaker's Ad Hoc Committee on Energy was created by voice vote. The Speaker, who was authorized to choose its members and its chairman, selected Thomas Ashley (D-Ohio), a prominent member of the Northeast–Midwest Congressional Coalition, as the new committee's chairman. While the Ad Hoc Committee on Energy was denied the authority to amend the pieces of energy legislation as they were reported by the House committees considering energy (to the relief of Sunbelt legislators), the committee was given the authority to offer amendments once the energy package reached the floor of the House.

Because the Ad Hoc Committee on Energy was denied authority to amend energy legislation when it was reported, Sunbelt legislators did not feel that their advantage, derived from their positioning in the committee structure, had been damaged to the point where they had to caucus like the northeasterners. They remained content to act independently of one another, confident in their individual abilities to defend their respective local interests.

THE CRUDE OIL EQUALIZATION TAX AND ITS HOME HEATING OIL REBATE

As a tax-related matter, the first legislative decision point reached by the crude oil equalization tax was the House Ways and Means Committee, chaired by Al Ullman (D-Oreg.).[21] Ullman, under or-

ders from Speaker O'Neill to complete all legislative action on the
energy bill by July 13, recognized that this deadline provided his
committee with less than sixty days to complete its work on the tax-
related portions of the energy bill. In order to comply with the
Speaker's edict, Ullman announced that hearings on the president's
energy program would begin on May 16, 1977, where the secretary
of the treasury, W. Michael Blumenthal and the president's chief
energy advisor, Dr. James Schlesinger, would inform the committee
of the implications of the president's proposals on the national
economy.

During the first day of what turned out to be three weeks of public
testimony, Blumenthal and Schlesinger were subjected to a barrage
of criticism, most of it directed at the president's standby gasoline
tax and the tax on gas-guzzling cars. During Blumenthal's testimony, however, one member of the Ways and Means Committee,
James Burke (D-Mass.), was particularly interested in the crude oil
equalization tax and its consumer rebate formula. As the second-
ranking Democrat on the Ways and Means Committee, Burke,
acting independently of the coalition and of the New England Caucus, announced to Secretary Blumenthal that "I represent the New
England section of the country on this committee"[22] and stated that
he wanted to know how the tax and rebate program worked, particularly since the rebate program allowed a refund to consumers
of home heating oil.

According to Blumenthal, under the president's crude oil equalization tax, domestic crude oil would be subject to an excise tax
equal to the difference between the current domestic controlled
price and the 1977 world market price, adjusted for inflation. The
tax would be applied in three annual stages beginning on January
1, 1978, and would become fully effective by 1980. The actual non-
taxed price of domestic crude oil would continue to be regulated
by the Federal Energy Administration under the provisions of the
Emergency Petroleum Allocation Act of 1973. The mandatory
price-control feature of this act was set to expire in May 1979, after
which the president would retain discretionary control over domestic oil prices until September 1981.[23]

Secretary Blumenthal went on to add that the president's proposal
also provided for the revenue generated by the oil equalization tax

to be refunded to consumers. These refunds were of two types: rebates for home heating oil and per capita rebates. The home heating oil rebate (equal to the crude oil equalization tax) would be offered to sellers of domestically refined distillate fuel that could be delivered to residential structures provided that the seller could prove that this saving had been passed on to the consumer. The second form of the rebate was to be computed by the secretary of the treasury. He was to estimate the total revenues generated from the crude oil equalization tax for the following year, subtract the amount rebated for home heating oil, the loss of revenue from business deductions of the tax, and the cost of administering the program and rebate the balance to the general public on a per capita basis as a credit against income taxes levied on income for the year.[24] According to Blumenthal, the crude oil equalization tax would generate $2.8 billion in 1978, $11.9 billion in 1979, and stabilize at approximately $12 billion by 1985. The home heating oil rebate would amount to approximately $48 million in 1978, rise to $957 million by 1981, and remain at that level thereafter. The remainder of funds, approximately $2 billion in 1978, rising to $7.4 billion by 1985, would be rebated on a per capita basis to all taxpayers as well as to individuals on social security and welfare.[25]

The object of the crude oil equalization tax, according to both Blumenthal and Schlesinger, was to encourage domestic conservation by forcing the price of fuel to rise. It was their contention that the president's crude oil equalization tax would reduce oil imports 2.5 to 2.8 million barrels of oil per day by what was estimated would be imported by 1985. While Presidents Nixon and Ford had also advocated a rise in fuel prices to promote domestic conservation of fuel, they would have allowed most of the increased revenues generated by the higher prices to go to the oil companies. President Carter, on the other hand, wanted to use the taxing mechanism so that the increased revenues generated by higher fuel prices would not be returned to the oil companies but to the Treasury Department and, ultimately, back to consumers. Since the northeastern states are high energy-consuming states and the energy-producing states are located in the Sunbelt, the president's position was supported by most of the representatives of the Northeast but not by very many Sunbelt representatives.

COTTER TO THE RESCUE

The markup session before the House Ways and Means Committee on the equalization tax was scheduled for June 14, 1977. Since only six weeks had passed since the introduction of the legislation, the Northeast–Midwest Congressional Coalition had had little time to prepare for the vote. In fact, the coalition's Task Force on Energy took six weeks to get organized, and it was not until June 13, 1977, just one day before the markup session on the crude oil equalization tax was to take place, that this task force made its first formal action—and a mild action it was—the issuance of an energy questionnaire to each of its members.

This questionnaire, designed to inform the staff of the task force (William Boxall and Larry Halloren) of which of the energy proposals the coalition's members wanted the task force to examine, was quickly filled out and returned to the task force by many coalition members. But none of the questionnaires was completed in time to provide any indication as to how the coalition's membership felt about the equalization tax. The staff, however, assumed (and the completed questionnaires substantiated their view) that the great majority of the coalition's members lacked sufficient information on the economic impact of the president's energy proposals to make a firm judgment on the regional impact of any of the president's proposals. Halloran and Boxall made this assumption because President Carter's energy staff was not able, when asked, to provide them with statistical evidence about who benefited and who was hurt by each of the energy proposals on a district-by-district basis. It was obvious to them that members of President Carter's energy staff had not done their homework on the energy proposals' regional economic impact. Moreover, because of Speaker O'Neill's July 13 deadline for completion of all standing committee action on the energy bill, the Congress would be prevented from receiving any in-depth studies of the energy bill from its own informational resources. Given this problem, Halloran and Boxall recognized that reliable information, on a district-by-district basis, of the economic impact of each of the president's proposals would provide the coalition with a considerable advantage over any of their potential adversaries as the energy bill went through the legislative process.

Therefore, they eagerly began to gather as much information as they could concerning the energy proposals' economic impact. While they were doing so, the New England Caucus' Economic Research Office, which was devoting almost all its efforts to the energy bill, was already in the process of completing some preliminary analyses on the energy bill's economic effect on New England. Because of the overlapping membership of the two organizations, these analyses were made available to Halloran and Boxall. Combining their own research with that of the New England Caucus, they discovered that since the Northeast is heavily dependent on expensive OPEC oil to fuel its economy, the Northeast already paid higher oil prices compared with the rest of the nation. Since the proposed equalization tax taxed domestic oil, the negative economic impact of the tax would be only marginally felt in the Northeast; the largest jump in oil prices would actually occur in the South and West, since their economies are more heavily dependent on domestic oil. The task force staff also discovered that 78 percent of all home heating oil was used in the Northeast-Midwest region.[26] For this reason, the staff recognized that the home heating oil rebate offered the coalition members an added incentive to support the president's crude oil equalization tax. The problem, however, was that the majority of the members of the House Ways and Means Committee were not from the Northeast, and only one member, William Brodhead, was also a member of the coalition's Energy Task Force. On the basis of sheer numerical strength, it was clear that the coalition faced an uphill battle to save the rebate, especially since the staff had not had time to put its findings into a coherent package suitable for presentation to those Ways and Means Committee members who might be expected to support the rebate plan.

On June 14, 1977, President Carter was given his first major energy victory as the Ways and Means Committee voted 21–16 to adopt the crude oil equalization tax. The next day, June 15, 1977, the committee considered the president's rebate provisions of the tax and overwhelmingly voted, by a show of hands, to reject the president's rebate plan, 20–4, condemning the rebate as New England porkbarrel.[27]

According to three aides who were present when the vote was cast on the rebate, its overwhelming defeat was caused, at least in part, by the fact that the vote was the last of the day and followed many hours of discussion and many votes on various tax provisions allowing preferential treatment for certain groups or areas. By the time the rebate was considered, many committee members felt that enough exceptions or terms of special treatment under the energy tax proposals had already been allowed. Compounding the situation was the lack of information concerning who would benefit under the rebate's provisions. According to these aides, nearly all of the Ways and Means members believed that New England would receive all of the rebate's funds. Because they were not the recipients of the rebate's subsidy, they voted it down. The vote was a matter of individual self-interest rather than an organized opposition to the interests of the northeastern states.

As soon as he learned of the vote on the home heating oil rebate, Stewart McKinney drafted a letter to Ways and Means Committee Chairman Ullman condemning its rejection. In the letter, sent on June 24, 1977, and cosigned by ten other coalition members,[28] McKinney wrote:

We believe the Committee's action, if based on the fear of regional advantage or undue complexity, is directly contrary to President Carter's stated goal that energy taxes fairly distribute the economic burdens of reduced petroleum consumption. . . . in effect, you have imposed an additional "cold weather tax" on every section of the country which must consume home heating oil, natural gas or propane to keep warm. . . . on behalf of the Northeast-Midwest Economic Advancement Coalition's Energy Task Force, we respectfully request that you reconsider your decision to eliminate the President's proposed residential heating rebate.[29]

In the meantime, the two New England representatives on the Ways and Means Committee, James Burke and William Cotter (who was a member of the coalition's steering committee), began to contact various members on the Ways and Means Committee informally in an effort to have the rebate plan reconsidered. Burke, who planned to retire at the end of the Ninety-fifth Congress, approached his colleagues on the committee as an elder statesman seeking their votes in return for past favors. The younger Cotter, on the other hand, armed with statistical evidence provided by the coalition's Energy Task Force staff, approached several selected members of the committee and informed them that their districts, as well as his own, would benefit by the home heating oil rebate. According to the staff of the task force, the three states of New York, New Jersey, and Pennsylvania, for example, stood to lose more money ($604 million) than the entire six-state New England region by 1980 ($407 million) if the rebate was not adopted.

As several members of the Ways and Means Committee began to change their minds about the rebate, Cotter decided to go public with the effort to reverse the earlier rejection of the rebate plan. Not only did Cotter make his efforts known; he also announced that unless the rebate was reinstated, the New England delegation would seriously consider voting as a bloc against the entire energy package. This announcement of course immediately caught the attention of House Speaker O'Neill, who was already worried about the prospects of the energy bill's passage on the House floor. In light of the coalition's letter to Ullman and his own experience within the New England Caucus, Speaker O'Neill had to take Cotter's threat seriously. Speaker O'Neill then had his staff contact Ullman's staff to see if the rebate could be restored without embarrassment to the Ways and Means Committee members, since they had already so overwhelmingly rejected the rebate. In the meantime, Cotter's and Burke's efforts on behalf of the rebate plan began to pay off as several of the committee's members informed Ullman that unless the home heating oil rebate was restored they would vote to reconsider the crude oil equalization tax and then vote against it. Since the latter tax had passed by only a 5-vote margin, only three members had to switch their votes to defeat the measure. Recognizing the closeness, and under pressure from the Speaker, Ullman suddenly discovered that unless he wanted to see the president's only major legislative success on energy overturned (making Ullman appear to have no control over his committee), the rebate had to be restored. To prevent any member from being caught voting two ways on the same measure, Ullman had a modified home heating oil rebate plan considered within the committee on June 28, 1977, and voted upon by voice rather than by recorded vote. This modified rebate plan, now called the Cotter/Burke amendment, was accepted without a dissenting voice.

O'NEILL'S ENERGY COMMITTEE CLEARS THE BILL FOR ACTION

After the crude oil equalization tax and its home heating oil rebate plan had cleared the Ways and Means Committee, it was sent to the Ad Hoc Committee on Energy on July 13 for consideration of possible floor amendments. The ad hoc committee was composed of forty members: twenty-seven democrats and thirteen Republicans, all hand-picked by Speaker O'Neill. The Speaker deliberately chose most of the members for the committee from among the members of the standing committees that held jurisdiction over energy-related matters. Among the leading members of the Ad Hoc Committee on Energy were Al Ullman, chairman of the Ways and Means Committee; Morris Udall, chairman of the Interior and Insular Affairs Committee; and John Dingell, chairman of the Commerce Committee's Energy and Power Subcommittee, which would consider the president's natural gas proposal. While the Speaker was careful not to snub anyone, he was equally careful to choose members of the committee that would approve of the president's energy proposals, based on their past voting records on the deregulation of oil and natural gas. Of the twenty-seven Democrats, for example, only five had voted in favor of the deregulation of natural gas prices in 1976 and only five had voted for the deregulation of oil prices in 1976.[30] As Paul Tsongas, a member of the ad hoc committee, stated:

> There is no sense putting together a committee that is going to vote "no" on everything. If anything doesn't make it past the committee it certainly is not going to make its way past the floor.[31]

As a result, the Ad Hoc Committee on Energy was, in contrast to the two principal standing committees handling the energy bill in the House, Commerce and Ways and Means, dominated by members representing energy-consuming districts. Of the forty ad hoc committee members, twenty were members of the Northeast–Midwest Congressional Coalition, including its chairman, Thomas Ashley, whereas only seven members represented the oil- and gas-producing states of Texas, Louisiana, and Oklahoma.

With the votes of those noncoalition members who represented energy-consuming districts combined with the coalition's votes, the president's crude oil equalization tax and its modified home heating oil rebate plan easily cleared the ad hoc committee with only minor amendments recommended, none of which affected the rebate.[32] On July 22, 1977, the ad hoc committee formally forwarded the president's energy bill to the House floor for final consideration (now H.R. 8444).[33]

THE OIL REBATE SURVIVES CHALLENGES ON THE HOUSE FLOOR

On July 29, 1977, debate on the national energy bill began on the floor of the House of Representatives. On August 4, 1977, the first of three challenges to the crude oil equalization tax and its home heating oil rebate emerged as James Jones (D-Okla.) introduced an amendment that would allow oil producers to recover part of the equalization tax if they made additional investments in exploring for new oil. Under the Jones amendment, oil producers would be required to invest at least 25 percent of their gross income on exploration. Ninety percent of expenditures over that level would be counted as a credit against the equalization tax.[34] Since this plowback to the Sunbelt-based oil companies would deprive northern energy consumers of their home heating oil rebate, the stage was set for a regional showdown. On this particular vote, the ideological concern over the intervention of the federal government on the price of fuel was not an issue. Party loyalty, however, was at issue because the president had firmly denounced any effort to plow back the receipts of the equalization tax to the oil companies.

The Jones amendment was defeated 198–223 (10 not voting, 2 vacancies). As expected, because the Jones amendment would have deleted the rebate plan, congressional members of the coalition voted against the Jones plowback amendment, 72–133, and the Sunbelt representatives voted for it, 88–61. But this apparent regional response to the Jones amendment was spurious; on closer examination, the vote on the Jones amendment was primarily based upon party, not regional differences. For example, coalition Democrats voted 11–119 against the Jones amendment, while the coalition's Republican members voted for it 61–14. The vote appears to be regionally defined only because Democrats greatly outnumbered Republicans within the coalition. Looking at the Sunbelt's vote on the Jones amendment, partisanship clearly emerges as the overriding factor. While Texas, Oklahoma and Louisiana did, understandably, vote for the Jones amendment (21–2, 6–0, and 7–0, respectively) the rest of the Sunbelt voted along party lines. Sunbelt Democrats (excluding Texas, Oklahoma and Louisiana) opposed the Jones amendment, 21–57, while Sunbelt Republicans supported the amendment, 40–1. In the House as a whole, of the 282 Democrats voting, only 74 bolted the party line; of the 139 Republicans voting, only 15 bolted their party line. There are several reasons why the party lines held so firmly. The Democrats, as the party in power, had already addressed and rejected this amendment during both the Ways and Means Committee's and the Ad Hoc Committee on Energy's consideration of the crude oil equalization tax. Adoption of the amendment at this time would not only have embarrassed the president; but, perhaps more important, adoption of this amendment would have been an affront to the leading members of the Ways and Means Committee and to the Ad Hoc Committee on Energy. These members held institutional power positions; thus, a Democrat aspiring to obtain power in the House did not want to cross them unless he or she had to. In addition, the party lines coincided to a great extent with regional and district self-interest. Democrats from the Northeast were already inclined to oppose the amendment, as were Democrats from the non-oil-producing states of the Sunbelt. In this regard, it is interesting to note that when regional and district self-interest opposed the party line, it was self-interest, not the party line that was adhered to. Of the 74 Democratic defectors, 62 were from oil-producing states in the Sunbelt. Of the 15 Republican defectors, 14 were from the energy-consuming coalition states.[35]

On August 5, 1977, two more attempts were made to kill the equalization tax and its rebate. The first, introduced by John Anderson (R-Ill.), a member of the coalition's Energy Task Force, would have substituted for the president's proposal a Republican-sponsored tax aimed at encouraging domestic oil production as well as conservation. This proposal would have removed price controls on upper-tier oil over a five-year period, removed all price controls immediately on new oil, and provided a 50 percent plowback credit to oil companies against the tax incurred as a result of the retention of the president's tax on lower-tier oil.[36]

The fact that John Anderson, a member of the coalition's Energy Task Force, introduced this amendment indicates the extent to which energy policy was tearing at the bipartisan solidarity of the coalition. Highlighting this inner division was Frank Horton (R-N.Y.), cochairman of the Northeast–Midwest Congressional Coalition, who stood on the floor of the House in support of the Republican amendment on the partisan and ideological grounds that the president's proposal:

offers only one solution to our national energy crisis. And it offers that solution over and over again. Government intervention. Mandate this, prohibit that, and tax this, that and the other thing.

. . . the American citizen is sinking in a quagmire of federal regulations while being smothered in an avalanche of paperwork.[37]

John Dingell (D-Mich.) stood to oppose the Republican substitution amendment on the floor of the House, declaring:

There is only one person that is going to get stung by this substitution—that is the American consumer. It will divert billions . . . of dollars to oil and gas producers and will drain billions . . . from American consumers.[38]

While Dingell's appraisal of the Republican substitute bill clearly squared the Snowbelt against the Sunbelt, the fact that the substitute bill was sponsored by the Republicans meant that partisanship as well as regionalism would effect the outcome of the vote. The fact that the substitute bill would also have decontrolled the price of many types of domestic oil meant that ideology would also affect the vote. For the coalition, Anderson's amendment, even more than the Jones plowback amendment of the day before, promised to divide its ranks, Realizing that a regional consensus was impossible, the coalition's Energy Task Force, which had not issued a formal recommendation on the Jones amendment, chose not to make a recommendation on this amendment either. The task force itself had become so hopelessly torn by partisan and ideological divisions that by this time it had ceased to exist as a forum for the exchange of ideas.

The Republican's substitute amendment was defeated along party lines, 147–273 (11 not voting, 2 vacancies). Republicans voted in favor of the amendment, 118–22, Democrats opposed it, 29–251. Again the influence of regional and district self-interest was at least somewhat in evidence as 15 of the 22 Republican defectors were members of the coalition, and 28 of the 29 Democratic defectors were from the energy-producing Sunbelt states. The coalition's voting behavior, as a whole, however, was once again split by party, as its Democrats voted 1–126 against the Republican amendment and its Republicans voted for it 61–15.[39]

Like the Jones plowback amendment of the previous day, the party line was used as a voting cue as information that clearly indicated the effect of adopting the amendment was not available. The potential adverse electoral consequences of overriding the president's program also worked to solidify Democratic ranks.

After the defeat of the Republican substitute amendment, a third and last effort was made to kill the equalization tax. Introduced by William Steiger (R-Wis.), another coalition member, this amendment would have recommitted the entire energy bill to the ad hoc committee with instructions to strike the equalization tax and report the bill back to the House floor otherwise unchanged. Under this less overtly partisan attempt to kill the president's proposal, those opposed to the tax on partisan or ideological grounds could still vote to kill the bill, while Democrats who were uncertain of the bill's ability to reduce oil consumption and were concerned about the tax's possible inflationary effect upon the economy could also vote against the tax while still voting in favor of the rest of the energy package.

Of the three attempts to defeat the equalization tax, Steiger's promised to divide not only the coalition but the Democratic party as well. Because of this danger, the party leadership actively attempted to keep the Democratic ranks closed in order to prevent a defeat of the president's centerpiece energy proposal.

The motion for recommittal was narrowly defeated, 209–219 (9 not voting, 2 vacancies). Of the 140 Republicans voting, 137 voted in favor of recommittal and only 3 were opposed. Of the 282 Democrats voting, 66 bolted the party position by voting in favor of recommittal. All 3 of the Republicans who voted against the motion were from the Northeast, while 58 of the 66 Democrats who voted in favor of recommittal represented Sunbelt districts. As in the prior two efforts to kill the tax, regional self-interest had some effect on the vote. The coalition, however, like the rest of the House, generally voted on this issue according to the party line. Seventy-one of the 79 coalition members voting to recommit the energy bill were Republicans; 120 of the 123 coalition members voting not to recommit were Democrats.[40]

The next vote taken on the House floor was on the entire energy package. It was adopted, 244–177. The crude oil equalization tax and its home heating oil rebate plan had survived several close votes on the floor of the House and within the House Ways and Means Committee. The tax and its rebate plan, however, still had to clear the Senate and its Sunbelt-dominated Finance Committee, and there it met defeat.

COMPLICATIONS IN THE SENATE: RUSSELL LONG AND THE FINANCE COMMITTEE

The seventeen-member Senate Finance Committee, chaired by Russell Long, had only four members representing states located in the Northeast-Midwest region. The Finance Committee was collectively, as friendly to the cause of the oil companies as any in the Congress. The vast majority of its members, including Chairman Long, represent states dependent upon energy producers as a source of employment and tax income. As the markup session on the House-passed energy tax-related items began on September 20, 1977, before the full committee, there was little doubt that the equalization tax was in trouble. The Finance Committee, as a committee representing energy-producing states, was naturally inclined to support decontrol of oil prices, not a crude oil equalization tax, especially not one that would rebate a portion of the tax to consumers of home heating oil (only two Finance Committee members, Abraham Ribicoff [D-Conn.] and Daniel Moynihan [D-N.Y.], represented states that would significantly benefit from the rebate). As a result, when the tax was brought up for consideration, Chairman Long made it clear that the home heating oil rebate and the per capita rebate plans would not be passed (or even voted on). He also indicated that the Finance Committee would kill the bill unless the administration agreed to plow back at least some of the revenues of the tax to energy producers in order to create greater incentives for energy production. To give the president some time to consider its ultimatum, the committee decided to postpone the final vote on the equalization tax until September 26. In the meantime, the president let the committee know that he would be willing to accept a plowback provision and the deletion of the rebate if that was the only means of getting the equalization tax passed in the Senate. Once the president had done this, however, several labor organizations and the Consumer Federation of America quickly announced that while they had supported the president's tax in the House, they could no longer do so if the rebate provisions to consumers were deleted. Now that various consumer groups were assailing the tax program as being too favorable to the oil interests and the oil interests were assailing the tax bill as being not favorable enough, the delicate balance between the consuming and producing interests upon which the crude oil equalization tax had managed to survive the House had been destroyed. As a result, the president's proposal had scant chance of surviving in the Senate.

On September 26 the Senate Finance Committee voted 10–6 to kill the president's crude oil equalization tax despite the fact that he had accepted their terms. Democratic Senators Harry Byrd (Va.), Floyd Haskell (Colo.), and Gaylord Nelson (Wis.) joined the committee's seven Republicans to kill the bill.[41]

CONCLUSION: REDISTRIBUTIVE ISSUES, THE COALITION'S ACHILLES' HEEL

The coalition's reluctance to take an aggressive role in the legislative battles over energy policy tells much about the limitations of caucus politics in general and particularly about bipartisan caucus politics. In the face of an issue that is sensitive in both ideological and partisan ways—the essence of redistributive politics—the bipartisan coalition could not function very well. Once ideology and partisanship were no longer overriding concerns and distributive politics was allowed to prevail, the coalition was able to function very well, as evidenced by its aggressive actions taken to save the home heating oil rebate plan. Clearly, the coalition's success as a lobbying force within the Congress is dependent both on the type of issue in question and on specific circumstances surrounding its passage. This conclusion is evident from a comparison of the activity undertaken by the coalition on the oil rebate plan (a distributive issue) with its nonactivity on the natural gas bill (a redistributive issue) and also from an examination of the coalition's activity on the housing and community development bill of 1977, another distributive issue (see Chapter 2).

At the same time the coalition was carefully avoiding a debate on the key components of the president's energy bill, it was aggressively attempting to revise the formula of the housing and community development bill in both committee and on the floor of the House. As noted earlier, the coalition's floor activity on the latter measure inspired the *National Journal* to call the coalition a "well-oiled bipartisan lobbying machine."[42] The coalition, however, hardly fitted this description as it carefully backed away even from recommending a vote on most of the energy proposals. The difference in the actions taken by the coalition lies in the nature of the two issues. Housing and community development was clearly identified within the coalition, thanks in large part to its informational resources, as a distributive issue that overrode partisan or ideological attachments. Energy, on the other hand, was less clearly identifiable as a distributive or, as Larry Halloran put it, a "give me" issue. On the contrary, most of the energy proposals were clearly identifiable as partisan issues; and certain components of the energy proposals, such as the deregulation of natural gas and oil prices, were identifiable as ideological issues. As large, controversial issues with ideological and partisan pressures, logrolling on these issues—between both Sunbelt and Snowbelt representatives, as well as within each of the regions—was nearly impossible.

While the coalition failed in the energy battle to live up to its image as created by the *National Journal* and other publications, it once again undertook activities that clearly set it apart from most other caucuses. Most caucuses monitor the legislative process and undertake activities similar to the coalition's behavior surrounding the natural gas proposal. It is true that the rebate was eventually killed by the Senate Finance Committee. But the coalition's efforts on its behalf provide another illustration that the legislative process, as well as congressional behavior, is being altered by the existence of the coalition. A striking example of the coalition's effect on congressional behavior is provided by the contrasting styles of the older James Burke and the younger William Cotter as they both attempted to save the home heating oil rebate. Burke approached his colleagues on the Ways and Means Committee on a personal level, asking for their support on the issue. Burke was, in effect, using the age-old technique of logrolling to get the rebate reconsidered. Cotter, on the other hand, did not (indeed could not, because of his junior status) approach his colleagues in the same personal way. Instead, with statistical information provided by the coalition, Cotter appealed directly to his colleagues' self-interest, asking for their votes, not as a personal favor to him, but as a favor for themselves. In this sense, the coalition has helped to usher in a new form of legislative behavior that both complements and rivals logrolling. The coalition has ushered in a new era of computer politics where hard, statistical information, which was less available in the past, now challenges logrolling as an accepted means of conducting congressional business. Today, thanks in large part to the coalition and caucuses like it, even junior members of Congress, like Cotter, have access to information and, as a result, power in the House.

Representatives Cotter's and Burke's efforts within the Ways and Means Committee also serve to highlight the organizational advantage the formation of the coalition has provided to the northeastern states. While Burke's unsolicited efforts were helpful, it is doubtful that he could have convinced enough committee members to switch their votes on the rebate plan to save it. What did save it was Cotter's threat to use the New England Caucus and the Northeast-Midwest Congressional Coalition as vehicles to mount opposition to the energy bill as a whole. Speaker O'Neill, who had already provided a means of circumventing the normal institutional advantage of the Sunbelt legislators, was compelled by Cotter's threat to intervene in the legislative process once again, this time on behalf of the rebate. Ullman, now under pressure from the Speaker, the New

England Caucus, and the coalition from outside his committe and from Burke and Cotter from within it, decided to go along on this issue. That the Sunbelt legislators, confident that their institutional advantage would yet again protect their interests, were not organized in an explicit caucus as were the Snowbelt legislators, no doubt made Ullman's decision to reconsider the rebate that much easier.

An examination of the role taken by the Northeast–Midwest Congressional Coalition in the legislative fate of the president's home heating oil rebate plan highlights not only the aggressive action taken by the coalition to protect the northeastern states' interests but also other ways in which interests of the northeastern states are represented in the Congress. Speaker O'Neill's role in the passage of the president's energy package in the House, and specifically the passage of the home heating oil rebate plan, indicate that the coalition often complements rather than dominates the representation of the northeastern states' interests in Congress. Burke's effort on behalf of the rebate is another example of the Northeastern states' ability to have their voices heard within the institutional power structure. Cotter's use of the coalition's information to influence the votes of his colleagues clearly worked to complement Burke's efforts. Together, they met with success; but if one or the other had not done what he did, the home heating oil rebate probably would never have been reported by the Ways and Means Committee.

CHAPTER NINE *The Coalition, the Congress, and the Intergovernmental Grant System: Challenging the Norms, Changing the Systems*

The Northeast–Midwest Congressional Coalition's intervention in the deliberations of friendly as well as hostile subgovernments during the Ninety-fifth Congress had a significant impact on many decisions that were reached at the subgovernment level, on how those decisions were reached, and on the intergovernmental grant system as well. Subgovernment decisions on distributive policies, for example, have historically had a low degree of visibility and a high degree of logrolling both within the subgovernment structure and on the floor of the House of Representatives.[1] The coalition's formulamanship skills, however, have successfully broadened the scope of conflict normally associated with distributive policies within several subgovernments. The coalition's informational resources made many Snowbelt representatives aware of what was occurring at the subgovernment level, thereby increasing the issue's visibility. It also convinced a number of subgovernment members that logrolling on distributive issues (both within subgovernment structures and on the House floor) was contrary to their interests. Although it cannot be said that the coalition altered the entire federal policymaking process concerning distributive issues, the coalition's efforts were clearly felt within several subgovernments, especially that of housing and community development. Decisions within these subgovernments were no longer routinely adopted on the floor of the House, and individuals within them were now more prone to question the cost benefits of logrolling versus challenging the status quo. Hannaford's amendment to the housing and community development bill was only one instance of a member's challenging the status quo. The Howard amendment, the two Cotter amendments, and the Jeffords and Ford amendments are examples of the coalition's efforts spurring a challenge to the status quo and the logrolling system.

In altering both the outcome and the manner in which legislative decisions were reached at the subgovernment level, the coalition obviously also altered the behavior of individual congressmen. In voting terms, the coalition's informational resources lessened the dependence of many of its members on their colleagues as voting cues on traditionally defined distributive policies and on those policies now seen as being redistributive along geographic lines. Also, evaluative information, which in the past was difficult to acquire, was now readily available to coalition members regardless of seniority or party label.

Not only was evaluative information useful for one's own enlightenment; it could also be used to attract political allies from other regions. As was indicated in the previous chapter, William Cotter used the evaluative information of the coalition's staff to elicit the support of other members of the Ways and Means Committee. In the past, Cotter could not have participated in "computer politics" because he would not have had access to this kind of information. While logrolling was still the norm, computer politics (the use of evaluative information to build a coalition based on self-interest as opposed to trusting another's judgement) provided the leverage within the Ways and Means Committee to reinstate the home heating oil rebate plan. In light of its effectiveness in this case, computer politics, as fostered by the coalition, will probably become a permanent fixture within the federal policymaking process. Computer politics, in turn, is (1) weakening the ability of the Congress to shape national policy and (2) insuring that the use of formulamanship (computer politics applied to formula grants) will play an increasingly important role in the determination of the regional allocation of federal funds. Given the Reagan administration's efforts to replace categorical grants with formula-based block grants, it is most probable that formulamanship will soon completely dominate the intergovernmental field.

THE COALITION AS AN ORGANIZATION

In light of the various articles that have been published concerning the coalition's role in the outcome of the Housing and Community Development Act of 1977, I reexamined the legislative evolution of this act to determine if the coalition was responsible, as these articles implied, for the changes in the legislation that enhanced the economic fortunes of the Northeast-Midwest region. I discovered that while the coalition was at the forefront of the effort to enact the administration-sponsored dual formula, a number of intervening variables refute the conclusion that it was solely responsible for the Snowbelt representatives' solid opposition to the Hannaford amendment.

This alternative view of the Hannaford amendment also raised some questions concerning the coalition as an organization. If its efforts were not necessarily responsible for the regional solidarity of the representatives of the Northeast-Midwest region, was the coalition, as the *National Journal* article indicated, a smoothly functioning machine,[2] or was it something less? Interviews with the representatives who led the coalition's efforts on the housing and community development bill (Michael Harrington, Stanley Lundine, and Paul Tsongas) as well as with the coalition's principal staff members (John Moriarty, Shelly Amdur, and Laurence Zabar) show that it was not by any means a machine. Of course, even its proponents did not describe the coalition as a monolithic machine with orders emanating from the top and obeyed by the masses at the bottom. Instead, they described an organization that was only loosely structured through its task forces. The coalition they spoke of was used as a forum for the interchange of ideas, information, and political strategies. While Harrington had become first among equals as far as the coalition was concerned, he possessed no rewards or penalties to influence the vote of any other coalition member or any action other than the one that member felt was in his own self-interest.

Structurally, during the Ninety-fifth Congress the coalition developed an inner circle of approximately thirty activists and a vast outer circle of what has been described as spectator members. The activists were convinced (though unfamiliar with the terms) that all policies were redistributive when viewed from the geographic perspective. The spectators were not convinced that district and regional interests were always identical. They were, however, willing to receive (but not necessarily follow) whatever political impulses (such as information, suggested votes, etc.) the activists sent them. When the spectators believed that the activists' regional policy options also enhanced their local interests and that logrolling for these policy options was unlikely, they would vote for the coalition's position. The preference among the spectators, however, was to logroll, even if, by doing so, their districts would receive less aid in the short-run than by supporting the coalition's position. Logrolling does not cause hard and bitter feelings among congressional members. It also provides subsidy security. Congressmen do not have to continually defend what they already receive. In a naturally combative and uncertain environment, most representatives like knowing that a given subsidy will continue. By rocking the boat with computer politics, one takes the risk of losing everything. Many felt that the risk was too great.

THE COALITION'S ACTIVISTS: THE OBJECTIVES

What had become clear in speaking with members of the coalition's inner circle was that the key to understanding the coalition as an organization was the relationship between its activist and spectator members. During the Ninety-fifth Congress, this relationship was a tenuous one. Despite the fact that 189 representatives from the coalition states had chosen to oppose the Hannaford amendment to the housing and community development bill and only five supported it, this fact did not indicate, as implied by the press, that the entire membership of the coalition would repeat this kind of regional solidarity in all issue areas, under all conditions. What this vote indicated was only that such an alignment was possible. In fact, subsequent votes on the House floor during the Ninety-fifth Congress indicated that the coalition's spectator members were quite willing to vote against amendments sponsored by the activists. The defeat of James Howard's amendment to the defense appropriations bill is just one such example.

The coalition's activists found it so difficult to obtain the spectator members' support of coalition positions simply because the spectator members often felt they had nothing to gain by offering their support. These spectator members were not convinced that all policies were redistributive along geographic lines; and for those who did accept this argument on a specific item of legislation, the geographic cleavage was not always seen as the most dominant one. In the federal procurement case, for example, most of the coalition's spectator members recognized that both their regional and their local interests would be hurt by the Maybank amendment. Nevertheless, many of them rejected the coalition's Howard amendment because the national security argument was seen as overriding regional or parochial interests. The fact that many of these same members later reversed themselves by supporting the Addabbo amendment during the Ninety-sixth Congress suggests, however, that the coalition is becoming more successful in its efforts to convince its spectator members that the geographic cleavage should be the dominant one.

Another reason the coalition's spectator members, especially those from marginal districts, were not always inclined to support the activists' views was that participating in computer politics provided little electoral security. After all, despite their leadership, Hannaford was defeated in 1978 and Harrington chose to retire. Also, computer politics raised the ire of many senior members of the House who were committed to (and benefited by) the traditional, logrolling style of politics. Representatives from marginal districts, therefore, had to choose between playing it safe by logrolling with their more senior members or risk having the more senior members work to cut off their portion of the federal government's economic resources.

A third reason the coalition's activists had difficulty in securing a regional response from its spectator members was that logrolling enabled many of them to attain a sufficient portion of the federal largesse to satisfy their own political and personal needs. These representatives—generally the region's more senior members—saw no reason to abandon a style of politics that had served them well in the past.

Despite all of these factors working against them, the coalition's activists clearly made progress in their efforts to increase the Northeast-Midwest's advantage already possessed in non-defense-related federal expenditures and to chip away at the Sunbelt states' enormous advantage concerning defense-related expenditures. In reaching these goals, the coalition's activists (1) intervened on the behalf of the region in the legislative deliberations of selected subgovernments dealing with regionally sensitive issues, (2) appealed those decisions reached at the subgovernment level that did not redress the imbalance of federal funds to the House floor, and (3) attempted to convince the coalition's spectator members that logrolling was contrary to their self-interest.

In more analytic terms, the coalition's activists sought to convince the spectator members, particularly those who held key institutional power positions in the House, of the following argument. All policies dealing with federal expenditures hold a regional implication and are, therefore, redistributive. Since all policies are redistributive, the reasons for logrolling are no longer in force. It is now in your interest to scrutinize the decisions being reached at the subgovernment level, to appeal decisions that do not redress the regional imbalance in the flow of federal funds, and to stop relying on the advice of a selected few cue givers within these subgovernments because that advice has proved to be contrary to the region's, and therefore the member's self-interest.

In essence, the coalition's activists, though not familiar with the terms, were arguing that a new dimension needed to be added to Theodore Lowi's classification of issues. Issues were no longer to be judged as being redistributive or nonredistributive according to whether or not they cut across class or group lines, since the geographic axis now had to be considered as well. Many issues previously considered distributive now had to be considered redistributive because they were seen as cutting across geographic lines. Anticipated congressional behavior, as a result, was to be adjusted accordingly.

THE COALITION AS A LOBBY: ITS EFFECT ON THE OUTCOME OF POLICY

The previous chapters have revealed that the coalition's efforts in the Ninety-fifth Congress followed a distinct pattern. In each of the issues examined, the coalition began with the identification of those issues that held a major regional implication. Once an issue was identified as having a major regional implication, Michael Harrington, in consultation with Staff Director John Moriarty, determined whether or not the coalition would take any action concerning the issue. This decision was based on the economic magnitude of the issue and, at least to some extent, on the prospects of achieving some measure of success in altering the legislative outcome of that policy.

Once the decision was made to address an issue, a member or several members of the staff were assigned by John Moriarty or Thomas Cochran to develop a paper that defined both the issue's regional implication and the impact of as many serious policy options as possible. When this information was gathered and processed into a usable format, Michael Harrington, usually in consultation with Moriarty, Frank Horton, and James Oberstar, then sought the assistance of two of three members of the coalition's inner circle of activists. These members would be responsible for determining which (if any) of the staff's proposed policy options the coalition should endorse and for developing and executing a strategy to get those options enacted. These selected activists (usually designated as cochairman of the issue's task force) also consulted with other members of the coalition's inner circle (principally those who joined the respective task force) to develop a consensus concerning which policy options to endorse. As soon as this consensus was reached, the coalition activists would then make a direct, unified input into the legislative deliberations of the subgovernment in question. If consensus was not achieved quickly (or if their efforts failed at the subgovernment level), however, the activists were then forced to appeal the decisions reached by the subgovernment to the floor of the House. Since the related norms of committee specialization and reciprocity worked against amendments opposed by any given subgovernment on most subsidy-related issues, the activists preferred to work on the subgovernment first and face a floor fight only if necessary.

The examination of the coalition's activities during the Ninety-fifth Congress makes it clear that its activists were responsible for initiating several changes in legislation that resulted in some improvement, from their standpoint, of the regional flow of funds. These changes, however, did not result from the coalition's ability to foster a regional response from its members on the House floor. The coalition's major floor effort during the Ninety-fifth Congress (the Howard amendment), for example, failed because the coalition could not elicit a regional response from its members. Most of these legislative changes were achieved at the subgovernment level. Once adopted within the committee, these legislative changes were then routinely adopted on the House floor because most representatives still considered the legislation, as a whole, to be distributive in nature. Thus, the adoption of the Lundine amendment was clearly initiated by the coalition and adopted by the House Banking Committee because of the coalition's efforts and superior formulamanship skills. When the committee's bill reached the House floor, it was challenged by some Sunbelt representatives who felt that the legislation was no longer distributive in nature. The Hannaford amendment, however, was soundly defeated because many Sunbelt representatives did not believe the legislation was redistributive and, instead of supporting the amendment, chose to logroll with their northeastern colleagues on the Banking Committee. The northeastern representatives, for their part, were benefited by both the Lundine amendment and the president's dual formula. They were naturally inclined as a group, therefore, to oppose the amendment.

An examination of the coalition's efforts at the subgovernment level during the Ninety-fifth Congress suggests that the coalition's ability to alter subgovernment decisions depended on three interdependent conditions: (1) if the coalition's activists viewed the issue under consideration as being redistributive over geographic lines alone (rather than over class and group lines as well), (2) if these activists themselves reached a consensus concerning what action to take, and (3) if the committee in question was dominated by representatives from the Northeast-Midwest region. In issues that met all three of these conditions (like the Lundine amendment), the coalition's efforts to amend legislative decisions at the subgovernment level usually met with unqualified success. In issue areas in which only the first two conditions were met (like the two Cotter amendments), however, the activists' efforts to improve the Northeast-Midwest's position met with varying degrees of success. In issue areas in which the first condition was not met (like the energy issue), the activists could not reach a consensus as to what action to take and abandoned all efforts to influence the decisions reached by those issue areas' subgovernments.

THE COALITION'S EFFECT ON THE FEDERAL POLICYMAKING PROCESS

Taken collectively, the coalition's efforts at altering legislative outcomes were responsible for providing the Northeast-Midwest region with hundreds of millions of dollars that would otherwise have gone to the Sunbelt. While this outcome represents a substantial amount of federal revenue, the coalition's efforts fell far short of its goal of changing the balance in the regional distribution of federal funds. It must be remembered, however, that this study has examined the coalition's efforts during the Ninety-fifth Congress, a period in which the coalition was still maturing as an organization, discovering which strategies were successful and which were not. It was a period in which the coalition's inner circle of activists was expanding and its spectator members were only beginning to recognize the utility of the coalition's reports and to question the costs and benefits of adhering to the related norms of committee specialization and reciprocity.

In recognition of the coalition's maturation during the Ninety-fifth Congress, a final judgment on its effect on the federal policymaking process and its outcomes cannot be made at this time. Without a doubt, the coalition will have a substantial impact both on future legislative decisions and on the manner in which those decisions are reached in future Congresses. During the Ninety-fifth Congress, the coalition's efforts met with only partial success in the legislative arena because it had not yet been able to radically alter the manner in which the federal policymaking process works.

The standard model of legislation in the House concerning those issues considered nonredistributive in nature is that it is initiated by the president in consultation with the legislative actors at the subgovernment level. Because the House has a number of issues to consider and nonredistributive policies were considered relatively cost free, these legislative actors were allowed to carry on their deliberations in relative isolation. This isolation, in turn, created a situation in which the members of each subgovernment, especially each subcommittee chairman, became the only legislative actors in the federal policymaking process who knew how "their" legislation worked and precisely what it accomplished. Because other members of the House were busy within their own subgovernments, each subcommittee chairman became (as spokesman for the subgovernment) the House specialist in that particular policy area. In deference to this expertise and in recognition of the fact that the legislation in question was considered relatively cost free, on the floor of the House other legislative actors deferred to all decisions made at the subgovernment level that were not flagrantly against their local interests. Subcommittee chairmen, recognizing that their subcommittee's decisions were not going to be overruled if they did not flagrantly oppose any significant number of representatives' local interests, made certain to avoid such overruling by giving all members of "their" subgovernment a significant piece of the subsidy pie. This sharing of the wealth prevented any of the subgovernment members from having a reason to appeal any of the subgovernment's decisions to the full House. When these decisions did reach the floor of the House, members of other subgovernments, lacking familiarity with the issue, would customarily seek out those members of the subgovernment who held interests similar to their own and ask them whether or not they should support the legislation before them. Since all members of the subgovernment received a significant piece of the subsidy pie, they usually told outside members that the subgovernment's decision was all right. And they usually accorded the same courtesy to members of other subgovernments. As a result, most subgovernment decisions concerning nonredistributive issues were routinely adopted by the full House. This is the essence of logrolling politics—division of labor leads to specialization, which in turn leads to reciprocity.

At the conclusion of the Ninety-fifth Congress, logrolling on nonredistributive policies was still the norm. There were several indications, however, that the coalition's efforts were helping to curtail the logrolling politics of the Congress; otherwise, the Lundine amendment would have never become law, nor would the Hannaford, Edwards, Howard, and Cotter amendments have been contested at all. These issues were contested because the coalition's information resources made many representatives more aware of what was happening at the subgovernment level and of the significance subgovernment decisions had for their local and regional interests. Because of this heightened awareness many representatives, such as Stanley Lundine, Paul Tsongas, and James Jeffords, were less willing than in the past to automatically logroll both at the subgovernment level and on the House floor. They now had other ways of obtaining relief for their districts than by trading votes. Now many representatives were thinking: "Though this legislation doesn't benefit my district, my support for it may bring me support for future measures favorable to my district. But can I best benefit my district by opposing this measure and joining a coalition whose members share my interests?" In the past, most representatives were forced to trust others, usually members of the subgovernment in question, to protect their interests. With the emergence of the coalition's evaluative information, however, many representatives realized that they had an opportunity to get a second opinion, the coalition's. As a result, for many of its members the coalition lessened their dependence upon their colleagues as voting cues.

The coalition's major impact on logrolling politics, however, was not through its increased use as a voting cue but through its use as a vehicle to intervene in the legislative deliberations at the subgovernment level. This intervention, coupled with the use of the coalition's evaluative information to attract additional support, fostered what I have referred to as computer politics. The emergence of computer politics, as practiced by William Cotter during consideration of the home heating oil rebate plan, by Stanley Lundine during consideration of his small-cities dual formula, and by Jeffords and Ford during consideration of Title 1 entitlement funds provided representatives from the Snowbelt a choice of legislative methods when seeking support for any given policy option. In the past, because access to evaluative information was limited, logrolling was the only method available for gathering support for any given piece of distributive legislation. Now, however, a representative can use computer politics to supplement or even replace logrolling in his efforts to achieve legislative success.

The success of computer politics, especially within friendly subgovernments, insures that computer politics will continue to supplement logrolling in future Congresses. Most of the representatives, from both the Sunbelt and the Snowbelt, however, will remain reluctant to abandon logrolling altogether. For Snowbelt representatives there will still be the fear that Sunbelt representatives (who constitute a growing majority of the House) will follow the advice of Hannaford and Edwards and challenge the decisions made by those subgovernments biased toward the Snowbelt. When one considers what has happened to the institutional power structure within the House in the past decade, this fear is understandable. It has been the Snowbelt that has been acquiring institutional power positions, not the Sunbelt. Many of the South's senior representatives retired during the 1970s. Their replacements, lacking seniority, will not be able to provide the South with the same institutional influence over legislation their predecessors did. Since 1970 the South has lost in the House the chairmanships of the Ways and Means, Armed Services, Rules, Agriculture, and Banking Committees. In the Senate, the turnover has been just as great. In 1970 southerners chaired eleven of the Senate's sixteen standing committees. In 1980 southerners held only three chairmanships of the then fifteen standing committees of the Senate. Thus, the 1980s will see more representatives from the Snowbelt attaining institutional power positions. At the same time, the total number of Snowbelt representatives will drop by 15 members following the 1982 reapportionment (from 213 to 198). These two trends—the gaining of institutional power positions and the decline in total representative due to relative population declines—indicate that in the coming decade it will be the Snowbelt, not the Sunbelt that will want to see subgovernment decisions go unchallenged on the floor of the House. It will be the Snowbelt, not the Sunbelt that will lack the numbers to prevent subgovernment decisions from being overturned. Thus, the coalition's successful efforts in supplementing logrolling politics with computer politics may actually turn into a political pandora's box: they are teaching the Sunbelt the very tactics its members will need in the coming years to defeat the Snowbelt. In this regard, as the coalition's victories piled up during the Ninety-fifth and Ninety-sixth Congresses many Sunbelt representatives decided that the time had come to act. On April 9, 1981, eighty Sunbelt members of the House of Representatives joined forces and formed the Sunbelt Council. The Sunbelt Council is a regionally based political caucus emulating the Northeast–Midwest Congressional Coalition. Its first priority for the Ninety-seventh Congress is to reinstate, in full, the Maybank amendment and to examine President Reagan's block grant proposals to insure that their formulas do not hurt the Sunbelt.[3] Computer politics is here to stay.

SOME LONG-TERM CONSEQUENCES: MORE DECENTRALIZATION AND LESS OBEDIENCE

In the early 1970s the Democrats in the House of Representatives enacted several reforms that resulted in a further decentralization of power in the House. Among these reform measures was the "subcommittee bill of rights," which increased the power of subcommittee chairmen at the expense of standing committee chairmen.[4] One by-product of these reforms' decentralizing effect on the House was to present conditions that were favorable to the formation of the coalition. Now that committee chairmen are weaker than in the recent past, many rank-and-file members of the House are no longer afraid to take positions contrary to the legislative interests of their respective committees' leaders. It has been said that apprenticeship is dead in the House and the Senate. Computer politics has served as a vehicle for many of these young members of the House to break the bonds of apprenticeship. Stanley Lundine and Paul Tsongas, for example, were only junior members of the House Banking Committee, yet by employing computer politics they both played central roles in the development of the housing and community development bill. Computer politics success, in terms of achieving short-term policy goals, insures that many rank-and-file members, and even some committee leaders, will engage in computer politics. Success, as the formation of the Sunbelt Council demonstrates, has a way of winning converts.

Two problems arise, however, when one considers the long-term consequences of the rise of computer politics. The first problem has to do with leadership; the second, with "justice." As for leadership, no matter what one thinks of logrolling, it has been—and remains—the grease that allows the wheels of government to run smoothly and quickly on distributive policies. Begin to remove the grease and the wheels will begin to squeak. This danger has already been evidenced by the rising incidence of House floor appeals by both Sunbelt and Snowbelt representatives. These challenges, both on the House floor and in subcommittee, are certain to cause delays; they also raise the question of just who is in charge. With more and more junior members engaging in computer politics, working independently of subcommittee, committee, and party leadership, the authority and thus the power of all three of these leadership positions is diminished. As James Jeffords, who played a key role in the Title 1 formula fight despite his junior and minority party status, said:

> When you get into a formula fight anyone who is willing to spend the necessary time to find out who benefits and who gets hurt has a decided advantage. If you know who you help and who you hurt you can organize your forces, if not, you're at the mercy of the committee chairman.[5]

The point is that Jeffords was not at the mercy of Carl Perkins, and one of the reasons he joined the coalition was to free himself from Perkins's and other committee leaders' domination.

Like the effect of the institutional reforms of the early 1970s, the resulting computer politics of the late 1970s and 1980s clearly promises to make the House an even more equalitarian institution than it is today. In the future committee and party leaders are going to find it even more difficult to control the behavior of their rank-and-file members. No one, not even the president, will be able to count on anyone's support unless the computer printout indicates that it is in that particular member's interest to go along. Leaders, in short, are going to find it increasingly difficult to lead as the rank and file become better prepared to act independently of their leaders. The Congress, and particularly the House, will be an increasingly difficult institution to manage during the middle and later years of the 1980s.

The second problem, one that in some respects is just as important as the leadership problem, is that of justice. Computer politics defines "justice" as being might makes right. In these chapters little is heard of discussions of what formula will produce the best results for the nation as a whole. Members of both sides are convinced that if their side is helped, then the nation is helped. In a sense, both sides are right. If the Sunbelt grows, so does the nation, and the same is true of the Snowbelt. But, to borrow a phrase from John Rawls, as computer politics has raised the "veil of ignorance" in the House, justice has somehow become lost. Now that everyone knows where they will be in society, everyone defines justice to suit themselves. To equate justice with power (or votes) is simply inadequate. I offer no solutions to this problem here. I merely point out the problem. Much more research is necessary to arrive at an understanding of what a just criterion of need is. As I have indicated, this is a statistician's nightmare, but the stakes are immensely high. One thing is certain, however: computer politics will not provide an adequate answer to this problem.

Notes

INTRODUCTION

1. Harold Lasswell, *Politics: Who Gets What, When and How* (New York: The World Publishing Company, 1958).

2. The name of the organization was originally the Northeast–Midwest Economic Advancement Coalition and was changed to the Northeast–Midwest Congressional Coalition in 1978. In 1976 sixteen states held membership in the coalition: Connecticut, Illinois, Indiana, Iowa, Maine, Massachusetts, Michigan, Minnesota, New Hampshire, New Jersey, New York, Ohio, Pennsylvania, Rhode Island, Vermont, and Wisconsin. Delaware and Maryland joined the coalition (membership is gained when any representative of a state requests membership) in 1978. These eighteen states are collectively treated as the Snowbelt in this analysis.

3. Sarah E. Warren, "The New Look of the Congressional Caucus," *National Journal* 10, 17 (29 April 1978), 677.

4. Burdett Loomis, "Congressional Caucuses and the Politics of Representation," in Lawrence Dodd and Bruce Oppenheimer, eds., *Congress Reconsidered*, 2d ed. (Washington D.C.: Congressional Quarterly Press, 1981), pp. 204–220.

5. Kirkpatrick Sale, *Power Shift* (New York: Random House, 1975), p. 5.

6. Ibid., pp. 5–7.

7. *The State of the Region* (Washington, D.C.: The Northeast–Midwest Congressional Coalition, January 1979), p. 2.

8. C. L. Jusenius and L. C. Ledebur, "A Myth in the Making: The Southern Economic Challenge and Northern Economic Decline," in E. Blaine Liner and Lawrence Lynch, eds., *The Economics of Southern Growth* (Research Triangle Park, N.C.: The Southern Growth Policies Board, 1977), pp. 131–173.

CHAPTER ONE

1. John Moore, "Washington Pressures/Business Forms Economic Study Group Unit to Support Bipartisan New England Caucus," *National Journal* 5, 7 (17 February 1973), 226.

2. Ibid., pp. 228–230.

3. Ibid., p. 230.

4. Ibid.

5. Ibid., pp. 230 and 231.

6. Ibid., p. 226.

7. Harrington was elected to the Congress in 1970. He campaigned vig-orously against the Vietnam War, yet was still assigned to the Armed Serv-ices Committee. His run-ins with his fellow committee members, exacer-bated by his straightforward, aggressive personality, resulted in his leaving the committee in 1973. In 1975 he won appointment to the special com-mittee investigating the CIA. When it was disclosed that the committee's chairman, Lucien Nedzi of Michigan, had not disclosed information he had been provided with a year earlier concerning the CIA, Harrington and several other committee members demanded that Nedzi resign from the committee. The House leadership finally had to intervene, and Nedzi and Harrington were removed from the committee. Later in the same year, Harrington was once again involved in a controversial situation when he disclosed classified information concerning United States involvement in the coup that brought the Chilean junta to power. Representative Robin Beard filed a motion to censure Harrington for his action, but it was tabled on a technicality. Source: Michael Barone, Grant Ujifusa, and Douglas Matthews, *The Almanac of American Politics 1978* (New York: E. P. Dut-ton, 1978), p. 385.

8. "Energy Brief Number 1: Energy and the Northeast" (Washington, D.C.: CONEG Policy Research Center, 1980), p. 2.

9. Robert Firestone and Bernard Weinstein, *Regional Growth and De-cline in the United States* (New York: Praeger Publishers, 1978), p. 26.

10. Michael Harrington, interviewed by Robert Dilger, 18 May 1979, Washington, D.C.

11. "Sunbelt Picks Up Seats but Chairmanships Down," Congressional Quarterly, *Weekly Reports* 35, 34 (20 August 1977), 1750.

12. Michael McManus, "Boston Detente at the North-South Summit," *Northeast-Midwest Agenda* (Summer 1978), p. 4.

13. Michael Harrington, interviewed by Robert Dilger, 18 May 1979, Washington, D.C.

14. David Maxfield and Ted Valen, "House Rejects Monies to Cut Arms Budget," Congressional Quarterly, *Weekly Reports* 34, 16 (17 April 1976), 932.

15. In Harrington's case, one of the bases slated for a major personnel reduction was Fort Devens, in Ayer, Massachusetts. While Ayer is located in Robert Drinan's district, many of Harrington's constituents worked or had friends or relatives who worked at the base.

16. Joel Havemann and Rochelle Stanfield, "A Year Later, the Frostbelt Strikes Back," *National Journal* 9, 27 (2 July 1977), 1028.

17. Twenty-eight of the forty-seven members of the House Banking, Finance and Urban Affairs Committee were members of the Northeast–Midwest Congressional Coalition.

18. John Moriarty, interviewed by Robert Dilger, 21 March 1979, Wash-ington, D.C.

19. Ashley represents Toledo, Ohio, and its suburbs. His district is heavily dependent on the automobile industry for jobs. This industry was in very poor condition following the Arab oil embargo in 1973 and had not significantly improved at this time. Moorhead represents Pittsburgh, Pennsylvania. This city's economy is dependent upon the steel industry for a large proportion of its jobs. Like the automobile industry, the steel industry was having difficulties at this time.

20. The three staff members were Staff Director John Moriarty, Shelly Amdur, and Laurence Zabar.

21. Havemann and Stanfield, "A Year Later," p. 1032.

22. Laurence Zabar, "Federal Procurement and Regional Needs: The Case of Defense Manpower Policy Number Four" (Washington, D.C.: The Northeast–Midwest Congressional Coalition, March 1977), p. 3.

23. While the comparative system of analysis employed here provides a desirable means of focusing the analysis for descriptive purposes, the problem of uniqueness remains. For example, I may have chosen five cases that overstate the coalition's influence. I chose to study the housing and community development, elementary and secondary education, and DMP-4 cases because I knew the coalition was contesting these policies. I did not know, however, (except for the housing and community development case) if the coalition's efforts were successful prior to engaging in research. Also, I chose the Carter urban proposals and his crude oil equalization tax for analysis because I believed the coalition should have contested these policies. I did not know prior to engaging in research, if the coalition was contesting these policies. The fact that it did, indicated that its activities were not restricted to just a few isolated policies. One could still argue that I may have unintentionally picked five cases that make the coalition and its computer politics seem more important than warranted. This methodological question is not dismissed lightly, but even if the coalition were active in only these five cases (which was not the case) I would still argue that their successful use of computer politics has altered the policy process (as evidenced by the formation of the Sunbelt Council–see Chapter 9).

CHAPTER TWO

1. Joel Havemann and Rochelle Stanfield, "Federal Spending: The North's Loss Is the Sunbelt's Gain," *National Journal* 9, 26 (26 June 1976), 880.

2. Havemann and Stanfield, "Federal Spending," p. 880. (According to this article, spending on defense accounted for nearly all the federal expenditure disparity between the regions.)

3. Richard Nathan, *The Plot that Failed* (New York: John Wiley and Sons, 1975), p. 102.

4. Richard Nathan, Paul Dommel, Sarah Liebschultz, Milton Morris

and Associates of the Brookings Institution, *Block Grants for Community Development* (Washington, D.C.: U.S. Department of Housing and Urban Development, January 1977), p. 76.

5. Daniel Elazar, "Cursed by Bigness or Toward a Post-Technocratic Federalism," in Daniel Elazar, ed., *The Federal Polity* (New Brunswick, N.J.: Transaction Books, 1974), p. 244.

6. Advisory Commission on Intergovernmental Relations, *Categorical Grants and Their Role and Design* (Washington, D.C.: U.S. Government Printing Office, May 1976), p. 92.

7. Kathryn Waters Gest, "House Boosts Share for Older Cities," Congressional Quarterly, *Weekly Reports* 35, 20 (14 May 1977), 891. (The term "subgovernment" was first used by Douglas Cater, *Power in Washington*, [New York: Random House, 1964]. It refers to the alliances often formed at the lower levels of government that influence program development.)

8. Nathan, Dommel, Liebschultz, Morris and Associates of the Brookings Institution, *Block Grants*.

9. Ibid., p. 140.

10. Shelly Amdur, interviewed by Robert Dilger, 6 December 1978, Washington, D.C. (The members who joined the Housing and Community Development Task Force were: Paul Tsongas (D-Mass.) and Stanley Lundine (D-N.Y.), cochairmen; Stewart McKinney (R-Conn.), Christopher Dodd (D-Conn.), J. William Stanton (D-Ohio), Michael Harrington (D-Mass.), Frank Horton (R-N.Y.), and James Oberstar (D-Minn.). Thomas Ashley declined membership on the task force because, as the Housing and Community Development Subcommittee chairman, he felt that he had to appear regionally unbiased. Otherwise, he felt he would have had a more difficult time communicating with the Sunbelt members of his subcommittee.)

11. Stanley Lundine's district runs along the western half of New York's border with Pennsylvania and includes many smaller cities like Elmira. Paul Tsongas's district lies to the north of Boston and includes the mid-sized cities of Lowell and Lawrence.

12. Kathryn Waters Gest, "Administration Targets Aid to Aging Cities," Congressional Quarterly, *Weekly Reports* 25, 10 (5 March 1977), 418.

13. Shelly Amdur, interviewed by Robert Dilger, 6 June 1978, Washington, D.C.

14. Several congressmen felt that the administration agreed to support the amendment because (1) Embry supported it and (2) there was a conscious effort not to antagonize potential supporters of Ted Kennedy, then rumored to be considering a run for the presidency.

15. There was no recorded vote on this amendment. Representative Lundine provided this information.

16. Shelly Amdur, interviewed by Robert Dilger, 6 December 1977, Washington, D.C.

17. The 3 opposing votes were cast by Mark Hannaford (D-Calif.), Richard Kelly (R-Fla.), and Charles Grassley (R-Iowa).

18. Mark Hannaford's district encompases the more prosperous half of the city of Long Beach and the middle-income suburbs of Lakewood and Bellflower. He was mayor of Lakewood prior to being elected to the Congress in 1974. He narrowly defeated his Republican opponent, Richard Lungren, 51 to 49 percent in 1976, and lost in 1978. Jerry Patterson's district lies in the eastern half of prosperous Orange County. His seat is considered relatively safe.

19. A "Dear Colleague" letter is sent to a number of congressmen and carries the salutation of "Dear Colleague" instead of "Dear Congressman X," for example.

20. Mark Hannaford and Jerry Patterson, letter concerning the Housing and Community Development Act of 1977, 4 May 1977.

21. Michael Harrington, Frank Horton, James Oberstar, and Stanley Lundine, letter concerning the adoption of the housing and community development bill of 1977, 5 May 1977.

22. Michael Harrington, Frank Horton, Stanley Lundine, Paul Tsongas, James Oberstar, and Stewart McKinney, letter concerning possible amendments to the housing and community development bill of 1977, 9 May 1977.

23. *Congressional Record* 123, 79 (10 May 1977), 4231 and 4232.

24. Ibid., p. 4236.

25. Ibid., p. 4239.

26. Ibid.

27. John Moriarty, address to an Ohio audience, 18 July 1977.

28. Kathryn Waters Gest, "Compromise Reached on Urban Aid Bill," Congressional Quarterly, *Weekly Reports* 35, 40 (1 October 1977), 2079.

29. Ibid.

30. This assessment of the reason Ashley opposed the Senate's impaction adjustment was provided in separate interviews by Paul Tsongas (D-Mass.) and Stanley Lundine (D-N.Y.).

31. Paul Tsongas, interviewed by Robert Dilger, 30 January 1979, Washington, D.C.

32. Mark Hannaford, interviewed by Robert Dilger, 12 December 1979, Washington, D.C.

33. Two stopgap extensions (P.L. 95–60 and 95–90) were passed during the deadlock in order to prevent several of the programs from running out of funds.

34. Paul Tsongas, interviewed by Robert Dilger, 1978 June, Worcester, Massachusetts.

35. Gest, "Compromise Reached on Urban Aid Bill," p. 2080.

36. Kathryn Waters Gest, "Urban Aid Bill Cleared," Congressional Quarterly, *Weekly Reports* 35, 41 (8 October 1977), 2135.

37. Ibid.

38. *Weekly Compilation of Presidential Documents* 13, 42 (17 October 1977), 1530.

39. *Congressional Record* 123, 79 (10 May 1977), 4233.

40. "The Pork-Barrel War Between the States," *U.S. News & World Report* 83, 23 (5 December 1977), 39–41.

41. Paul Tsongas, interviewed by Robert Dilger, 1978 June, Worcester, Massachusetts.

42. "The Pork-Barrel War Between the States," p. 39.

43. Michael Harrington and Frank Horton, "Rescuing the Region," *New York Times*, 1 July 1977, p. A23.

44. Michael Harrington, Frank Horton, and James Oberstar, Letter to the White House Delegates to the Conference on Balanced Growth, 23 January 1978.

CHAPTER THREE

1. Horace Sutton, "Sunbelt vs. Frostbelt: A Second Civil War?" *Saturday Review* (15 April 1978), 33.

2. Mark Hannaford interviewed by Robert Dilger, 12 December 1978, Washington, D.C.

3. Alan Ehrenhalt, "Regionalism in Congress: Formulas Debated," Congressional Quarterly, *Weekly Reports* (20 August 1977), 1748.

4. Robert Firestone and Bernard Weinstein, *Regional Growth and Decline in the United States* (New York: Praeger Publishers, 1978), pp. 60 and 61.

5. Mark Hannaford, interviewed by Robert Dilger, 12 December 1978, Washington, D.C.

6. The Speaker of the House, Thomas O'Neill, Jr., was from Massachusetts.

7. Mark Hannaford, interviewed by Robert Dilger, 12 December 1978, Washington, D.C.

8. Reuben Askew, Introduction to *The Economics of Southern Growth*, ed. E. Blaine Liner and Lawrence Lynch (Research Triangle Park, N.C.: The Southern Growth Policies Board, 1977), pp. 3 and 4.

9. Joel Havemann and Rochelle Stanfield, "A Year Later the Frostbelt Strikes Back," *National Journal* 35, 27 (2 July 1977), 1030.

10. The Southern Growth Policies Board, *Southern Growth, Problems and Promises*, newsletter (Fall 1977), p. 6.

11. Ibid., p. 3.

12. Bernard Weinstein, interviewed by Robert Dilger, 30 January 1979, Washington, D.C.

13. "Southern Growth Board Protests Fund Study," *National Journal* (27 August 1977), 1356.

14. E. Blaine Liner and Lawrence Lynch, eds., *The Economics of Southern Growth* (Research Triangle Park, N.C.: The Southern Growth Policies Board, 1977).

15. C. L. Jusenius and L. C. Ledebur, "A Myth in the Making: The Southern Economic Challenge and Northern Economic Decline," in E. Blaine Liner and Lawrence Lynch, eds., *The Economics of Southern Growth* (Research Triangle Park, N.C.: The Southern Growth Policies Board, 1977), pp. 131–173. (Jusenius and Ledebur define the South as the fourteen member-states of the Southern Growth Policies Board: Alabama, Arkansas, Florida, Georgia, Kentucky, Louisiana, Mississippi, North Carolina, Oklahoma, South Carolina, Tennessee, Texas, Virginia, and West Virginia.)

16. Ibid., p. 173.

17. Ibid., p. 139.

18. Ibid.

19. Ibid., pp. 148–159.

20. Ibid., pp. 133–135.

21. Firestone and Weinstein, *Regional Growth and Decline in the United States*, p. 5.

22. Jusenius and Ledebur, "A Myth in the Making," pp. 134 and 135.

23. Ibid., p. 161.

24. Ibid.

25. Bernard Weinstein, interviewed by Robert Dilger, 30 January 1979, Washington, D.C.

26. Report of the President's Commission for a National Agenda for the Eighties, *Urban America in the Eighties* (Washington D.C.: U.S. Government Printing Office, 1980).

27. Ibid., p. 13.

28. Ibid., p. 28.

29. Michael Harrington, Frank Horton, and James Oberstar, Letter to the White House Delegates to the Conference on Balanced Growth, 23 January 1978.

30. Bernard Weinstein, "Cost of Living Adjustments for Federal Grants-in-Aid: A Negative View" (Washington, D.C.: The Southern Growth Policies Board, February 1979), p. i.

CHAPTER FOUR

1. At the outset of the Ninety-fifth Congress the average seniority of the sixty activists was 3.00 terms. The average for the spectators was 4.18 terms. Source: Congressional Quarterly, *Almanac* (1977).

2. Twenty percent of the activists were from marginal districts (12/60), while 15 percent of the spectators were from marginal districts (defined as less than 55 percent of the general election vote).

3. Richard Fenno, *Congressmen in Committees* (Boston: Little, Brown and Co., 1973), p. 1.

4. The sixteen members of the Education Task Force were: John Anderson (R-Ill.), Mario Biaggi (D-N.Y.), Jonathan Bingham (D-N.Y.), Michael Blouin (D-Iowa), Shirley Chisholm (D-N.Y.), Joshua Eilberg (D-Pa.), William Ford (D-Mich.), James Jeffords (R-Vt.), John LaFalce (D-N.Y.), Joseph LeFante (D-N.Y.), Stanley Lundine (D-N.Y.), Edward Markey (D-Mass.), Austin Murphy (D-Pa.), Albert Quie (R-Minn.), Frank Thompson (D-N.Y.), and Leo Zeferetti (D-N.Y.).

5. John Martin, *Regional Inequities in Federal Education Aid: Case of ESEA Title 1* (Washington, D.C.: The Northeast–Midwest Research Institute, 6 March 1978), p. 2.

6. "President Signs $25.2 billion Education Bill," Congressional Quarterly, *Almanac* (1974), p. 447. The four dissenting votes were cast by William Ford (D-Mich.), James O'Hara (D-Mich.), Robert Huber (R-Mich.), and Earl Landgrebe (R-Ind.).

7. The committee also reduced the payment rate from 50 percent of the national or state expenditure per pupil to 40 percent; changed the definition of poverty to the Orshansky Index, which included a family's nutritional requirements in defining need; and guaranteed each county, through a hold harmless clause, 85 percent of its previous level of funding. (Molly Orshansky was an economist at the Social Security Administration.)

8. "President Signs $25.2 Billion Education Bill," p. 449.

9. Ibid., p. 450.

10. Ibid., pp. 451 and 452.

11. Ibid., p. 460.

12. Congressional Quarterly, *Almanac* (1974), p. 30-S.

13. "President Signs $25.2 Billion Education Bill," p. 460.

14. Ibid., pp. 473 and 441.

15. "Massive Aid to Education Programs Extended," Congressional Quarterly, *Almanac* (1978), p. 560.

16. David Peterson, "Issue Paper Number 1: Elementary and Secondary Education Act," (Washington, D.C.: The Southern Growth Policies Board, 13 December 1977).

17. Martin, *Regional Inequities in Federal Education Aid*, p. 52.

18. Peterson included as southern states the fourteen members of the Southern Growth Policies Board plus Delaware, Maryland, and the District of Columbia.

19. Peterson, "Issue Paper Number 1," p. 2.

20. Ibid.

21. Ibid.

22. John Martin, interviewed by Robert Dilger, 21 November 1978, Washington, D.C.

23. Ibid.

24. Ann Elmore, interviewed by Robert Dilger, 21 November 1978, Washington, D.C.

25. John Martin, interviewed by Robert Dilger, 21 November 1978, Washington, D.C.

26. Ibid.

27. Harrison Donnelly, "Bill Tilts Education Funds Away from the South," Congressional Quarterly, *Weekly Reports* 36, 23 (10 June 1978), 1480.

28. Ibid., p. 1481.

29. Martin, *Regional Inequities in Federal Education Aid*, p. 24.

30. Ibid., pp. 13–17.

31. Fenno, *Congressmen in Committees*, p. 87.

32. Norman Ornstein, "Causes and Consequences of Congressional Change," in Norman Ornstein, ed., *Congress in Change* (New York: Praeger Publishers, 1975), and Lawrence Dodd and Bruce Oppenheimer, eds., *Congress Reconsidered* (New York: Praeger Publishers, 1977).

33. Roberta Stanley, interviewed by Robert Dilger, 6 December 1978, Washington, D.C.

34. John Martin, interviewed by Robert Dilger, 21 November 1978, Washington, D.C.

35. Ann Elmore, interviewed by Robert Dilger, 21 November 1978, Washington, D.C.

36. Roberta Stanley, interviewed by Robert Dilger, 6 December 1978, Washington, D.C.

37. John Martin, interviewed by Robert Dilger, 21 November 1978, Washington, D.C.

38. No record of this vote was taken, and none of the participants interviewed could recall what the Sunbelt/Snowbelt split was on the vote or who broke the tie.

39. Donnelly, "Bill Tilts Education Funds Away from the South," p. 1480.

40. Ibid., p. 1479.

41. *Congressional Record* 124, 104 (12 July 1978), 6580–6582.

42. *Congressional Record* 124, 104 (12 July 1978), 6580.

43. Congressional Quarterly, *Almanac* (1978), pp. 134 and 135-H.

44. The ten Snowbelt states aided by the Edwards amendment were: Delaware, Indiana, Iowa, Maine, Maryland, Minnesota, New Hampshire, Ohio, Rhode Island, and Vermont.

45. Donnelly, "Bill Tilts Education Funds Away from the South," p. 1479.

46. Martin, *Regional Inequities in Federal Education Aid*, p. 8.

47. Kathryn Waters Gest, "Senate Rejects Anti-Busing Effort, Parochial School Aid, Passes Education Bill," Congressional Quarterly, *Weekly Reports* (26 August 1978), 2243.

48. Harrison, Donnelly, "Massive Aid to Education Programs Extended," Congressional Quarterly, *Weekly Reports* 36, 44 (4 November 1978), 3207.
49. Ibid.
50. *Congressional Record* 124, 104 (12 July 1977), 6580.
51. Michael McManus, "Boston Detente at the North-South Summit," *Northeast-Midwest Agenda* (Washington, D.C.: The Northeast–Midwest Congressional Coalition, Summer 1978), p. 4.

CHAPTER FIVE

1. The eight were: Chisholm (D-N.Y.), Diggs (D-Mich.), Drinan (D-Mass.), Edwards (D-Calif.), Hays (D-Ind.), Nowak (D-N.Y.), Pattison (D-N.Y.), and Solarz (D-N.Y.).
2. The Office of Defense Mobilization, *Defense Manpower Policy Number Four*, 7 February 1952.
3. U.S. Congress, Senate, Select Committee on Small Business, *Hearings*, 92d Cong., 1st sess., Washington, D.C.: U.S. Government Printing Office, 10 October 1973, p. 48.
4. The Office of Defense Mobilization, *Defense Manpower Policy Number Four*, 7 February 1952.
5. Ibid.
6. Laurence Zabar, "Federal Procurement Policy: The Case of Defense Manpower Policy Number Four" (Washington, D.C.: The Northeast–Midwest Research Institute, 28 March 1977), p. 4.
7. Ibid.
8. Ibid., p. 2.
9. Ibid., p. 3.
10. Laurence Zabar, "Targeting Contracts to Areas of Need: A Review of Civilian Compliance with Defense Manpower Policy Number Four" (Washington, D.C.: Northeast–Midwest Research Institute, 10 October 1977), p. 3.
11. Zabar, "Federal Procurement Policy," pp. 15 and 16.
12. Laurence Zabar, interviewed by Robert Dilger, 18 December 1978, Washington, D.C.
13. U.S. Congress, House, Small Business Committee's Subcommittee on Minority Enterprise and General Oversight, *Hearings*, 95th Cong., 1st sess., Washington, D.C.: U.S. Government Printing Office, 2 June 1977, p. 55.
14. Zabar, "Targeting Contracts to Areas of Need," p. 9.
15. Ibid.
16. Ibid., pp. 10–13.
17. Ibid., p. 13.

18. Michael Harrington, Frank Horton, and James Oberstar, Letter to the White House Delegates to the Conference on Balanced Growth, 23 January 1978, p. 2.

19. U.S. Congress, House, Small Business Committee's Subcommittee on Minority Enterprise and General Oversight, *Hearings*, 95th Cong., 1st sess., Washington, D.C.: U.S. Government Printing Office, 2 June 1977, p. 34.

20. *Congressional Record* 124, 124 (8 August 1978), 8086.

21. Laurence Zabar, interviewed by Robert Dilger, 18 December 1978, Washington, D.C.

22. Robert Towell, "New Carrier, Vertical Jet Research Funded," Congressional Quarterly, *Weekly Reports* 36, 31 (5 August 1978), 2016.

23. Congressional Quarterly, *Almanac* (1978), pp. 164 and 165-H.

24. *Area Trends in Employment and Unemployment*, U.S. Department of Labor (January–March 1978), pp. 2–19.

25. *Congressional Record* 124, 124 (8 August 1978), 8084.

26. *Weekly Compilation of Presidential Documents* 14 (15 August 1978), 1432.

27. Richard Fenno, *Congressmen in Committees* (Boston: Little, Brown and Co., 1973), pp. 123–127.

28. Congressional Quarterly, *Weekly Reports* (20 September 1980), 2802 and 2803.

CHAPTER SIX

1. Martin Donsky, "Carter Fiscal Plan Faces Overhaul in Congress," Congressional Quarterly, *Weekly Reports* 36: 20 (20 May 1978), 1268.

2. Michael Harrington and Frank Horton, "Regionalism for the Sake of the Nation," *Northeast-Midwest Agenda* (Washington D.C.: The Northeast–Midwest Congressional Coalition, Summer 1978), p. 1.

3. Richard Nathan and Paul Dommel, "The Strong Sunbelt Cities and the Weak Coldbelt Cities," *Toward a National Urban Plan*, Report to the House Banking, Finance and Urban Affairs Committee, 95th Cong., 1st sess., Washington, D.C.: U.S. Government Printing Office, April 1977, p. 19.

4. Michael Moriarty, interviewed by Robert Dilger, 27 March 1979, Washington, D.C.

5. Michael Harrington, "On the Future of Northeastern Cities" (Washington, D.C.: The Northeast–Midwest Congressional Coalition, 20 July 1978), p. 2.

6. John DeGrove, "The Impact of Federal Grants-in-Aid on the South and Its Cities" (Research Triangle Park, N.C.: The Southern Growth Policies Board, September 1977), p. 2.

7. Ibid., p. 48.

8. Martin Tolchin, "Carter Says He Opposes 'Special Favors' to Aid City," *New York Times*, 31 March 1976, p. 20.

9. Charles Mohr, "Carter Qualifies Pledge to Cities," *New York Times*, 30 June 1976, p. 20.

10. Ibid.

11. Barry Hager, "Carter Aides Proud of Urban Policy Process," *Congressional Quarterly, Weekly Reports* 36, 13 (1 April 1978), 784.

12. Ibid.

13. Rochelle Stanfield, "The Carter Urban Strategy—Principles in Search of a Policy," *National Journal* 10, 8 (25 February 1978), 306.

14. Ibid., p. 304.

15. Kevin White, televised comments on *Congressional Outlook* (Washington, D.C.: Congressional Quarterly, Inc., 8 December 1978). The foreign policy concerns mentioned referred to the Middle East peace talks between Egypt and Israel.

16. Tolchin, "Carter Says He Opposes 'Special Favors' to Aid City," p. 20.

17. Donna Shalala, interviewed by Robert Dilger, 21 September 1979, Washington, D.C.

18. Ibid.

19. Frank Godfried, interviewed by Robert Dilger, 21 September 1979, Washington, D.C.

20. Stanfield, "The Carter Urban Strategy," p. 308.

21. Susanna McBee, "Carter Aides Favor Middle Ground on Aid to Decaying Cities," *Washington Post*, 12 January 1978, p. A4.

22. Stanfield, "The Carter Urban Strategy," p. 308.

23. Ibid., p. 307.

24. Susanna McBee, "Urban Policy Outlined for Carter," *Washington Post*, 25 December 1977, p. A4.

25. Ibid.

26. Hager, "Carter Aides Proud of Urban Policy Process," p. 783.

27. Michael Harrington, memorandum to Stuart Eizenstat, 10 January 1978.

28. McBee, "Urban Policy Outlined for Carter," p. A4.

29. James Carter, memorandum to Stuart Eizenstat and Patricia Harris, 25 January 1978.

30. Urban and Regional Policy Group, internal memorandum, no date.

31. At this point in time, the "Coalition" actually meant Michael Harrington and the staff rather than the entire membership.

32. The other congressional members were: Thomas Ashley (D-Ohio), Les AuCoin (D-Oreg.), Robert Edgar (D-Pa.), Frank Horton (R-N.Y.), Stanley Lundine (R-N.Y.), Stuart McKinney (R-Conn.), Donald Mitchell (R-N.Y.), Parren Mitchell (D-Md.), Leon Pannetta (D-Calif.), and Henry Reuss (D-Wis.).

33. Hager, "Carter Aides Proud of Urban Policy Process," p. 784.

34. Ibid., p. 785.

35. Martin Donsky, "Carter Urban Policy: A 'Smorgasbord,'" Congressional Quarterly, *Weekly Reports* 36, 13 (1 April 1978), 779.

36. Ibid., p. 785.

37. Donna Shalala, interviewed by Robert Dilger, 21 September 1979, Washington, D.C.

38. Donna Shalala, "A Pilgrim's Progress: Moving Toward a National Urban Policy," address at Trinity College, Hartford, Connecticut, 20 April 1978.

39. Joel Havemann and Rochelle Stanfield, "A Year Later, the Frostbelt Strikes Back," *National Journal* 9, 28 (2 July 1977), 1028.

40. Patricia Dusenbury, interviewed by Robert Dilger, 15 March 1979, Research Triangle Park, North Carolina.

CHAPTER SEVEN

1. Susanna McBee, "Urban Policy Outlined for Carter," *Washington Post*, 25 December 1977, p. A4.

2. Martin Donsky, "Carter Fiscal Plan Faces Overhaul in Congress," Congressional Quarterly, *Weekly Reports* 36, 20 (20 May 1978), 1267.

3. "Congress Overrides Ford's Job Bill Veto," Congressional Quarterly, *Almanac* (1976), p. 68.

4. If a jurisdiction had a 5 percent unemployment rate, it had 0.5 percent excess unemployment. A jurisdiction with 6 percent unemployment had 1.5 percent excess unemployment. The allotment formula transformed the difference between 5 and 6 percent (20 percent) into a 300 percent difference (0.5 to 1.5 percent) when the money was distributed.

5. Patricia Dusenbury, "Issue Paper Number 7: The Supplemental Fiscal Assistance Act of 1978" (Research Triangle Park, N.C.: The Southern Growth Policies Board, 19 June 1978), p. 6.

6. The national unemployment rate did fall below 6 percent in April 1978 and remained below 6 percent for the rest of fiscal 1979.

7. Donsky, "Carter Fiscal Plan Faces Overhaul in Congress," p. 1267. (The president also proposed to eliminate state governments from the program. This raised the ire of the National Governors' Conference, which opposed the bill because none of its revenues would pass through the governors' hands.)

8. Dusenbury, "Issue Paper Number 7," p. 3.

9. Ibid., pp. 7 and 8. (The coalition's states were to receive 55.61 percent of the Carter proposal's funds in fiscal 1979.)

10. U.S. Congress, House, the Government Operations Committee's Subcommittee on Intergovernmental Relations, *Hearings*, 95th Cong., 2d

sess., Washington, D.C.: U.S. Government Printing Office, 5 May 1978, p. 177.

11. Ibid., p. 26.

12. Ibid., p. 47.

13. Donsky, "Carter Fiscal Plan Faces Overhaul in Congress," p. 1268.

14. Petition to L. H. Fountain concerning the Supplemental Fiscal Assistance Act, 1 August 1978.

15. Those voting to table the measure: Fountain (D-N.C.), Fuqua (D-Fla.), English (D-Okla.), Levitas (D-Ga.), Brooks (D-Tex.), Cunningham (R-Wash.), and Broun (D-Ohio). Those voting not to table the motion: Jenrette (D-S.C.), Blouin (D-Iowa), Aspin (D-Wis.), Wydler (R-N.Y.), Horton (R-N.Y.), and Waxman (D-Calif.).

16. Martin Donsky, "Countercyclical Aid Bill Dies in Adjournment Crush," Congressional Quarterly, *Weekly Reports* 36, 42 (24 October 1978), 3038. (The Senate bill would have allocated approximately $500 million in fiscal 1979 and $340 million in fiscal 1980.)

17. The Senate's countercyclical aid bill easily passed the Senate (44–8) on 23 September 1978.

18. Donsky, "Countercyclical Aid Bill Dies in Adjournment Crush," p. 3038.

19. Jack Brooks and L. H. Fountain, letter concerning the Supplemental Fiscal Assistance Act of 1978, 10 October 1978.

20. Martin Donsky, "Carter's Urban Package Floundering on Hill," Congressional Quarterly, *Weekly Reports* 36, 30 (29 July 1978), 1960. (The urbank is not a bank in the sense of having marble floors and tellers. The bank is a source of funds available by application to the Department of Commerce Economic Development Administration.)

21. Rochelle Stanfield, "An Urbank Sounds Good, but Few Can Agree on What It Should Do," *National Journal* 9, 38 (17 September 1978), 1450.

22. Donsky, "Carter's Urban Package Floundering on Hill," p. 1961.

23. U.S. Congress, House, the Banking, Finance and Urban Affairs Committee's Subcommittee on Economic Stabilization, *Hearings*, 95th Cong., 2d sess., Washington, D.C.: U.S. Government Printing Office, 1 August 1978, p. 61.

24. Patricia Dusenbury, "Issue Paper Number 8: National Development Bank" (Research Triangle Park, N.C.: The Southern Growth Policies Board, 15 August 1978), p. 2.

25. U.S. Congress, House, the Banking, Finance and Urban Affairs Committee's Subcommittee on Economic Stabilization, *Hearings*, 95th Cong., 2d sess., Washington, D.C.: U.S. Government Printing Office, 1 August 1978, p. 88.

26. Dusenbury, "Issue Paper Number 8," p. 4. (The ten states referred to are: Connecticut, Illinois, Indiana, Massachusetts, Michigan, New Jersey, New York, Ohio, Pennsylvania, and Rhode Island.)

27. Twenty-eight of the Banking, Finance and Urban Affairs Committee's forty-seven members were members of the coalition, and the committee's chairman, Henry Reuss, was an active member of the coalition. The committee's Subcommittee on Economic Stabilization was also chaired by an active member of the coalition, William Moorhead, and was primarily composed of individuals from the coalition's states. Eleven of the subcommittee's sixteen members were from the Northeast-Midwest region.

28. Donsky, "Carter's Urban Package Floundering on Hill," p. 1960.

29. Michael Moriarty, interviewed by Robert Dilger, 21 March 1979, Washington, D.C. (Internal memoranda dated prior to congressional action on the president's urban proposals also indicated that the coalition did not expect the national development bank proposal to pass.)

30. *Legislative Report*, newsletter (Washington, D.C.: National Council for Urban Development, 14 April 1978), p. 6.

31. Martin Donsky, "Urban Policy Criticism Reflects Regional Rivalries," Congressional Quarterly, *Weekly Reports* 36, 14 (8 April 1978), 834. (The then current law provided for a permanent investment tax cretit of 7 percent and was temporarily raised to 10 percent in 1975.)

32. Shelly Amdur, Samuel Friedman, and Rebecca Staiger, "Investment and Employment Tax Credits" (Washington, D.C.: The Northeast–Midwest Research Institute, June 1978).

33. On this issue, Representatives Harrington (D-Mass.), Edgar (D-Pa.), Reuss (D-Wis.), Florio (D-N.Y.), and Cotter (D-Conn.) were actively involved. To a somewhat lesser extent, Representatives Holtzman (D-N.Y.), Horton (R-N.Y.), and Simon (D-Ill.) were involved.

34. According to the report by Shelly Amdur et al., the $200 million tax credit represented a loss in federal revenues of $41 million, while the $1.4 billion tax credit represented a loss in federal revenues of $13.1 million.

35. Donsky, "Urban Policy Criticism Reflects Regional Rivalries," p. 834.

36. U.S. Congress, House, Budget Committee's Task Force on State and Local Government, *Hearings*, 95th Cong., 2d sess., Washington, D.C.: U.S. Government Printing Office, 3 April 1978, p. 222.

37. Ibid., p. 220.

38. Sixty-seven percent of the 12,000 qualifying areas under the 5 percent targeted tax credit were located in the coalition's states, according to the Shelly Amdur et al. report.

39. Of the twenty-three members who voted for the Cotter amendment, thirteen were members of the coalition. Of the thirteen opposing, six were members of the coalition. This split, according to several legislative aides who were interviewed and were present at the time of the vote, was due to the fact that several members from the Sunbelt voted in favor of the amendment to "load it up" so that when the bill reached the floor of the House it would be easier to defeat it. Also, several coalition members voted against the amendment because the amendment was introduced after it had been agreed that no further amendments would be considered.

40. Chris Conte, "Taxes: House Hands Carter Another Defeat," Congressional Quarterly, *Weekly Reports* 36, 32 (12 August 1978), 2095.

41. Chris Conte, "Finance Committee Tax Bill Moves to Floor," Congressional Quarterly, *Weekly Reports* (30 September 1978), 2607.

42. The Northeast–Midwest Senate Coalition was formed on June 9, 1977, but had not operated as a political lobby group until this vote. Prior to this vote, the Senate Coalition served as an information resource concerning legislation of interest.

43. The Metzenbaum amendment was identical to the Cotter amendment except that buildings to be renovated had to be in use twenty years instead of five years.

44. The eight were: Chaffee (R-R.I.), Glenn (D-Ohio), Heinz (R-Pa.), Leahy (D-Vt.), Pell (D-R.I.), Stafford (R-Vt.), Anderson (D-Minn.), and Javits (R-N.Y.).

45. *Congressional Record* 124, 162 (7 October 1978), 17552.

46. Ibid., p. 17553.

47. Ibid., pp. 17555 and 17556.

48. Senator Muskie voted against the Metzenbaum amendment because as chairman of the Senate Budget Committee he felt that he must oppose all efforts to spend federal dollars that were not already accounted for in the budget. Senator Roth, a fiscal conservative, has almost always voted against any amendment that would increase domestic federal spending.

49. *Congressional Record* 124, 162 (7 October 1978), 19174.

50. Ibid., p. 13561.

51. Public Law 94-369, Local Public Works Capital Development and Investment Act of 1976.

52. Michael Harrington, "On the Future of Northeastern Cities" (Washington, D.C.: The Northeast–Midwest Congressional Coalition, 20 July 1978), p. 2.

53. U.S. Congress, Senate, the Environment and Public Works Committee's Subcommittee on Regional and Community Development, *Hearings*, 95th Cong., 2d sess., Washington, D.C.: U.S. Government Printing Office, 15 June 1978, p. 24.

54. Ibid., p. 48.

55. Rochelle Stanfield, "Rough Handling for Urban Programs," *National Journal* 10, 38 (23 September 1978), 1504.

56. *Congressional Record* 124, 143 (14 September 1978), 15104.

57. Ibid., p. 15107.

58. Ibid., p. 15115.

59. Ibid., p. 15116.

60. Ibid.

61. Ibid.

62. Ibid.

63. Neal R. Peirce and Jerry Hagstrom, "The Growing Movement to Take the Jobs to the People," *National Journal* 10, 13 (1 April 1978), 517.

CHAPTER EIGHT

1. Margaret Thompson, ed., *Energy Policy* (Washington, D.C.: Congressional Quarterly, Inc., April 1979), p. 3-A.
2. Ibid.
3. Ibid., p. 4-A.
4. Ibid.
5. A Gallup poll conducted in early April 1977 indicated that most Americans did not view the energy situation as being very serious.
6. Mercur Cross, "Carter Takes to Television for Energy Plea," Congressional Quarterly, *Weekly Reports* 35, 17 (23 April 1977), 753.
7. Ibid.
8. Ibid., p. 752.
9. Ibid., pp. 751–753.
10. Ibid., p. 752.
11. Ibid., p. 751.
12. Ibid., p. 750.
13. Robert Rankin, "Carter's Energy Plan: A Test of Leadership," Congressional Quarterly, *Weekly Reports* 35, 17 (23 April 1977), 727.
14. Cross, "Carter Takes to Television for Energy Plea," p. 750.
15. The eleven other representatives were: Joseph Addabbo (D-N.Y.), John Anderson (R-Ill.), Robert Drinan (D-Mass.), Hamilton Fish, Jr. (R-N.Y.), Floyd Fithian (D-Ind.), Michael Harrington (D-Mass.), Frank Horton (R-N.Y.), James Oberstar (D-Minn.), Richard Ottinger (D-N.Y.), Phillip Ruppe (R-Mich.), and Robert Walker (R-Pa.).
16. William Boxall, interviewed by Robert Dilger, 8 June 1979, Washington, D.C.
17. Larry Halloran, interviewed by Robert Dilger, 8 June 1979, Washington, D.C.
18. Neal R. Peirce and Jerry Hagstrom, "Western States Join in Forming a United Energy Front," *National Journal* 9, 1 (5 February 1977), 208.
19. Patricia Rice, "Energy Conditions in the South: 1975" (Research Triangle Park, N.C.: The Southern Growth Policies Board, September 1977), p. 1.
20. Rankin, "Carter's Energy Plan: A Test of Leadership," p. 770.
21. The U.S. Constitution specifically indicates that all tax-related legislation must originate in the House. For this reason, all legislative consideration of the energy bill was delayed by the Senate Finance Committee until the House Ways and Means Committee had completed its work on the bill.
22. U.S. Congress, House, Ways and Means Committee, *Hearings*, 95th Cong., 1st sess., Washington, D.C.: U.S. Government Printing Office, 16 May 1977, p. 216.
23. Thompson, ed., *Energy Policy* p. 44-A.
24. U.S. Congress, House, Ways and Means Committee, *Hearings*, 95th

Cong., 1st sess., Washington, D.C.: U.S. Government Printing Office, 16 May 1977, p. 143.

25. Ibid., pp. 121 and 122.

26. "Regional Energy Impact Brief No. 4" (Washington, D.C.: The Northeast–Midwest Congressional Coalition, January 1978), p. 1.

27. The transcript of the proceedings indicates that Burke and Cotter wanted to be recorded as having opposed the rejection of the home heating oil rebate plan. (A special thanks to Mr. Pat Baker of the Ways and Means staff for checking the transcript for this information.)

28. The ten were: Michael Harrington (D-Mass.), Robert Drinan (D-Mass.), Ronald Sarasin (R-Conn.), Frank Horton (R-N.Y.), Hamilton Fish, Jr. (R-N.Y.), Floyd Fithian (D-Ind.), James Oberstar (D-Minn.), Antony Moffett (D-Conn.), Joseph Addabbo (D-N.Y.), and Richard Ottinger (D-N.Y.). (William Brodhead did not sign the letter, as he was a member of the Ways and Means Committee and felt that signing the letter would be inappropriate.)

29. Stewart McKinney, letter to Al Ullman concerning the rejection of the home heating oil rebate plan, 24 June 1977.

30. Richard Corrigan, "House Committee Offers Shelter to Carter's Energy Program," in Richard Fenno, ed., *Congress: New Rules, New Leaders, Old Problems* (Washington D.C.: The Government Research Corporation), p. 44.

31. Ibid., p. 41.

32. William Archer (D-Tex.) did attempt to delete the home heating oil rebate plan during the Ad Hoc Committee on Energy's consideration of the crude oil equalization tax on July 21, 1977. Archer's amendment was defeated, 26–12, as Ullman defended the rebate as necessary to insure the fairness necessary for the president's energy program to be adopted. (Source: Northeast–Midwest Congressional Coalition, internal memorandum, 22 July 1977.)

33. Before the energy bill was considered on the House floor, the House Rules Committee provided a modified closed rule to govern floor debate on the bill. This rule made it very difficult to amend the energy bill and mandated a final, single vote on the entire bill.

34. Robert Rankin, "House Gives Carter Major Energy Victory," *Congressional Quarterly, Weekly Reports* 35, 32 (6 August 1977), 1628.

35. *Congressional Quarterly, Almanac* (1977), p. 138-H.

36. *Congressional Record* 123, 135 (5 August 1977), 8800.

37. Ibid., pp. 8806 and 8807.

38. Ibid., p. 8809.

39. *Congressional Quarterly, Almanac* (1977), p. 140-H.

40. Ibid.

41. Robert Rankin, "Natural Gas Filibuster Ties Up the Senate," *Congressional Quarterly, Weekly Reports* 35, 40 (1 October 1977), 2060.

42. Joel Havemann and Rochelle Stanfield, "A Year Later, the Frostbelt Strikes Back," *National Journal* 9, 27 (2 July 1977), 1028.

CHAPTER NINE

1. Randall Ripley and Grace Franklin, *Congress, the Bureaucracy and Public Policy* (Homewood, Ill.: The Dorsey Press, 1980), pp. 87–120.

2. Joel Havemann and Rochelle Stanfield, "A Year Later, the Frostbelt Strikes Back," *National Journal* 9, 27 (2 July 1977), 1028.

3. Jeane Mann, interviewed by Robert Dilger, 1 May 1981, Washington, D.C.

4. Norman Ornstein, "Causes and Consequences of Congressional Change: Subcommittee Reforms in the House of Representatives, 1970–73," in Norman Ornstein, ed., *Congress in Change* (New York: Praeger Publishers, 1975), pp. 88–114. (The "subcommittee bill of rights" formally institutionalized the party caucus role in selecting subcommittee chairmen within each standing committee, granted subcommittee's fixed jurisdictions, guaranteed powers, referral of all appropriate legislation, a budget, and staff. Also, each Democratic committee member was guaranteed a choice of one subcommittee, according to seniority.)

5. James Jeffords, interviewed by Robert Dilger, 18 January 1979, Washington D.C.

Selected Bibliography

BOOKS

Arnold, R. Douglas. *Congress and the Bureaucracy*. New Haven: Yale University Press, 1979.

Bauer, Raymond; de Sola Pool, Ithiel; and Dexter, Louis. *American Business and Public Policy*. New York: Atherton Press, 1963.

Clapp, Charles, L. *The Congressman: His Work as He Sees It*. New York: Doubleday and Company, 1964.

Clark, Joseph S. *The Senate Establishment*. New York: Hill and Wang, 1963.

Dexter, Lewis A. *How Organizations Are Represented in Washington*. Indianapolis: Bobbs-Merrill, 1969.

Dodd, Laurence, and Oppenheimer, Bruce, eds. *Congress Reconsidered*. New York: Praeger Publishers, 1977.

Elazar, Daniel. *American Federalism*. New York: Thomas Y. Crowell, 1972.

Evans, Rowland, and Novak, Robert. *Lyndon B. Johnson: The Exercise of Power*. New York: New American Library, 1966.

Fenno, Richard F. *Congressmen in Committees*. Boston: Little, Brown and Co., 1973.

Fiorina, Morris. *Congress: Keystone of the Washington Establishment*. New Haven: Yale University Press, 1977.

Firestone, Robert, and Weinstein, Bernard. *Regional Growth and Decline in the United States*. New York: Praeger Publishers, 1978.

Fox, Harrison, and Hammond, Susan Webb. *Congressional Staffs: The Invisible Force in American Lawmaking*. New York: The Free Press, 1977.

Froman, Lewis A. *Congressmen and Their Constituencies*. Chicago: Rand McNally, 1963.

Key, V. O., Jr. *Politics, Parties and Pressure Groups*. 5th ed. New York: Thomas Y. Crowell, 1964.

Kingdon, John. *Congressmen's Voting Decisions*. New York: Harper and Row, 1973.

Kofmehl, Kenneth. *Professional Staffs of Congress*. West Lafayette, Ind.: Purdue Research Foundation, 1962.

Kuhn, Thomas S. *The Structure of Scientific Revolutions*. Chicago: The University of Chicago Press, 1962.

Lindblom, Charles E. *The Policy-Making Process.* Englewood Cliffs, N.J.: Prentice Hall, 1968.

Liner, E. Blaine, and Lynch, Lawrence, eds. *The Economics of Southern Growth.* Research Triangle Park, N.C.: The Southern Growth Policies Board, 1977.

Matthews, Donald R. *U.S. Senators and Their World.* New York: Random House, 1960.

—— and Stimson, James. *Yeas and Nays: Normal Decision-Making in the U.S. House of Representatives.* New York: John Wiley and Sons, 1975.

Mayhew, David R. *Congress: The Electoral Connection.* New Haven: Yale University Press, 1976.

——. *Party Loyalty among Congressmen.* Cambridge: Harvard University Press, 1966.

Nathan, Richard P. *The Plot that Failed.* New York: John Wiley and Sons, 1975.

Orstein, Norman, ed. *Congress in Change.* New York: Praeger Publishers, 1975.

Peabody, Robert, and Polsby, Nelson, eds. *New Perspectives in the House of Representatives.* Chicago: Rand McNally, 1971.

Phillips, Kevin. *The Emerging Republican Majority.* New York: Arlington House, 1969.

Ripley, Randall B. *Congress: Process and Policy.* New York: W. W. Norton, 1975.

——, ed. *Public Policies and Their Politics.* New York: W. W. Norton, 1966.

—— and Franklin, Grace. *Congress, the Bureaucracy and Public Policy.* Revised ed. Homewood, Ill.: The Dorsey Press, 1980.

Sale, Kirkpatrick. *Power Shift.* New York: Random House, 1975.

Shannon, Wayne W. *Party, Constitutency and Congressional Voting.* Baton Rouge: Louisiana State University Press, 1968.

Thompson, Margaret, ed. *Energy Policy.* Washington, D.C.: Congressional Quarterly, Inc., 1979.

Truman, David, ed. *The Congress and America's Future.* Englewood Cliffs, N.J.: Prentice-Hall, 1973.

——. *The Congressional Party.* New York: John Wiley and Sons, 1959.

Turner, Frederick Jackson. *The Significance of Sections in American History.* New York: Henry Holt and Company, 1932.

Turner, Julius, and Edward Schneier, Jr. *Party and Constituency:*

Pressures on Congress. 2d rev. ed. Baltimore: The Johns Hopkins University Press, 1970.

Wilson, Woodrow. *Congressional Government.* New York: World Publishing Company, 1885.

ARTICLES AND PAPERS

Advisory Commission on Intergovernmental Relations. *Categorical Grants: Their Role and Design.* Washington, D.C.: U.S. Government Printing Office (May 1977).

———. *Community Development: The Workings of a Federal Local Block Grant.* Washington, D.C.: U.S. Government Printing Office (June 1976).

———. *Significant Features of Fiscal Federalism.* Washington, D.C.: U.S. Government Printing Office (October 1980).

Amdur, Shelly; Friedman, Samuel; and Staiger, Rebecca. "Investment and Employment Tax Credits: An Assessment of Geographically Sensitive Alternatives." Washington, D.C.: The Northeast–Midwest Research Institute (June 1978).

Beer, Samuel H. "The Modernization of American Federalism." *Publius* 3, 2 (Fall 1973): 49–95.

Brunson, E. Evan, and Dusenbury, Patricia. "National Urban Policy: Issue Paper #6." Research Triangle Park, N.C.: The Southern Growth Policies Board (June 1978).

Butler, Warren H. "Administering Congress: The Role of the Staff." *Public Administration Review* 26 (March 1966): 3–13.

Congressional Outlook. *Urban Policy #110.* Washington, D.C.: Congressional Quarterly, Inc., December 8, 1978.

DeGrace, John. "The Impact of Federal Grants-in-Aid on the South and Its Cities." Research Triangle Park, N.C.: The Southern Growth Policies Board (September 1977).

DeVaul, Diane. "Two Urban Initiatives: A Report Card." Washington, D.C.: The Northeast–Midwest Research Institute (March 1979).

Dusenbury, Patricia. "Issue Paper #5: Comprehensive Employment and Training Grants to State and Local Governments (CETA)." Research Triangle Park, N.C.: The Southern Growth Policies Board (May 1978).

———. "Issue Paper #7: Supplemental Fiscal Assistance to State and Local Governments." Research Triangle Park, N.C.: The Southern Growth Policies Board (June 1978).

————. "Issue Paper #8: National Development Bank." Research Triangle Park, N.C.: The Southern Growth Policies Board (August 1978).

————. "Issue Paper #9: Urban Development Action Grants." Research Triangle Park, N.C.: The Southern Growth Policies Board (n.d.).

————. "Regional Targeting." Research Triangle Park, N.C.: The Southern Growth Policies Board (February 1979).

Ehrenhalt, Alan. "Regionalism in Congress: Formulas Debated." Congressional Quarterly, *Weekly Reports* 35, 34 (20 August 1977): 1747–1752.

"Federal Spending: The North's Loss Is the Sunbelt's Gain." *National Journal* 8, 26 (26 June 1976): 878–891.

Focus on Regional Cooperation: North-South Summit. Washington, D.C.: The Northeast-Midwest Congressional Coalition (August 1978).

"Frostbelt Forces Launch Tax Credit Campaign." *National Journal* 10, 47 (25 November 1978): 1919.

George, Alexander. "Case Studies and Theory Development: The Method of Structured, Focused Comparison." Manuscript.

Harrington, Michael. "On the Future of Northeastern Cities." Remarks before the National League of Cities Northeast Regional Conference, July 20, 1978.

———— and Horton, Frank. "Rescuing the Region." *New York Times.* July 1, 1977.

Havemann, Joel, and Stanfield, Rochelle. "A Year Later, the Frostbelt Strikes Back." *National Journal* 9, 27 (2 July 1977): 1028–1037.

Haywood, Charles. "Financing Growth in the South." Research Triangle Park, N.C.: The Southern Growth Policies Board (September 1977).

Herbers, John. "West Taking South's Place as Most Alienated Area." *New York Times.* March 18, 1979.

Hogan, William, and Johnson, Julia. *The State of the Region.* Washington, D.C.: The Northeast–Midwest Research Institute (January 1979).

Lijphart, Arend. "Comparative Politics and the Comparative Method." *American Political Science Review* 65, 3 (September 1971): 682–693.

Liner, E. Blaine. "The Snowbelt and the Seven Myths." Research

Triangle Park, N.C.: The Southern Growth Policies Board (January 1978).

────── and Godschalk, David. "Shifting Urban Policy Targets: Impacts on North Carolina and the South." Research Triangle Park, N.C.: The Southern Growth Policies Board (1978).

Lowi, Theodore. "American Business, Public Policy, Case Studies and Political Theory." *World Politics* 16, 4 (July 1964): 677–715.

Manley, John. "Congressional Staffs and Public Policy Making: The Joint Committee on Internal Revenue Taxation." *Journal of Politics* 30 (1968): 1046–1067.

Markusen, Ann R., and Fastrup, Jerry. "The Regional War for Federal Aid." *The Public Interest* 53 (Fall 1978): 87–99.

Moore, John. "Washington Pressures/Business Forms Economic Study Unit to Support Bipartisan New England Caucus." *National Journal* 5, 7 (17 February 1973): 226–233.

Nathan, Richard; Dommel, Paul; Liebschultz, Sarah; Morris, Milton and Associates. *Block Grants for Community Development.* Washington, D.C.: U.S. Department of Housing and Urban Development, 1977.

"Northeast/Midwest Coalition Says Pentagon Shortchanges Region." Congressional Quarterly, *Weekly Reports* 35, 39 (24 September 1977): 2054.

Patterson, Samuel C. "The Professional Staffs of Congressional Committees." *Administrative Science Quarterly* 15 (1970): 22–37.

Peterson, David. "Issue Paper #1: Elementary and Secondary Education Act." Washington, D.C.: The Southern Growth Policies Board (February 1978).

──────. "The Relative Need of States and Regions for Federal Aid." Research Triangle Park, N.C.: The Southern Growth Policies Board (March 1979).

Peirce, Neal R., and Hagstrom, Jerry. "The Growing Movement to Take the Jobs to the People." *National Journal* 11, 13 (1 April 1979): 517–519.

──────. "Regional Groups Talk About Cooperation, but They Continue to Feud." *National Journal* 10, 21 (27 May 1978): 844 and 845.

──────. "Western States Join in Forming a United Energy Front." *National Journal* 9, 6 (5 February 1977): 208–210.

"Pork-Barrel War Between the States." *U.S. News & World Report* (5 December 1977): 39–41.

Reynolds, Alan. "Of Biting and Feeding." *New York Times*. August 23, 1977.

Rice, Bradley. "Searching for the Sunbelt." *American Demographics* 3, 3 (March 1981): 22–23.

Rice, Patricia. "Energy Conditions in the South, 1975." Research Triangle Park, N.C.: The Southern Growth Policies Board (September 1977).

Rich, Spencer. "Sunbelt and Far West Rising Further in the House." *Washington Post*. January 30, 1980.

Sassaman, Jan. "A Regional Analysis of Four Natural Gas Pricing Alternatives." Washington, D.C.: The Northeast–Midwest Research Institute (May 1978).

Stanfield, Rochelle. "Lies, Damn Lies and Statistics." *National Journal* 9, 12 (19 March 1977): 435.

————. "Playing Computer Politics with Local Aid Formulas." *National Journal* 10, 49 (9 December 1978): 1977–1981.

————. "Toward an Urban Policy with a Small Town Accent." *Publius* 9, 1 (1978): 31–44.

Sullivan, Michael, and Zabar, Laurence. "The Use of Federal Procurement in Revitalizing the Economy of Youngstown, Ohio." Washington, D.C.: The Northeast–Midwest Research Institute (April 1978).

Sutton, Horace. "Sunbelt versus Frostbelt: A Second Civil War?" *Saturday Review* (15 April 1978): 28–37.

"The Second War Between the States." *Business Week* (17 May 1976): 92–97.

Travis, Paul, and Zabar, Laurence. "A Case of Inequity: Regional Patterns in Defense Expenditures, 1950–1977." Washington, D.C.: The Northeast–Midwest Research Institute (August 1977).

Verba, Sidney. "Some Dilemmas in Comparative Research." *World Politics* 20, 1 (October 1967): 111–127.

Warren, Sarah. "The New Look of the Congressional Caucus." *National Journal* 10, 17 (29 April 1978): 677–679.

Weinstein, Bernard. "Cost-of-Living Adjustments For Federal Grants-In-Aid: A Negative View." Research Triangle Park, N.C.: The Southern Growth Policies Board (February 1979).

————. "Economic War on the Sunbelt?" *The Wall Street Journal*. January 29, 1979.

Zabar, Laurence. "Federal Procurement and Regional Needs: The Case of Defense Manpower Policy Number Four." Washington, D.C.: The Northeast–Midwest Research Institute (March 1977).

————. "Congressional Guide to Federal Procurement." Washington, D.C.: The Northeast–Midwest Research Institute (February 1979).

————. "Targeting Contracts to Areas of Need: A Review of Civilian Agency Compliance with Defense Manpower Policy Number Four." Washington, D.C.: The Northeast–Midwest Research Institute (October 1977).

Index